Roy E. Myers
Mathematics Department
The Pennsylvania State University

MICROCOMPUTER GRAPHICS FOR THE IBM PC

Addison-Wesley Publishing Company
Reading, Massachusetts • Menlo Park, California • New York
Don Mills, Ontario • Wokingham, England • Amsterdam • Bonn
Sydney • Singapore • Tokyo • Madrid • Bogotá
Santiago • San Juan

Library of Congress Cataloging in Publication Data

Myers, Roy E.
Microcomputer graphics for the IBM PC.

Includes index.
1. Computer graphics. 2. IBM Personal Computer—Programming. I. Title. II. Title: Microcomputer graphics for the I.B.M. P.C.
T385.M933 1984 001.64'43 83-21545
ISBN 0-201-05158-3

Cover design by Marshall Henrichs
Set in 11 point Times Roman by Techna Type, Inc., York, PA

ISBN 0-201-05158-3
EFGHIJ-HA-897
Fifth Printing, May 1987

Contents

Programs

Preface

Work in computer graphics began in the 1950s. While major advances have been made since then, few people have been able to use computer graphics. For years the cost of equipment has kept graphics out of the reach of most computer users. The microcomputer has changed that. A microcomputer graphics system can be purchased for a few thousand dollars. Businesses, educational institutions, and individuals are finding that computer graphics are accessible, and that they can be useful, interesting, challenging, and fun.

While the graphics systems associated with low-cost microcomputers are far from the state of the art, they provide reasonable images in a reasonable time for a programmer of modest talents. More sophisticated graphics systems have capabilities which microcomputers do not provide. In order to achieve quality images, the microcomputer graphics programmer must compensate for the limitations of the graphics hardware and the graphics language.

It is the intention of this book to provide the mathematical and programming techniques that are central to microcomputer graphics.

The basis for all discussion is the IBM PC. It is assumed that the reader will have access to this computer, will be developing programs using BASIC (version 2.0 or later), and will be using the color/graphics interface. All example programs are designed for use on the IBM PC, and are written in Advanced BASIC; many may be adapted for use with other languages and microcomputers.

No attempt has been made to teach programming in BASIC. It is assumed that the reader is familiar with the language, and has access to the IBM PC BASIC manual. The program examples are written to illustrate graphics techniques, not programming techniques; moreover, they are not intended to be model programs. The astute programmer will find ways to improve the execution time and ways to make the programs more elegant. All programs have been tested and checked for errors. If one does not perform as described, this is more than likely the result of a typing error. It is possible to adapt the example programs for use in individual applications, but far better to use them as a learning tool. When the mathematical and programming techniques are well understood, they can be used as the basis for many types of applications.

Since the applications of computer graphics are many and varied, an attempt has been made to have example programs which reflect this diversity. Thus the examples include business graphics, an animated game, three-dimensional images, and other displays for esthetic and practical purposes.

Computer graphics is a broad and interesting field of study. This book is intended as an introduction to the subject. From here you can go on to specialized applications like computer-assisted design, high-speed animation via assembly language programming, or interfacing BASIC graphics programs with data analysis programs for business, scientific, or engineering applications.

As you read this book, remember that you will learn more if you try each example as you read, and you will learn even more if you extend the examples. Experiment. That is the best way to learn the capabilities and limitations of the computer and the graphics language.

ACKNOWLEDGMENT

Thank you, Karen.

Chapter 1

Introduction to Computer Graphics

The term computer graphics does not have a common meaning to all people. To some it may bring video arcade games to mind; to others, a flight simulator for training aircraft pilots. To an architect, computer graphics provides a means of planning and displaying drawings for the design of a building. An engineer might use computer graphics to design and analyze an electrical circuit or a bridge.

The uses of computers for graphics purposes are many and varied. It is the intent of this book to consider the mathematical and programming techniques necessary to generate graphics images on a low-cost microcomputer. The IBM PC is used as the basis of discussion and all examples are written in advanced BASIC. In this chapter, we will consider example programs which illustrate both the capability of the computer and the programming processes which are described in later chapters.

> **NOTE:** In this chapter, the example programs use techniques which will be described in later parts of the book. Don't be concerned about programming details yet. Enjoy the graphics.

RASTERS AND PIXELS

The IBM PC uses a raster display for graphics. This means simply that the display screen consists of a collection of horizontal lines, and each raster line is made up of dots called *pixels* (picture elements, or *pels*). In the IBM PC's high-resolution graphics mode there are 200 raster lines, each containing 640 pixels. The raster lines are numbered 0 to 199; the pixels within each line are numbered from 0 to 639. Each pixel is thus identified by two numbers: the number of the raster line and the number of the pixel within the line. Images are generated on the graphics screen by turning pixels on and off.

At the heart of a raster scan computer graphics language must be the ability to turn on individual pixels (i.e., plot points). In IBM PC BASIC the PSET and PRESET statements perform this duty. PSET (X,Y) will turn on the pixel in the X position of raster line Y. For example, PSET (0,0) will turn on the dot in the upper left of the screen; PSET (639,199) will turn on the dot in the lower right corner of the high-resolution graphics screen. PRESET (X,Y) will turn the specified dot off.

SPACE

While most of the images we will be generating consist of more than a few dots, our first example program develops an image using only the PSET statement.

Program P1-1: SPACE

```
10 'PROGRAM P1-1  (SPACE)
20 'Plots randomly selected points
100 '================================
110 RANDOMIZE TIMER
120 KEY OFF: SCREEN 2: CLS
130 FOR I = 1 TO 100
140  X = 640*RND: Y = 200*RND
150  PSET (X,Y)
160 NEXT I
```

In the SPACE example above, stars are plotted in positions randomly selected by line 140, providing a new star scene each time the program is run.

> **NOTE:** If your version of BASIC does not have the TIMER function, just leave line 110 out of the program. It will still work, but will give the same star pattern every time the program is run.

BOUNCING BALL

As a second example of a program based primarily on the PSET statement, consider the following simulation of a bouncing ball.

Program P1-2: BOUNCING BALL

```
10 'PROGRAM P1-2  (BOUNCING BALL)
20 'Simulates a ball bouncing off floor and walls
100 '===================================================
110 KEY OFF: SCREEN 2: CLS
120 DX = 6: X = 7: Y = 0: A = 1: V = 0
130 LINE (0,0) - (0,191)
140 LINE - (639,191)
150 LINE - (639,0)
160 PSET (X,Y): PSET (X+1,Y)
170 IF Y = 190 THEN V = -V: IF V = 0 THEN V = -19
180 IF X = 637 OR X = 1 THEN DX = - DX
190 V = V + A
200 PRESET (X,Y): PRESET (X+1,Y)
210 Y = Y + V: X = X + DX
220 GOTO 160
```

The "ball" is provided by line 160. In order to increase the visibility of the ball, two dots are plotted side by side. Lines 130–150 provide "walls" and a "floor" for the ball to bounce against. As the ball moves, the horizontal movement is controlled by a constant velocity, DX; the vertical movement is controlled by a variable velocity, V, together with a constant acceleration, A. The "movement" of the ball is simulated by plotting a dot [PSET (X,Y), in line 160], then erasing it [PRESET (X,Y); line 200]. The position (X,Y) of the ball is changed (line 210) and the ball is plotted in the new position. "Bounces" off the walls and floor are controlled by lines 170 and 180. To maintain the action, line 170 accelerates the ball when its bounce is low (Y = 190 and V = 0).

The LINE statements of lines 130–150 will, of course, draw line segments connecting the specified points. Thus LINE (0,0)–(0,191) draws a line down the left side of the screen. LINE–(639,191) draws a line *from the last plotted point* [which was (0,191)] to the point (639,191). Similarly, LINE–(639,0) draws a line connecting points (639,191) and (639,0). The LINE statement has other options. Several will be demonstrated in later programs.

PRESET and PSET may be less obvious in their effect than LINE. For the present we will say that PSET draws a dot (turns on a pixel) at a specified location, using the current foreground color (none has been specified; the default is white). PRESET (X,Y) also draws a dot at location (X,Y), but uses the background color for drawing. Of course, drawing a dot in the background color has the effect of erasing the dot.

DRAW

The PSET, PRESET, and LINE statements provide the ability to generate a wide variety of graphics images. However, they are not the only graphics statements available in IBM PC BASIC. Example program P1-3 gives an example of the use of the DRAW statement to provide animation of a simple image. The DRAW statements in lines 150 and 180 make use of coded instructions contained in those lines and in the string ST$, which is defined in lines 130 and 140. Further examples of the use of DRAW are given in Chapter 3.

Program P1-3: PULSATE

```
10 'PROGRAM P1-3  (PULSATE)
20 'Uses DRAW graphics
100 '====================================
110 KEY OFF: SCREEN 1,0: CLS
120 SC = 2: INC = 2
130 ST$ = "BH4 R2 D8 L2 U2 R8 D2 L2 "
140 ST$ = ST$ + "U8 R2 D2 L8 U2"
150 DRAW "BM 160,100;C1;S=SC;XST$;"
160 OLDSC = SC: SC = SC + INC
170 IF SC = 2 OR SC = 40 THEN INC = - INC
180 DRAW "BM 160,100;C0;S=OLDSC;XST$;"
190 IF INKEY$ <> "" THEN END
200 GOTO 150
```

GREMLIN

Program P1-4 provides graphics in yet another mode: character graphics on the text display screen. The program makes use of the graphics characters (listed in Appendix G of the IBM PC BASIC reference manual) to draw a small gremlin. The components of the gremlin are specified by string variables defined on lines 130–190. To draw the gremlin, we PRINT the corresponding components on the screen (lines 330–360).

NOTES AND SUGGESTIONS

1. When printing the components of the gremlin we precede and follow each component by two spaces (defined in S$). As a result, we are able to animate the image horizontally across the screen. The spaces serve to erase the previous image as a component is printed in a new location.

2. Program P1-4 also makes use of a procedure called page flipping to achieve smoother animation. To see the benefits of page flipping, insert an apostrophe before SCREEN in line 320 and run the program again.

3. Character graphics and page flipping receive more attention in Chapter 5. This particular example is repeated there as Program P5-3, where the animation techniques are discussed.

Program P1-4: GREMLIN

```
10 'PROGRAM P1-4  (GREMLIN)
20 'Animated character graphics
100 '=======================================
110 KEY OFF: SCREEN 0,1,0: COLOR 4,1,14
120 WIDTH 40: LOCATE ,,0: CLS: SCREEN ,,1: CLS
130 S$ = CHR$(32) + CHR$(32)
140 A$ = CHR$(8) + CHR$(8)
150 B$ = CHR$(219) + CHR$(219)
160 C$(0) = CHR$(188) + CHR$(186)
170 D$(0) = CHR$(32) + CHR$(200)
180 C$(1) = CHR$(186) + CHR$(200)
190 D$(1) = CHR$(188)
200 A = 2: B = 34: C = 1
210 '=======================================
220 FOR I = A TO B STEP C
230  GOSUB 320
240  FOR K = 1 TO 50: NEXT K
250 NEXT I
260 FOR L = 1 TO 30
270  GOSUB 320
280 NEXT L
290 SWAP A,B: C = -C
300 GOTO 220
310 '=======================================
320 SCREEN ,,J,1-J
330 LOCATE 5,I: PRINT S$ + A$ + S$
340 LOCATE 6,I: PRINT S$ + B$ + S$
```

```
350 LOCATE 7,I: PRINT S$ + C$(J) + S$
360 LOCATE 8,I: PRINT S$ + D$(J) + S$
370 J = 1 - J
380 IF INKEY$ <> "" THEN SCREEN 0,1,0,0: END
390 RETURN
```

SPACESHIP

The program below draws a child's version of a spaceship.

Program P1-5: SPACESHIP

```
10 'PROGRAM P1-5  (SPACE SHIP)
20 'Uses LINE to draw a simple shape
100 '==================================
110 KEY OFF: SCREEN 2: CLS
120 LINE (250,180) - (250,50)
130 LINE - (320,20)
140 LINE - (390,50)
150 LINE - (390,180)
160 LINE (390,120) - (470,180)
170 LINE - (170,180)
180 LINE - (250,120)
```

Programs of this sort are valuable for establishing a working understanding of the graphics screen. A rough line drawing on a page of graph paper will provide a model from which to write the program.

COLORED LINES

The next program is brief, and simple in design. It drops colored lines at random locations on the screen. This is the first program to use the medium-resolution screen (SCREEN 1). This screen provides 200 raster lines, each containing 320 pixels. Further, while colors are not permitted on the high-resolution graphics screen (SCREEN 2), a variety is available here.

Lines 130 and 140 select random endpoints for line segments drawn by line 160. Different colors are used in drawing the line segments.

Program P1-6: COLORED LINES

```
10 ' PROGRAM P1-6  (COLORED LINES)
20 ' Drops random colored lines
100 '===================================
110 KEY OFF: SCREEN 1,0: CLS
120 RANDOMIZE TIMER
130 X1 = 320*RND: Y1 = 200*RND
140 X2 = 320*RND: Y2 = 200*RND
150 C = C + 1
160 LINE (X1,Y1) - (X2,Y2), C MOD 4
170 IF C < 400 THEN GOTO 130
180 COLOR B MOD 16: CLS
190 B = B + 1: C = 0
200 GOTO 130
```

We turn now to a designer program.

Program P1-7: MOIRE

```
10 'PROGRAM P1-7  (MOIRE)
20 'Draws overlapping random patterns
100 '================================
110 KEY OFF: SCREEN 1,0: CLS: A = 5
120 X1 = 320*RND: Y1 = 200*RND
130 C = C + 1: IF C = 4 THEN C = 0: P = 1 - P: IF P THEN
B = B + 1: IF B = 16 THEN B = 0
140 COLOR B,P: Y = 199
150 FOR X = 0 TO 319 STEP A
160  LINE ( X,199) - (X1,Y1),C: LINE - (319 - X,0),C
170 NEXT X
180 FOR Y = 0 TO 199 STEP A
190  LINE (319,199 - Y) - (X1,Y1),C: LINE - (0,Y),C
200 NEXT Y
210 FOR I= 1 TO 500 : NEXT I
220 IF INKEY$ <> "" THEN END
230 GOTO 120
```

The results of overlapping colored lines can be very pleasing, as illustrated in the above program. Line 120 determines a random center for the design. This program draws consecutive designs over one another, changing colors between designs (lines 130 and 140). Line 210 provides a brief pause to allow time to view a pattern before drawing over it.

CURVE

Points and straight line segments will be the components of all our graphics images. We will be able to draw curves only by approximating them by straight line segments. The following example illustrates the technique.

Program P1-8: CURVE

```
10 'PROGRAM P1-8  (CURVE)
20 'STRAIGHT LINES - - > CURVE
100 '==============================
110 KEY OFF: SCREEN 2: CLS
120 FOR Y = 0 TO 199 STEP 4
130  LINE (0,Y) - (639*Y/199,199)
140 NEXT Y
150 IF INKEY$ = "" THEN 150
```

Clearly, only straight line segments are plotted (line 130). The image created yields an approximation to a curve, in the same manner as a string sculpture.

SPIRAL BAND

We have a CIRCLE statement available (and will use it in Program P1-10). However, there are times when it is better to calculate points on a circle directly. Several methods for doing this are presented in Chapter 7. Program P1-9 uses one of these methods to draw a sequence of concentric circles. As points on a circle are calculated, they are connected by short line segments of varying colors. The result is a colorful spiralling circular band.

The variables defined in lines 120–140 are used in calculating the points on the circle (line 180) and plotting the line segments (line 200). The color used is controlled by line 190.

Program P1-9: SPIRAL BAND

```
10 ' PROGRAM P1-9  (SPIRAL BAND)
20 ' Draws a colorful circular band
100 '===================================
110 KEY OFF: SCREEN 1,0: CLS
```

```
120 DT = .1: C = COS(DT): S = SIN(DT)
130 SC = 5/6: CX = 160: CY = 100
140 X = 0: Y = 90
150 PSET (X + CX,SC*Y + CY)
160 FOR J = 1 TO 20
170  FOR I = 1 TO 63
180   T = X *C-Y*S: Y = Y*C+X*S: X = T
190   CO = CO + .5
200   LINE - (X + CX,SC*Y + CY),CO MOD 4
210  NEXT I
220  Y = Y - 2
230 NEXT J
```

ANIMATION

For the last example of this chapter, we will draw a car on the medium-resolution graphics screen and have it move across the screen. The program uses several new statements and variations on old ones. CIRCLE is used in lines 180, 200, and 220 to provide the wheels and rounded trunk of the car. PAINT (lines 190, 210, 230) fills the interior of the circles with a specified color. Finally, the data which define the car are stored in an array by the GET statement (line 260) and PUT repositions the car in new locations across the screen, simulating animation.

Program P1-10: ANIMATED CAR

```
10 'PROGRAM P1-10  (ANIMATED CAR)
20 'Simple animation
100 '===================================
110 PI = 3.141593
120 KEY OFF: SCREEN 1,0: COLOR 1,4: CLS
130 'Draw a car.
140 LINE (25,19) - (80,35),2,BF
150 LINE (25,5) - (50,20),2,BF
160 LINE (3,33) - (82,35),2,BF
170 LINE (32,7) - (48,18),,BF
180 CIRCLE (25,35),20,2,-PI/2,-PI
190 PAINT (22,32),2
200 CIRCLE (25,35),8
210 PAINT (25,35)
220 CIRCLE (70,35),8
```

```
230 PAINT (70,35)
240 'Store it.
250 DIM A(268)
260 GET (1,5)-(84,55),A
270 'Move it.
280 FOR I = 1 TO 200
290  PUT (I,5),A,PSET
300 NEXT I
```

SUMMARY

The intention of this chapter has been to provide short examples of programs which generate graphics images. Although the programs are not very sophisticated, several make use of methods which may not be immediately clear. These techniques will be explained in the chapters that follow. As you progress through this book, these programs should become transparent. You should soon be able to improve on them.

Chapter 2

Graphics Characteristics of the IBM PC

The IBM PC has several means of generating graphic images in BASIC. Each of these methods has been used in at least one example in Chapter 1. This chapter will describe the behind-the-scenes operations that are taking place.

We can classify graphics commands into two basic categories: those which produce images on the text screen, and those which create images on one of the graphics screens. The primary emphasis of this book will be on the latter, but we will begin with a discussion of text screen graphics, or character graphics.

CHARACTER GRAPHICS

The text screen provides graphics capabilities which are not available on the graphics screens; however, it also has some severe limitations. The primary disadvantages of text screen graphics are that we cannot turn on an individual pixel and cannot draw line segments connecting arbitrary points. The primary advantages are that certain types of graphics displays can be created quite quickly, with wide color selection and with smooth animation. Further, such programs are relatively easy to design.

Display modes are specified by the SCREEN statement, which has the format

```
SCREEN [mode] [,[burst] [,[apage] [,vpage]]]
```

Text mode is selected if *mode* = 0. *Burst* determines whether characters are to be printed in color (*burst* = nonzero, when in text mode) or in black and white (*burst* = 0, when in text mode). *Apage* and *vpage* identify the active screen page (the page to be used for PRINTing) and the visual screen page (the screen which is displayed). This suggests that more than one text page is available. In fact, when WIDTH is set to 80, there are four pages available (vpage or apage = 0 to 3) and eight pages are available when WIDTH is 40 (vpage or apage = 0 to 7). If no values are specified for *apage* or for *vpage,* the default value of 0 is used.

MEMORY USAGE BY TEXT PAGES

When the Color/Graphics card is being used, both the text and the graphics screens draw their display from memory locations &HB8000–&HBBFFF. Table 2.1 shows the areas of memory used by each of the pages of the text screen.

Table 2.1 Memory Usage by SCREEN 0 (when Color/Graphics card is in use)

	40-column display		**80-column display**
page	*memory locations*	*page*	*memory locations*
0	&HB8000–&HB87FF	0	&BH8000–&HB8FFF
1	&HB8800–&HB8FFF	1	&HB9000–&HB9FFF
2	&HB9000–&HB97FF	2	&HBA000–&HBAFFF
3	&HB9800–&HB9FFF	3	&HBB000–&HBBFFF
4	&HBA000–&HBA7FF		
5	&HBA800–&HBAFFF		
6	&HBB000–&HBB7FF		
7	&HBB800–&HBBFFF		

To see how memory is used by the text screens, run the following program:

Program P2-1: TEXT PEEK

```
10 'PROGRAM P2-1  (TEXT PEEK)
20 'Text page memory usage
100 '============================
110 SCREEN 0,1,0,0: CLS: WIDTH 80
120 COLOR 7,0
130 PRINT "A"
140 DEF SEG = &HB800
150 PRINT PEEK(0), PEEK(1)
```

> **NOTE:** If you are not familiar with identifying segments of memory through the use of the DEF SEG statement, consult Appendix 2 of this book.

The program should display the letter A in the upper left of the screen, and the numbers 65 and 7 on the next line. The 65 is the ASCII code for A (see IBM PC BASIC manual, Appendix G), and 7 is the code of the foreground color (white) which is being used. (Note that two bytes of memory are used to identify one character. One byte identifies the ASCII code; the second identifies the color in which the character is displayed.)

Change line 120 to **120 COLOR 7,1** and run the program again. This time the numbers 65 and 23 should be printed and the letter A should be white on a blue background. Change line 120 to **120 COLOR 7,2** and run the program. Now the numbers printed are 65 and 39. Do you see what is occurring? The first number [PEEK (0)] gives the ASCII code of the character displayed. The second number [PEEK(1)] is a code which identifies the color (foreground/background) used for the display. This code is given by

```
128*(blink) + 16*(background) + (foreground)
```

for background color codes 0–7 and foreground color codes 0–15. If blink = 1 the character will blink in the foreground color; if blink = 0 the character does not blink.

We can use this information to display characters on the text screen. Program P2-2 prints the characters available on the PC (see Appendix G of the IBM PC BASIC manual), using varied foreground and background colors.

Program P2-2: RAINBOW TEXT

```
10 'PROGRAM P2-2  (RAINBOW TEXT)
20 'Control text screen display with pokes
100 '======================================
110 SCREEN 0,1,0,0: CLS: WIDTH 80
120 DEF SEG = &HB800
130 FOR I = 0 TO 255
140 POKE 2*I,I: POKE 2*I+1,I
```

```
150 NEXT I
160 LOCATE 10,1: 'Get cursor out of the way
```

Note that two memory locations are needed to identify a character. Each even numbered text page memory location (2∗I) will contain the ASCII code of a character to be displayed. The following odd-numbered location (2∗I + 1) will contain the character color code, as described by the formula above.

We can use this information to print messages on the screen. Program P2-3 gives an example.

Program P2-3: TEXT SCREEN ADDRESSING

```
10 'PROGRAM P2-3  (TEXT SCREEN ADDRESSING)
20 'Prints message using ASCII codes
100 '========================================
110 SCREEN 0,1,0,0: CLS: WIDTH 80
120 DEF SEG = &HB800
130 FOR I = 518 TO 521
140  READ X: 'Get ASCII codes
150 'Store ASCII codes and color code
160  POKE 2*I,X: POKE 2*I+1,73
170 NEXT I
180 FOR I = 595 TO 604
190  READ X: 'Get ASCII codes
200 'Store ASCII codes and color code
210  POKE 2*I,X: POKE 2*I+1,201
220 NEXT I
230 '========================================
240 'ASCII codes for message
250 DATA 84, 69, 88, 84
260 DATA 65, 68, 68, 82, 69, 83, 83, 73, 78, 71
```

Lines 250 and 260 contain the ASCII codes for the characters to be printed. These are read in lines 130–220 and stored in memory locations within the text page. Lines 130–170 store the first four characters in positions 38–41 of the sixth line of text (518 = 6∗80 + 38; 521 = 6∗80 + 41). Lines 180–220 store the last ten characters in positions 35–43 of the seventh line of text (595 = 7∗80 + 35; 604 = 7∗80 + 44). The color code specified in line 160 (POKE 2∗I + 1,73) will use background color 4, and color 9 for the foreground (73 = 4*16 + 9). The color code specified in line 180 (POKE 2*I + 1, 201) will use blinking foreground color 9 and color 4 for background (201 = 1*128 + 4*16 + 9).

NOTES

1. If you have done a little arithmetic as we go along, you have noticed that with the 80-column display mode 4000 bytes of memory are needed [(80 characters)*(25 lines)*(2 bytes per character)]. Table 2.1 indicates that 4096 bytes are allocated. The last 96 are not needed or used. Similarly, with the screen in the 40-column display mode, 2048 bytes are allocated, but only 2000 are needed.
2. The above discussion is intended to outline the use of memory by the text display screens. It is not generally efficient to display messages in the manner of Program P2-3, but it is useful to know how memory is used by the computer.
3. The characters that are displayed on the text screen are identified by the ASCII values which are stored in alternate memory locations. For example, the characters which are displayed on the text screen, page 0, are identified by the ASCII codes stored in memory locations &HB8000, &HB8002, &HB8004, etc. The color used for the display of a character is determined by the contents of the next successive memory location. Thus the color code in &HB8001 controls the color of the character whose ASCII code is stored in memory location &HB8000, and the color code in &HB8003 controls the color of the character whose ASCII code is in &HB8002.
4. Changes in the contents of the even-numbered memory locations (&HB8000, &HB8002, etc.) will change the characters displayed, but will not change the colors used. Changes in the contents of the odd-numbered locations (&HB8001, &HB8003, etc.) will change the colors used for display, but will not change the characters which are displayed.

   Some rather nice and dramatic effects can be arranged by displaying a full page of text, then changing color codes to highlight or hide (set color codes so that foreground color = background color) certain parts of the text.
5. The use of memory for displaying 40-column text is similar to the

way 80-column text is displayed. Modify the above programs for 40-column text; see what happens.

TEXT SCREEN GRAPHICS VS. GRAPHICS SCREENS

This concludes the discussion of graphics for the text screen (SCREEN 0). Text screen graphics does permit the use of a broad choice of color combinations and allows the use of multiple pages, which makes animation smoother. Further, the graphics characters can be PRINTed on the text screen quickly, and a large collection of predefined characters is provided. There are clear merits to the use of character graphics, and PC graphics would be weaker without this capability.

There are also limitations to the use of text screen graphics. No provision is made for addressing individual dots, or for drawing lines and curves. Further, it is not possible to add symbols to the character set. As a result, there are limitations to the type of images which can be developed.

The use of the graphics screens (SCREEN 1 and SCREEN 2) removes the limitations of the text screen that were stated above. Points, lines, and curves can be drawn. Further, character graphics are still available. Although the special characters (with ASCII codes larger than 127) are not provided, they can be defined by the programmer.

Are there limits in the use of the graphics screens? Yes, of course. While a wide range of color combinations is available, it is not as varied as that for the text screen. In fact, only four colors can be displayed at one time on the medium-resolution screen (SCREEN 1), and the high-resolution screen (SCREEN 2) provides only black and white. This is a minor inconvenience, however.

Another limitation is that the graphics screens do not provide multiple pages. That is unfortunate. While provision for a second graphics page would require an additional 16K of dedicated memory, it would give some useful graphics flexibility.

MEMORY USAGE BY GRAPHICS SCREEN 2

If the computer display is in the SCREEN 2 mode, the image shown on the screen is a bit-by-bit display of the contents of the graphics page of

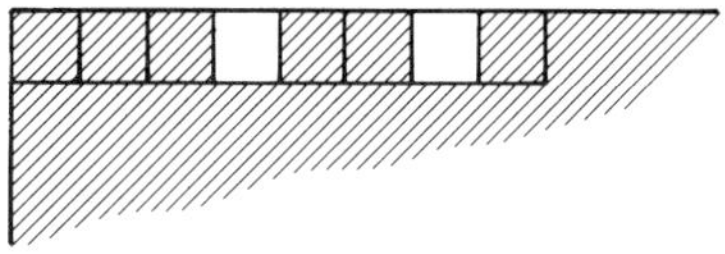

Figure 2.1

memory. This graphics page consists of memory locations numbered &HB8000–&HBBFFF (decimal 753664–770047). The same range of memory is used whether the display is showing SCREEN 1 or SCREEN 2. (This area of memory is also used for display of SCREEN 0 by the Color/Graphics card.) We will first consider the use of memory by SCREEN 2.

When in SCREEN 2 mode, the top left screen position is controlled by memory location &HB8000. In fact, the eight bits of this memory location are displayed as the first eight dots on the top line of SCREEN 2 display. Bit 8 controls the leftmost dot, bit 7 controls the second dot, and so forth. As an example, assume memory location &HB8000 contains the number 18 (to assure this, DEF SEG = &HB800: POKE 0,18). The binary representation of 18 is 00010010. The graphics display should be as indicated in Figure 2.1.

The pixels along the topmost line of SCREEN 2 are a display of the 80 bytes numbered &HB8000–&HB804F. Program P2-4 makes use of this numbering scheme to animate a dot, which moves across the top of the screen.

Program P2-4: GRAPHICS SCREEN POKES

```
10 'PROGRAM P2-4  (GRAPHICS SCREEN POKES)
20 'Animates a dot using POKE
100 '====================================
110 KEY OFF: SCREEN 2: CLS
120 DEF SEG = &HB800
130 FOR K = 0 TO 79
140  FOR I = 0 TO 8
150   READ X: POKE K,X
160  NEXT I
170  RESTORE
```

```
180 NEXT K
190 DATA 128, 64, 32, 16, 8, 4, 2, 1, 0
```

By sequentially storing the numbers 128, 64, 32, 16, 8, 4, 2, 1, and 0 in a memory location, the program will first display the leftmost bit of the memory location, then the second bit, then the third, etc. Finally, by storing a 0 in the memory location, the bits are all turned off. The program then stores the same sequence of numbers in the next memory location.

Since the topmost line of pixels is controlled by the 80 bytes of memory starting with location &HB8000, it might seem that the 81st byte would control the first 8 pixels in the second row. Not so. The 81st through 160th bytes control the *third* row of pixels, and the 161st through 240th bytes control the *fifth* row of pixels. This pattern will continue down the screen.

The first eight pixels on the second row are controlled by memory location &HBA000. (Note that &HBA000–&HB8000 = &H2000, or decimal 8192.) The 640 pixels in the second row of the screen are controlled by the 80 bytes starting at location &HBA000. The next 80 bytes control the fourth row of pixels, and so forth.

In general, if a pixel in row R is controlled by memory location M, then the pixel directly below is controlled by memory location M + 8192 if R is even, and by M − 8112 (8112 = 8192 − 80) if R is odd. (Similarly, we can calculate the address of the dot above a given location.)

Program P2-5 illustrates the vertical addressing of SCREEN 2 by displaying a sequence of backslash characters along the left screen boundary.

Program P2-5: GRAPHICS SCREEN ADDRESSING

```
10 'PROGRAM P2-5  (GRAPHICS SCREEN ADDRESSING)
20 'Illustrates addressing of SCREEN 2
100 '=====================================
110 KEY OFF: SCREEN 2: CLS
120 DEF SEG = &HB800
130 FOR K = 0 TO 100
```

```
140   READ X: POKE K*80,X
150   READ X: POKE K*80+8192,X
160   I = I + 1: IF I = 4 THEN I = 0 : RESTORE
170 NEXT K
180 DATA 128, 64, 32, 16, 8, 4, 2, 1
```

MEMORY USAGE BY GRAPHICS SCREEN 1

The medium-resolution graphics screen (SCREEN 1) permits display of 320 pixels on each line of the screen. Since this is half the number provided in high-resolution graphics (SCREEN 2), it may seem that fewer bytes of memory will be needed. However, since SCREEN 1 display includes the possibility of color graphics, it is necessary to provide memory space for storage of color codes.

This new set of requirements for control of the pixels in medium resolution is satisfied by assigning two bits to each pixel. As a result, each byte in the graphics page of memory controls the display of 4 pixels. Figure 2.2 shows the assignment of bits for memory location &HB8000 to the first four pixels in the top row of SCREEN 1. Each pixel on the graphics screen is similarly under the control of two bits of a byte of memory.

The contents of these two bits can then be read as a binary number which identifies the color of the pixel. If the binary number is 00, then the pixel is displayed in color 0 of the currently specified palette. (In this case the pixel appears in the background color and looks like it is turned off.) If the binary number is 01 the pixel is displayed in color 1 of the current palette. If the binary number is 10 (decimal 2) the pixel is displayed in color 2, and if the binary number is 11 (decimal 3) the pixel is displayed in color 3 of the current palette.

	bit number							
memory location &HB8000	8	7	6	5	4	3	2	1
display screen								
pixel number	1		2		3		4	

Figure 2.2

To illustrate, say we want to have the upper left dot displayed in color 1 of the currently specified palette. The number 1, in binary form, is 01. This is the bit pattern we want in the two bits associated with the upper left screen pixel. If all other pixels under the control of memory location &HB8000 are to appear in the background color, location &HB8000 should be made to contain the bit pattern 01000000 (decimal 64).

If the upper left pixel is to appear in color 2 (binary 10) of the current palette, then memory location &HB8000 will contain the bit pattern 10000000 (decimal 128). If the pixel is to appear in color 3, then &HB8000 will contain 11000000 (decimal 192). [In each of these examples the other pixels under the control of &HB8000 will appear in the background color, since they are displayed in color 0 (binary 00).]

Program P2-6 stores a sequence of numbers in memory location &HB8000. As a result, each of the four pixels which it controls will display each of the four colors in the current palette.

Program P2-6: COLOR CODING

```
10 'PROGRAM P2-6  (COLOR CODING)
20 'Illustrates color control
100 '================================
110 KEY OFF: SCREEN 1,0: CLS
120 DEF SEG = &HB800
130 FOR P = 0 TO 1
140  COLOR 0, P
150  FOR I = 0 TO 15
160   LOCATE 8,1: PRINT "pixel";INT(I/4)
170   PRINT "palette color";3-(I MOD 4)
180   PRINT "palette number"; P
190   READ X: POKE 0,X
200    IF INKEY$ = "" THEN 200
210  NEXT I
220  RESTORE
230 NEXT P
240 DATA 192, 128, 64, 0
250 DATA 48, 32, 16, 0
260 DATA 12, 8, 4, 0
270 DATA 3, 2, 1, 0
280 DATA 16, 12, 8, 4, 3, 2, 1
290 IF INKEY$ = "" THEN 290
```

Although most of the graphics presented in this book will not use the above information directly, there are occasions when it aids in producing a specific image. In general, however, it is useful to know some of the underlying structure of the graphics display. Such knowledge provides a better understanding of the capabilities and limitations of BASIC.

Chapter 3

The Graphics Language of IBM PC BASIC

BASIC provides a wide range of graphics capabilities. The following examples illustrate the use and capabilities of the graphics statements. The descriptions which accompany the programs explain the use of commands and point out some of the options that are available. For more complete descriptions, consult Chapter 4 of the IBM PC BASIC manual.

In each of these programs it is assumed that you are using advanced BASIC (BASICA), and that the display is providing color graphics via the Color/Graphics adapter. Since the image obtained will be dependent on the display screen you may find it necessary to vary the color selections to get good results on your display.

SCREEN, KEY, CLS, COLOR, PSET, PRESET, LINE

Although the IBM PC provides three display modes, we will no longer be using the text screen for graphics. The medium-resolution graphics mode (SCREEN 1) and the high-resolution graphics mode (SCREEN 2) will be used for all display purposes. Each of these has been used in earlier examples, and the characteristics of each has been described; therefore, we will be brief here.

The selection of display mode is made by the SCREEN statement which, for graphics purposes, has one of the following formats:

```
SCREEN 1 [,burst]
SCREEN 2
```

Burst is a color parameter. Burst = 0 means color is turned on, while Burst = 1 (or any other nonzero value) turns color off, so that only black and white images are produced. Burst is not an option when selecting the high-resolution display mode, since that mode is not capable of displaying colors. Note also that the *apage* and *vpage* options are not available when selecting either of the graphics screens. Those options are for use with the text screen only.

Recall from Chapter 2 that SCREEN 1 and SCREEN 2 each use the same range of memory (&HB8000–&HBBFFF) for display purposes. There is really only one graphics page, but two modes of displaying that page. When the mode is selected, several other options are also determined. For example, SCREEN 1 identifies WIDTH as 40, while SCREEN 2 sets WIDTH to be 80. If we want labels of various size on each screen, we must make special provisions for them. (This can be done by POKEing bit patterns into specific memory locations. An easier alternative is to use DRAW graphics, as described later in this chapter.)

KEY and CLS are not exclusively graphics commands, but they certainly affect the graphics display. In most instances, we would want to invoke KEY OFF early in the program so that the soft key display does not distract from the graphics image.

The CLS statement may be used several times within a program to provide a clear screen for the development of images. Notice that it is not necessary to use CLS to change the whole screen background color, as was the case in the text mode. If colors are changed by the COLOR statement, then the background color is immediately changed. This is because the graphics mode interprets the display page of memory in a different way than text mode. (Refer to Chapter 2, Memory Usage by Graphics Screen 1.)

The COLOR statement cannot be used in association with SCREEN 2 display mode. When used with medium resolution graphics, the format is

```
COLOR [background] [, palette].
```

While background color can be set to one of 16 values (0 through 15), only two palettes are available. The selection of a palette identifies three colors which may then be selected for the foreground color. As a result, at any one time, at most four colors can be displayed on the screen. When drawing lines, circles, or points, or when painting regions of the screen, we can choose a color of 0, 1, 2, 3 to draw in the background color (0) or one of the three others in the currently specified palette. Tables 3.1 and 3.2 show the color selections available.

Table 3.1 Background Colors

0	Black	8	Gray
1	Blue	9	Light Blue
2	Green	10	Light Green
3	Cyan	11	Light Cyan
4	Red	12	Light Red
5	Magenta	13	Light Magenta
6	Brown	14	Yellow
7	White	15	High-intensity White

Table 3.2 Palette Color Selections

Palette 0		**Palette 1**	
Color 0	Background	Color 0	Background
Color 1	Green	Color 1	Cyan
Color 2	Red	Color 2	Magenta
Color 3	Brown	Color 3	White

The most fundamental of the graphics statements are PSET and PRESET. They make it possible to turn individual pixels on and off. While it is convenient to use LINE and CIRCLE statements when programming graphics displays, it would be possible to get by with only PSET or PRESET.

The format of these statements is

```
PSET (x,y) [,color]
PRESET (x,y) [,color]
```

where (x,y) refers to the point that is to be turned on or off, and *color* identifies the color chosen from the present palette. Actually, these statements always turn dots on; the dot appears to be turned off if the color is the same as that of the surrounding dots.

Note: While the COLOR statement is not acceptable when in the high-resolution graphics mode, PSET and PRESET may still specify a color. In this mode, colors 0 or 2 will select black, and colors of 1 or 3 will select white.

It may seem that PSET and PRESET each performs the same function: They each turn on dots. The difference between them is evident only if no color is specified. Then PSET will use a default color of 3 (1 in SCREEN 2) while PRESET will use a default value of 0.

> **NOTE:** Programs P1-1 and P1-2 illustrate the use of PSET and PRESET.

The first example program in this chapter draws the simple image shown in Figure 3.1. The house is a free-hand drawing on graph paper. In preparation for producing the image on the graphics screen, a coordinate system is established [(0,0) in the upper left-hand corner of the graph paper] and coordinates are listed for each line segment endpoint.

Line 120 of Program P3-1 identifies SCREEN 2 (the high-resolution graphics screen) as the drawing and display screen. KEY OFF clears text line 25, which is a distraction in graphics displays. CLS then clears the screen, in preparation for drawing.

Program P3-1: SIMPLE HOUSE

```
10 'PROGRAM P3-1  (SIMPLE HOUSE)
20 'Uses SCREEN, KEY, LINE
100 '==============================
110 'Set screen parameters
120 SCREEN 2: KEY OFF: CLS
200 '==============================
210 'Simple house
220 LINE (40,40) - (60,10)
230 LINE - (160,10)
240 LINE - (170,35)
250 LINE - (170,80)
260 LINE - (140,85)
270 LINE (140,40) - (160,10)
280 LINE (40,40) - (140,85),,B
```

> **NOTE:** The statement SCREEN 2 will clear the screen if the screen previously displayed was other than the high-resolution graphics screen. In that case, CLS is not needed.

Screen 2 provides the highest resolution graphics available on the IBM PC. The display screen is a 640 × 200 dot matrix. The upper left corner is identified as position (0,0) and the lower right as (639,199). Any individual dot (pixel) can be addressed (and thus turned ON or OFF).

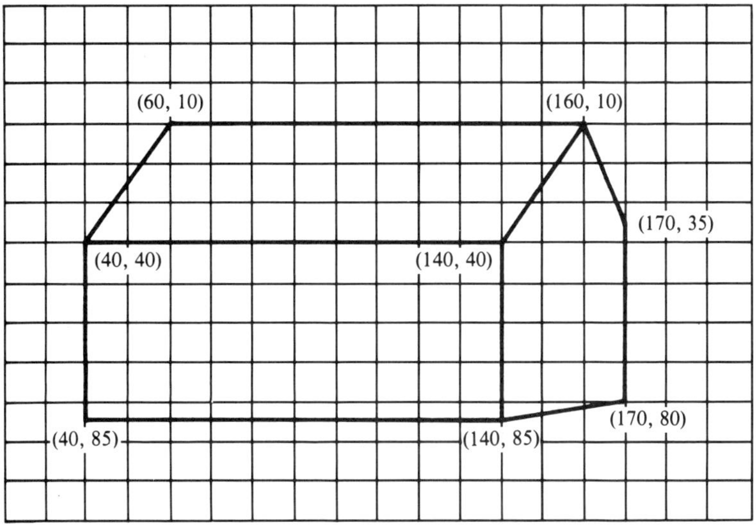

Figure 3.1

The line segments are drawn by the LINE statements of program lines 220–280 of Program P3-1. The LINE statement is quite versatile. Its format is

```
LINE [x1,y1)] - (x2,y2) [,[color][,B[F]]
[,style]]
```

We will illustrate the use of each of the options in the programs that lie ahead.

The statements in program lines 220 and 270 draw the line segments connecting the endpoints specified there. Program lines 230–260 draw continuation lines which connect the most recently plotted point to the point specified in the program line.

Program line 280 uses an option available for the LINE statement. The B option draws a box with horizontal and vertical sides as determined by the specified coordinates, which are interpreted as the coordinates of the diagonal corners of the box. (The BF option will be illustrated in Program P3-3.)

Since no color has been specified for the LINE statements in this program, the default color of white is used. In SCREEN 2 mode the only color choices are black and white. (There are times when we might want to use black to draw a line. For example, in an interactive or animated image, we might want to erase part of a previously drawn line.)

Style is used to specify a pattern to be used when a line is drawn. The pattern is specified by a 16-bit binary number. To design a line style, start with a row of 16 blocks (the bit positions). Put 0s in the bit positions which are to be off and 1s in the bit positions which are to be on. When the pattern is decided, convert the resulting binary number to its hexadecimal or decimal form. When that number is entered as the style parameter in a LINE statement, the corresponding pattern will be used when drawing the indicated line or box. (Don't try to use a line style with the filled box (BF) option. Better still, try it; no harm can come from experimenting, but a lot of learning will occur.)

The selection of a line style is illustrated in Figure 3.2.
The line style this pattern identifies will result in alternating short and long dashes.

To have the hidden edges of the house drawn in this dashed mode, add the following lines to Program P3-1:

```
290 LINE (60,10)-(70,35),,,&HF33C
300 LINE (40,85)-(70,80),,,&HF33C
310 LINE (70,35)-(170,80),,B,&HF33C
```

RELATIVE COORDINATES

So far the images we have drawn were identified by the screen coordinates of the endpoints of the line segments to be drawn. The coordinates given were identified relative to the screen origin (0,0) at the upper left of the screen. There are occasions when it is not convenient to give the coordinates relative to the origin, but it would be better to give coordinates relative to some other point. This is possible, using relative coordinate specification of points.

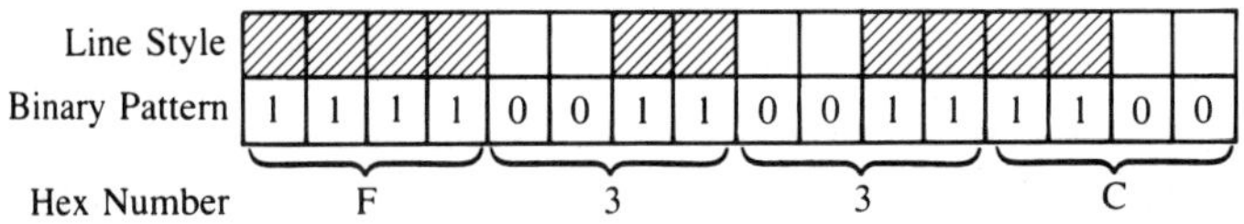

Figure 3.2 Line Styling

The notation STEP (A,B) identifies a point which is displaced A units horizontally and B units vertically from the last point referenced.

Program P3-2 is an extension of P3-1, and uses relative coordinates within a subroutine that draw windows at specified locations on the house. Subroutines are convenient for drawing graphics components which are repeated at several locations in an image; relative coordinates are especially useful in such subroutines.

Program P3-2: HOUSE WITH WINDOWS

```
10 'PROGRAM P3-2  (HOUSE WITH WINDOWS)
20 'Uses relative coordinates
100 '====================================
110 'Set screen parameters
120 SCREEN 2: KEY OFF: CLS
200 '====================================
210 'Simple house
220 LINE (40,40) - (60,10)
230 LINE - (160,10)
240 LINE - (170,35)
250 LINE - (170,80)
260 LINE - (140,85)
270 LINE (140,40) - (160,10)
280 LINE (40,40) - (140,85),,B
290 PSET (55,45): GOSUB 350
300 PSET (84,45): GOSUB 350
310 PSET (113,45): GOSUB 350
320 END
330 '====================================
340 'Window drawing subroutine
350 LINE - STEP (12,16),,B
360 LINE STEP (-6,0) - STEP (0,-16)
370 LINE STEP (-6,8) - STEP (12,0)
380 RETURN
```

Before calling the subroutine, the location of the upper left corner of the window is identified by the PSET statement. Within the subroutine line 350 draws a box extending 12 units horizontally and 16 units vertically from the specified corner. Lines 360 and 370 draw vertical and horizontal divisions in the window.

NOTES

1. The relative form of specifying points is available for use with the LINE, CIRCLE, PSET, and PRESET statements.
2. In BASIC 2.0, the WINDOW statement causes relative coordinate specification of points to be misinterpreted. However, this is corrected in BASIC 2.1. Although relative coordinates provide a convenient means of identifying points, they must be used with care.

WINDOW

Although the resolution of the high-resolution screen is desirable, the image we have generated with Program P3-1 occupies only the upper left corner of the screen. If we want it to fill a larger portion of the screen, we could go back to the beginning and identify the line segment endpoints using a different scale; or, we could use the WINDOW statement:

```
WINDOW [[SCREEN] (x1,y1) - (x2,y2)]
```

This will redefine the display screen coordinate system. Insert the following line into Program P3-1:

```
130 WINDOW SCREEN (0,0) - (190,90)
```

The upper left corner is now identified as (0,0) (no change here), and the lower right corner is (190,90). All other points are scaled proportionately. As a result, the image that is drawn will fill a larger portion of the screen.

We have proposed using the SCREEN option of WINDOW. With this option specified, the positive direction of the vertical axis is *downward* (as it is without the WINDOW statement). If the SCREEN option is not specified, the positive direction of the vertical axis is *upward*. The statement

```
WINDOW (0,0) - (190,90)
```

would identify the lower left corner as (0,0) and the upper right as (190,90).

With the SCREEN option included, the resulting display screen coordinate system is referred to as a *left-hand* coordinate system. With the SCREEN option left out, the coordinate system is called a *right-hand* system. While left-hand coordinate systems are frequently used on graphics computers, many people prefer the right-hand system. WINDOW provides that option, and other features as well.

Note that if line 130 is entered as

```
130 WINDOW (0,0) - (190,90)
```

and nothing else is changed, the resulting coordinate system will cause the house to be drawn upside down.

NOTES AND SUGGESTIONS

1. The WINDOW statement is not available on versions of BASIC prior to version 2.0.

2. The coordinates specified by the WINDOW statement are referred to as *world* coordinates, since they refer to the "world" the programmer is describing. The built-in screen coordinates are referred to as *physical* coordinates. More will be said on this matter in the comments which accompany Program P3-5.

3. WINDOW changes the scale of the display screen, and hence changes the scale of the displayed image. It does not affect the size of text characters that are PRINTed on the graphics screen. Experiment with the following replacements for line 130. Can you predict the results **before** running the program?

   - 130 WINDOW (−100, −100) − (200,200)
   - 130 WINDOW SCREEN (20,20) − (90,90)
   - 130 WINDOW SCREEN (0,0) − (639,199)

   After trying the above, try some of your own. Note that on some occasions no part of the house will be visible on the screen.

4. Beginning graphics programmers frequently have difficulty with WINDOW. We will use it periodically to maintain familiarity. Be sure you can use it well now. A poor understanding of WINDOW will make the going rougher when we get to VIEW (later in this chapter).

5. With a WINDOW in effect, try adding the dashed line mode (line styling) to display the hidden line segments which define the rear of the house. Note that the line style is not scaled by the choice of window parameters.

PAINT

Program P3-3 is an extension of Program P3-1. We are now using SCREEN 1 for display purposes in order to provide color images (line 120). Note that the WINDOW statement, as discussed above, is added in line 130. Line 140 identifies a background color of 1 (BLUE) and identifies palette 0 for foreground selections.

Program P3-3: PAINTED HOUSE

```
10 'PROGRAM P3-3  (PAINTED HOUSE)
20 'Adds COLOR, PAINT
100 '============================
110 'Set screen parameters
120 SCREEN 1,0: KEY OFF: CLS
130 WINDOW SCREEN (0,0) - (190,90)
140 COLOR 1,0
200 '============================
210 'Simple house
220 LINE (40,40) - (60,10)
230 LINE - (160,10)
240 LINE - (170,35)
250 LINE - (170,80)
260 LINE - (140,85)
270 LINE (140,40) - (160,10)
280 LINE (40,40) - (140,85),,B
300 '============================
310 'Painted house
320 PAINT (100,70),2,3
330 PAINT (150,70),2,3
340 TIL1$ = CHR$(187) + CHR$(238)
350 PAINT (100,30),TIL1$,3
360 LINE (65,65) - (80,84),0,BF
370 LINE (0,60) - (40,60)
380 LINE (170,60) - (190,60)
390 PAINT (150,88),1,3
400 LINE (101,65) - (120,75),3,B
410 TIL2$ = CHR$(0)+CHR$(20)+CHR$(20)+CHR$(20)+CHR$(20)
420 PAINT (113,70),TIL2$,3
```

As lines 220–280 draw the outline of the house, the lines are drawn in color 3 of palette 0, so the color should be brown. Brown does not show well on many color monitors, so you may not actually see a brown image on yours. Note that color 3 was not specified for drawing purposes. It is the default color, which the computer uses if no color is identified.

We next paint the sides of the house (lines 320, 330) using the PAINT statement. It has the format

```
PAINT (x,y) [[,paint] [,boundary] [,back-
ground]]
```

Let's consider these parameters individually. *Background* allows painting (actually tile painting) over an already painted area. We will not be using this option in the current example. (See note 7 on page 35.)

Boundary identifies the color of the boundary of the region to be painted. The boundary may be a sequence of lines, arcs, or other painted regions. The coordinates (x,y) identify a point within the region. The entire region is painted over in the color specified by *paint*.

Lines 320 and 330 paint the sides of the house. In each case the PAINT statement identifies a point within the region to be painted, then specifies the paint color (2 in these cases) and the boundary color (3 here). The choice of point is arbitrary, but it must be within a region which is totally enclosed by a boundary of the specified boundary color.

Lines 340 and 350 demonstrate an option which is available for the PAINT statement: *tiling*. Line 340 defines a string TIL1$ which specifies the tiling pattern used in line 350. The pattern used here is essentially a checkerboard, with alternating color 2 (red in this palette) and color 3 (brown in this palette) pixels.

Figure 3.3 shows how the checkerboard pattern is translated into the string TIL1$.

The tiling pattern defined by TIL1$ covers a rectangular area which is four pixels wide and two pixels high. When the pattern is called for by the PAINT statement of line 350, it is repeated throughout the interior of the specified region.

Tiling Pattern

Color	Color	Color	Color
2	3	2	3
3	2	3	2

Binary Pattern

10	11	10	11
11	10	11	10

Decimal

187
238

TIL1$ = CHR$(187) + CHR$(238)

Figure 3.3 Tiling pattern for house roof

Tiling Pattern				Binary Pattern				Decimal
Color	Color	Color	Color					
0	0	0	0	00	00	00	00	0
0	1	1	0	00	01	01	00	20
0	1	1	0	00	01	01	00	20
0	1	1	0	00	01	01	00	20
0	1	1	0	00	01	01	00	20

TIL2$ = CHR$(0) + CHR$(20) + CHR$(20) + CHR$(20) + CHR$(20)

Figure 3.4 Tiling pattern for window.

Line 360 illustrates another way of coloring a region. The BF option of the LINE statement provides a filled box with the specified points as diagonal corners. The color specified here is the background color (color 0), which is blue in this case.

Next, lines 370 and 380 draw horizontal lines from the screen boundaries (as identified in the WINDOW statement) to the sides of the house. Line 390 then paints the region below these lines in color 1 (which is green in palette 0).

To provide some contrast, line 400 draws a box for a window, and lines 410 and 420 paint the interior in a tiling pattern. Figure 3.4 shows how the tiling pattern is defined.

NOTES AND SUGGESTIONS

1. Note that there is no need to change the WINDOW (line 130) from its form in Program P3-1, although the SCREEN has been changed.

2. The statement COLOR 1,0 identifies both a background color (color 1, which is BLUE) and a palette of colors for the foreground (in this case, palette 0). See the table on the inside front cover for a list of the colors available for background and palette colors.

   Note that only four colors may be displayed on the medium-resolution graphics screen at any one time: the background color and the three colors available in the currently specified palette. You may recall the wider selection which was available on the text screen (SCREEN 0).

3. Paint tiling is a way of providing increased variety within the four-color restriction.

4. Paint tiling is not available in versions of BASIC prior to version 2.0.

5. The tiling pattern is not scaled by changes in the WINDOW parameters.

6. The tiling patterns identified by TIL1$ and TIL2$ were arbitrarily chosen. Design some of your own.

7. We have not used the *background* option of the PAINT statement. To see its effect, first redefine TIL2$ in line 400 as **TIL2$ = CHR$(0) + CHR$(170) + CHR$(170).** The tiling pattern will consist of one horizontal line in color 0, then two lines in color 2. Since the background color is also in color 2, the tiling pattern will not be repeated; when the tiling pattern coincides with the background for two successive lines, the tiling is terminated.

   The *background* attribute of PAINT provides a way to have the tiling continue. Rewrite the end of Program P3-3 as follows:

```
410 TIL2$ = CHR$(0) + CHR$(170) + CHR$(170)
420 TIL3$ = CHR$(170)
430 PAINT (113,70),TIL2$,3,TIL3$
```

   With the background attribute identified with the background color, the tiling pattern will continue until the pattern fills the region bounded by color 3, as specified. If TIL2$ is defined as

```
TIL2$ = CHR$(0) + CHR$(170) + CHR$(170) +
CHR$(170)
```

   the tiling will terminate without filling the region, even if the background attribute is specified. Giving the background attribute will cause PAINT to continue if no more than two lines of the tiling pattern match the background.

8. The tiling patterns above have been specified in decimal. They could also be given in hexadecimal form.

9. A line which was drawn using a line style is not an effective boundary for a region that is to be painted.

CIRCLE

Program P3-4 adds a car to the picture. The new part of the program (lines 520–610) uses the BF option of the LINE statement, along with two variations of CIRCLE, to draw the car. Lines 580 and 600 draw full circles with center at the specified point and radius 6. The circles are painted by lines 590 and 610. These circles are the wheels of the car.

Program P3-4: HOUSE AND CAR

```
10 'PROGRAM P3-4  (HOUSE AND CAR)
20 'Adds CIRCLE
100 '==============================
110 'Set screen parameters
120 SCREEN 1,0: KEY OFF: CLS
130 COLOR 1,0: PI = 3.141593
140 WINDOW SCREEN (0,0) - (190,90)
200 '==============================
210 'Simple house
220 LINE (40,40) - (60,10)
230 LINE - (160,10)
240 LINE - (170,35)
250 LINE - (170,80)
260 LINE - (140,85)
270 LINE (140,40) - (160,10)
280 LINE (40,40) - (140,85),,B
300 '==============================
310 'Painted house
320 PAINT (100,70),2,3
330 PAINT (150,70),2,3
340 TIL1$ = CHR$(187) + CHR$(238)
350 PAINT (100,30),TIL1$,3
360 LINE (65,65) - (80,84),0,BF
370 LINE (0,60) - (40,60)
380 LINE (170,60) - (190,60)
390 PAINT (150,88),1,3
400 LINE (101,65) - (120,75),3,B
410 TIL2$ = CHR$(0)+CHR$(20)+CHR$(20)+CHR$(20)+CHR$(20)
420 PAINT (113,70),TIL2$,3
500 '==============================
510 'Add car to image
520 LINE (15,75) - (51,84),0,BF
530 LINE (15,68) - (32,78),0,BF
540 LINE (51,82) - (53,84),0,BF
550 LINE (20,69) - (31,74),1,BF
560 CIRCLE (15,84),14,0,-PI/2,-PI
570 PAINT (13,82),0
580 CIRCLE (15,83),6
590 PAINT (15,83)
600 CIRCLE (43,83),6
610 PAINT (43,83)
```

Line 560 uses an option of CIRCLE to draw a quarter circle. The center (15,84), radius (14), and color (0) are given. The last two parameters provide the starting (PI/2) and ending (PI) angles of the arc to be drawn (PI is defined in line 130). These starting and ending angles must be given in radian measure (for a summary of radian measure, see Appendix 5).

The minus signs which prefix the starting and ending angles cause radius lines to be drawn, which connect the circle center to the ends of the arc. Without these minus signs the arc would still be drawn but the radial lines would be missing.

Line 570 paints the interior of the quarter circular region defined in line 560, using color 0 of the current palette.

NOTE: The CIRCLE statement has many options. The format of the statement is

```
CIRCLE (x,y),r [,color, [start,end [,aspect]]]
```

Program P3-4 identified values for each of the options except *aspect*. When aspect is not identified, a default value of 5/6 is assigned when SCREEN 1 is in use and the value of 5/12 when SCREEN 2 is in use. These choices are made because of the relative scaling of the display screens. The default values of aspect are chosen to guarantee that the circle drawn is indeed circular.

Choosing aspect value other than the default values will generate an ellipse. We will give some attention to ellipses in Chapter 7. For the present it would be good to experiment with some ellipses. You could position one in the sky as a blimp, for example.

VIEW

Program P3-5 is the last in this sequence of example programs. The drawing of house and car is still done in lines 200–610, but an additional line (620) is added, which turns the drawing routine into a subroutine. Line 150 defines a viewport (VIEW) and line 160 calls the subroutine. Line 170 defines a new viewport and line 180 calls the subroutine again.

Program P3-5: NEIGHBORHOOD

```
10 'PROGRAM P3-5  (NEIGHBORHOOD)
20 'Adds VIEW
100 '==============================
```

```
110 'Set screen parameters
120 SCREEN 1,0: KEY OFF: CLS
130 WINDOW SCREEN (0,0) - (190,90)
140 COLOR 1,0: PI = 3.141593
150 VIEW (160,100) - (319,199)
160 GOSUB 220
170 VIEW (0,100) - (160,199)
180 GOSUB 220
190 END
200 '=============================
210 'Simple house
220 LINE (40,40) - (60,10)
230 LINE - (160,10)
240 LINE - (170,35)
250 LINE - (170,80)
260 LINE - (140,85)
270 LINE (140,40) - (160,10)
280 LINE (40,40) - (140,85),,B
300 '=============================
310 'Painted house
320 PAINT (100,70),2,3
330 PAINT (150,70),2,3
340 TIL1$ = CHR$(187) + CHR$(238)
350 PAINT (100,30),TIL1$,3
360 LINE (65,65) - (80,84),0,BF
370 LINE (0,60) - (40,60)
380 LINE (170,60) - (190,60)
390 PAINT (150,88),1,3
400 LINE (101,65) - (120,75),3,B
410 TIL2$ = CHR$(0)+CHR$(20)+CHR$(20)+CHR$(20)+CHR$(20)
420 PAINT (113,70),TIL2$,3
500 '=============================
510 'Add car to image
520 LINE (15,75) - (51,84),0,BF
530 LINE (15,68) - (32,78),0,BF
540 LINE (51,82) - (53,84),0,BF
550 LINE (20,69) - (31,74),1,BF
560 CIRCLE (15,84),14,0,-PI/2,-PI
570 PAINT (13,82),0
580 CIRCLE (15,83),6
590 PAINT (15,83)
600 CIRCLE (43,83),6
610 PAINT (43,83)
620 RETURN
```

The effect of VIEW is to define a rectangular region of the display screen as *active*. When VIEW is set, drawing will take place only on the active region.

The statement **VIEW (160,100)–(319,199)** identifies the lower right quarter of the screen as being active. The currently defined WINDOW is mapped onto this viewport. (In our earlier images, you might consider that while VIEW was not specified, the entire screen was established as the viewport.) As a result, the point on the screen which usually would be identified with (physical) coordinates (160,100) now has (world) coordinates (0,0). The point on the screen which would usually be identified with (physical) coordinates (319,199) now has (world) coordinates (190,90). WINDOW and VIEW work together to identify the active part of the screen and to establish a new coordinate system there.

NOTES AND SUGGESTIONS

1. VIEW has another option: SCREEN. When written as

```
VIEW SCREEN (160,100)-(319,199)
```

the currently specified WINDOW is mapped onto the entire graphics screen, but the only part of an image that will be visible is the part which lies within the viewport (lower right quarter of the screen). Insert option SCREEN in lines 150 and 170 to see the effect. In order to have the PAINT work properly, you should also add the two lines

```
322 PAINT (45,70),2,3
392 PAINT (45,88),1,3
```

2. Note that both VIEW and WINDOW provide opportunities for scaling an image.
3. Experiment with other viewports and windows. Arrange to draw two houses at the bottom of the screen and three smaller ones at the top of the screen.
4. VIEW does not scale paint tilings or labels.
5. The complete format for VIEW is

```
VIEW [[SCREEN] [(x1,y1) - (x2,y2)[,[color]
[,[boundary]]]]]
```

If no options are specified, VIEW returns to a full screen viewport.

The *color* option, when selected, will fill the viewport with the color specified. The color is chosen from the currently specified palette.

The *boundary* option also identifies a color from the current palette. This color is used to draw a box around the viewport. If *boundary* is not specified, no box is drawn.

DRAW

The DRAW statement provides a complete graphics language in itself. The range of options is very wide, to the extent that they could not be addressed adequately in a few pages. Rather than attempt to do so, we give here example programs which are intended to suggest the power of this statement and the type of applications it provides.

The images provided by DRAW could be called *string graphics*, because the DRAW statement is always applied to a string. The string is actually a set of coded commands. To illustrate, the statement **DRAW "R5 U10 L5 D10"** is an instruction to draw to the right five units, then up ten units, then left five units, then down ten units. A rectangle would result.

In addition to the up, down, right, and left instructions, it is possible to direct diagonal movement, movement to any arbitrary point, and movement with or without plotting. Further, a defined string, such as ST$ = "R5 U10 L5 D10" can be rotated, scaled, and concatenated with other strings. The images, or portions of them, can be colored and painted. As suggested above, the range of possibilities is very broad. Refer to DRAW in the IBM PC BASIC reference manual for a complete list of options.

Program P3-6 uses the DRAW statement to define and produce the upper-case Greek letter sigma (Σ). While this character is provided for the text screen, it is not readily available for either of the graphics screens. We define the symbol by first mapping it on graph paper, as shown in Figure 3.5. It is drawn within a 7×7 grid, and we use the lower left corner of the grid as a base reference point.

Program P3-6: SIGMA

```
10 'PROGRAM P3-6  (SIGMA)
20 'Uses DRAW to print a character on the graphics
screen
100 '=====================================
110 SCREEN 1: CLS: KEY OFF
120 SIGMA$ = "BE5 U1 L5 F3 G3 R5 U1 BD1 BR3"
130 PSET (10,20):'Set position
140 DRAW SIGMA$
150 PSET (10,190),2:'Set position and color
160 FOR I = 1 TO 5
170  DRAW SIGMA$
180 NEXT I
```

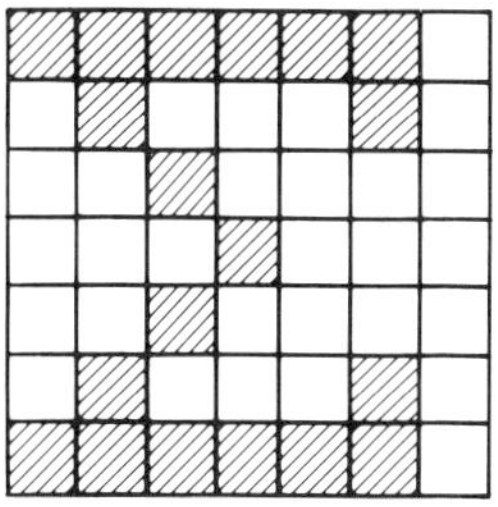

Figure 3.5

Next, the character pattern is translated to a string. First move, without drawing, from the base reference point to the top right of the character (BE5). Then move up one unit (U1), left five (L5), diagonally down and right three units (F3), diagonally down and left three units (G3), then right five (R5), and finally up one unit (U1). This completes the character. In order that the character can easily be used with a sequence of other characters, we add two more instructions: BD1 and BR3. These last two do not draw (because of the presence of B), but identify the last referenced point to be the appropriate starting point for another character.

Putting the above instructions together, we can define the string SIGMA$ = "BE5 U1 L5 F3 G3 R5 U1 BD1 BR3". The character can then be printed at any screen location by specifying the location at which the lower left corner of the character should be located, then DRAWing the string SIGMA$. Program P3-6 places the character near the upper left corner of the screen, then displays a sequence of five characters at the bottom of the screen.

Using the DRAW statement in this way permits us to place strings at any location on the graphics screens.

The DRAW statement also has an option that allows a string to be rotated by a specified angle before it is drawn. The angle (Turning Angle) must be specified in degrees, in the range −360 to +360. (This option is not available in versions of BASIC prior to Version 2.0.) To see this option at work, replace line 170 of Program P3-6 by

```
170 DRAW "TA 20;XSIGMA$;"
```

This uses SIGMA$ as a substring. Before the character is drawn, it is rotated through an angle of 20 degrees.

The angular rotation of a shape which is defined by a string provides capabilities which are not duplicated through other graphics techniques.

NOTES AND SUGGESTIONS

1. Notice that PSET can be used to identify the position at which a string is to be drawn. Unfortunately, PSET also draws a dot. The reason for using PSET here is to show that it is available. It actually serves to identify the most recently referenced position. LINE, CIRCLE, and PRESET would have similar effects. The most recently referenced position is reset by DRAW to the end position of its string.

2. An alternate way of positioning the string for drawing is to use the BM option. To see it at work, replace line 130 with

   ```
   130 DRAW "BM 10,20"
   ```

   BM results in a move (M) without drawing (B) to the specified location.

3. Shapes to be drawn by DRAW can be stored in string arrays, then accessed by number. This is done in Program P5-6 to access images for animation.

Program P3-7 shows another application of the DRAW statement. In this case the string to be drawn is quite simple: a single R40 (draw right 40 units). The string is drawn repeatedly. First it is drawn three times, with turning angles of 0, 120, and 240 degrees. The net result is a triangle. Next the screen is cleared, and the string is drawn four times, with turning angles of 0, 90, 180, and 270 degrees to yield a square. Again the screen is cleared, and the sequence continues. Although the first frame (the triangle) is small, the later images grow quite large. This program illustrates the approximation of a circle by regular polygons.

Program P3-7: POLYGONS --> CIRCLE

```
10 'PROGRAM P3-7   (POLYGONS --> CIRCLE)
20 'Uses DRAW to draw polygons
100 '====================================
110 SCREEN 1,0: CLS: KEY OFF: COLOR 0,1
120 ST$ = "R40"
130 FOR N = 3 TO 20
140  CLS
150  DRAW "BM140,199"
160  FOR ANGLE = 0 TO 359 STEP 360/N
170   DRAW "C3;TA=ANGLE;XST$;"
180  NEXT ANGLE
```

```
190   FOR I = 1 TO 500: NEXT I
200 NEXT N
```

Program P3-8 provides another illustration of the use of the DRAW statement. It draws a sequence of 20 randomly placed five-pointed stars. The design of the stars is based on Figure 3.6.

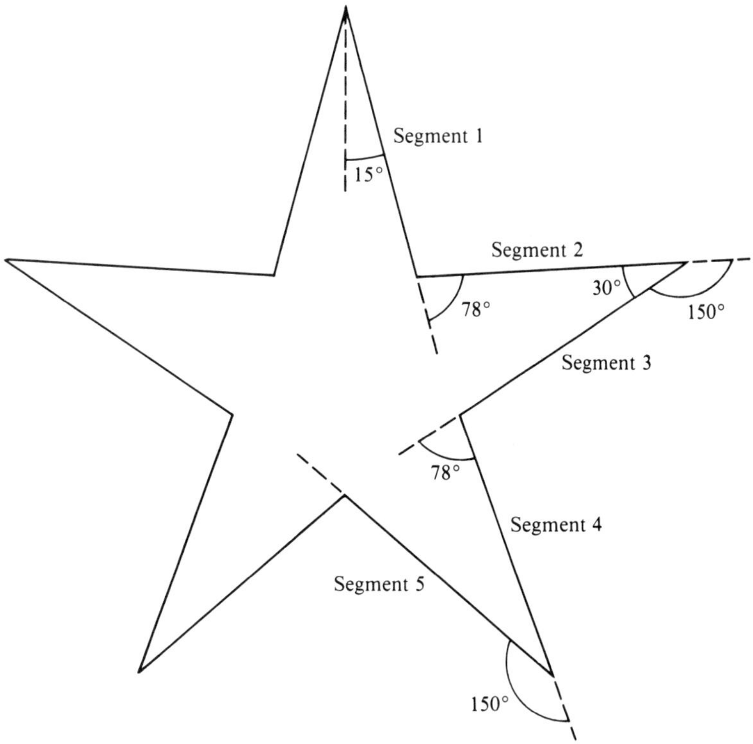

Figure 3.6

Program P3-8: STARS

```
10 'PROGRAM P3-8  (STARS)
20 'DRAW produces stars
100 '===============================
110 RANDOMIZE TIMER
```

```
120 SCREEN 1,0: COLOR 1,0: CLS: KEY OFF
130 ST$ = "D10"
140 FOR N = 1 TO 20
150 X = 320*RND: Y = 200*RND
160 GOSUB 210
170 NEXT N
180 END
190 '==================================
200 'STAR subroutine
210 A = 15
220 DRAW "BM =X;,=Y;"
230 FOR I = 1 TO 5
240  DRAW "C3;TA=A;XST$;"
250  A = A + 78
260  DRAW "TA=A;XST$;"
270  A = A - 150
280 NEXT I
290 RETURN
```

A string ST$ = ‘‘D10’’, which consists of a single draw down ten units is used for each of the ten line segments of the star. The variable A identifies the turning angle which is applied to the string as it is drawn. For segment 1, A is 15°. To change A so that the direction of movement is correct for segment 2, we add 78° to A (rotate through an additional counterclockwise angle to 78° degrees). Then, to change to the correct direction for segment 3, we subtract 150° (clockwise—therefore, subtract). The directions for segments 3 and 4 differ by a counterclockwise 78° and segments 4 and 5 differ by a clockwise 150°. Since there is a pattern here, it is programmed into a FOR–NEXT loop (lines 230–280 of Program P3-8).

The next example of the use of DRAW produces an axis system with tic marks along the axes. The tic marks are defined by the two strings TIC$ and TIK$, which are defined in lines 130 to 140 of Program P3-9. Each provides a horizontal line segment of five units' length and a vertical tic mark. The vertical tic mark is twice as high in TIK$ as in TIC$. By DRAWing TIK$ after four occurrences of TIC$, we can create a scale marking off units and multiples of five units. (The units actually represent a distance of five pixels.) This placement of tic marks is handled by the nested loops of lines 170–220.

Program P3-9: AXIS SYSTEM

```
10 'PROGRAM P3-9  (AXIS SYSTEM)
20 'DRAW graphics for axes
100 '==================================
110 SCREEN 1,0: CLS: KEY OFF:COLOR 0,1
120 WINDOW SCREEN (-64,-64) - (64,64)
130 TIC$ = "R5 NU2 ND2"
140 TIK$ = "R5 NU4 ND4"
150 FOR A = 0 TO 359 STEP 90
160  DRAW "BM160,100"
170  FOR I = 1 TO 5
180   FOR J = 1 TO 4
190    DRAW "TA=A;XTIC$;"
200   NEXT J
210   DRAW "TA=A;XTIK$;"
220  NEXT I
230 NEXT A
240 CIRCLE (0,0),20
```

An outer loop (lines 150–230) increments the turning angle through multiples of 90 degrees. As a result, four lines of tic marks are drawn: two for the positive and negative horizontal axis, and two for the vertical axis. After the axes are completed, line 240 places a circle on the graph.

There are other ways of generating axes, but this method is fairly quick and easy to program. The example also provides an opportunity to point out several characteristics of the DRAW statement.

NOTES

1. The WINDOW statement in line 120 was placed there to show that DRAW does not take notice of it.
2. The line of tic marks, when rotated, is scaled so that vertical units are equivalent to horizontal units (with no effort by the programmer). This is evidenced by the fact that the circle of line 240, which is centered at the intersection of the axes, intersects each axis on the same tic mark. Note that the CIRCLE statement does take note of WINDOW.
3. The rotated string is subject to some anomalies. First, look along the

vertical axis. Note that the tic marks are occasionally spaced further apart. This is because the scaling (to equate horizontal and vertical units) does not always match the pixel positions. If you are using BASIC 2.0, note that at the intersection of the axes the positive and negative horizontal axes do not meet at exactly the same level. Further, the lower half of the tic marks on the negative horizontal axis have a slight offset. These anomalies are certainly not major problems, but you should be aware of them when using rotations. (On some screens, they may barely be noticeable.)

4. The rotation, controlled by lines 150, 190, and 210, could be provided without the use of the turning angle option. Instead, use

```
150 FOR A = 0 TO 3
190 DRAW "A=A;XTIC$;"
210 DRAW "A=A;XTIK$;"
```

Note that WINDOW (line 120) provides equal numbers of horizontal and vertical units on the display screen. This does not mean that a horizontal unit is equivalent to a vertical unit. To show that they are unequal, replace line 240 with

```
240 CIRCLE (15,15),15
```

The resulting circle will not be tangent to each of the axes, as it would be if the horizontal and vertical units were equivalent. Try again, using

```
240 CIRCLE (15,20),15
```

The reason for this seeming discrepancy is due to what is called the display screen *aspect ratio.* This topic will be discussed in the Chapter 5 section, Scaling the Screen.

RELATIVE MOVES

The designation of distances used by the DRAW statement is typically in relative form. That is, a statement like **DRAW "U5"** is an instruction to draw upward five units *from the current location.* The only absolute measurements given are those associated with the M option. The statement **DRAW "M 20,20"** will draw from the present screen location to the point (20,20).

It is also possible to have M designate relative moves. This is done if the coordinates given are prefixed by a + or a − sign. For example, **DRAW "M +20,20"** will draw from the present screen location to the point which is 20 units to the right and 20 units lower on the screen.

Program P3-10 makes use of relative moves as it defines a string (LOGO$) which consists of the three triangles of the Addison-Wesley logo ( ). T1$ defines a triangle with vertex pointing downward and is used for each of the two lower triangles. T2$ is used for the upper triangle. (In BASIC 2.1, T2$ is not needed, since it is T1$ rotated through 180°. In BASIC 2.0 the rotation is not precise enough, and T2$ is needed.) Note the concatenation of T1$, T2$, and other strings to form LOGO$.

Note the use of the paint option available to DRAW (lines 130, 140).

Program P3-10: A-W LOGO

```
10 'PROGRAM P3-10  (A-W LOGO)
20 'Relative moves in DRAW
100 '=======================================
110 SCREEN 1,0: COLOR 1,0
120 KEY OFF: CLS
130 T1$ = "R20;M-10,15;M-10,-15;BM+5,5;P2,3"
140 T2$ = "R20;M-10,-15;M-10,15;BM+5,-5;P2,3"
150 LOGO$ = T1$+"C3 BM+19,-5"+T1$+"C3 BM-17,-8"+T2$
160 DRAW LOGO$
```

PMAP, POINT, AND SCREEN

The WINDOW statement permits rescaling of the screen and is a very convenient tool. However, changing the coordinates by which pixels are identified can lead to confusion. The coordinate system established by WINDOW is referred to as the *world* coordinate system, and the coordinate system established by the VIEW statement is referred to as the *physical* coordinate system. It is important that the two systems not be confused and that the relationships between the two be well understood.

Within a program there may be occasions when world coordinates are more convenient, and other occasions when physical coordinates are preferred. PMAP and POINT provide a way to obtain the physical coordinates of a point whose world coordinates are known, or to obtain the world coordinates of a point whose physical coordinates are known.

If a given point has physical coordinates (PX,PY) and world coordinates (WX,WY), then

PX = PMAP(WX,0) WX = PMAP(PX,2)
PY = PMAP(WY,1) WY = PMAP(PY,3)

POINT(*n*) can be used to obtain the physical coordinates (PX,PY) and world coordinates (WX,WY) of the last referenced point:

PX = POINT(0) WX = POINT(2)
PY = POINT(1) WY = POINT(3)

Program P3-11 illustrates the use of PMAP and POINT to position a symbol and a label on a windowed screen. Note the need for this: DRAW does not recognize WINDOWed coordinates. To properly position an image produced by DRAW, it is necessary to identify the reference point in screen coordinates. Likewise, PMAP and POINT can be useful in positioning labels which are to be PRINTed on the screen.

Program P3-11: LABELLED GRAPH

```
10 'PROGRAM P3-11  (LABELLED GRAPH)
20 'Uses PMAP, POINT
100 '========================================
110 KEY OFF: SCREEN 2: CLS
120 ARROW$ = "BM +0,-2;NM-4,-4;NM+4,-4;M-0,-15"
130 WINDOW (-6,-4) - (6,5)
140 LINE (0,-4) - (0,5)
150 LINE (-6,0) - (6,0)
160 '========================================
170 FOR X = -6 TO 6 STEP .1
180  Y = 4*X/(X*X+1)
190   IF MAX < Y THEN MAX = Y: XP = X
200   IF MIN > Y THEN MIN = Y: XQ = X
210   IF FL = 0 THEN PSET (X,Y): FL = 1
220  LINE - (X,Y)
230 NEXT X
240 '========================================
250 PX = PMAP(XP,0): PY = PMAP(MAX,1)
260 DRAW "BM =PX;,=PY;TA-20;XARROW$;"
270 V = INT(POINT(1)/8) + 1
280 H = INT(POINT(0)/8) + 2
290 LOCATE V,H: PRINT "MAX"
```

```
300 '=========================================
310 PX = PMAP(XQ,0): PY = PMAP(MIN,1)
320 DRAW "BM =PX;,=PY;TA-160;XARROW$;"
330 V = INT(POINT(1)/8) + 2
340 H = INT(POINT(0)/8) + 3
350 LOCATE V,H: PRINT "MIN"
360 LOCATE 1,1
```

Line 180 defines the graph which is drawn. Chapter 7 presents methods for producing other images like this one. Note how lines 190 and 200 identify the highest (MAX) and lowest (MIN) points of the curve. Lines 250, 260, and 310, and 320 use this information to determine the placement of arrows which call attention to these points. When the arrow is drawn, its endpoint is used by POINT (lines 270, 280 and 330, and 340) to identify the location at which a label is printed (lines 290, 350).

Program P5-2 uses SCREEN (Y,X) to determine whether a moving shape (a ball) has collided with a target block or with the shape which served as the game player's paddle. SCREEN (Y,X) yields the ASCII code of the character which is displayed in the specified screen position. A variant of the function, SCREEN (Y,X,Z), will (if Z is nonzero) yield the color code of the character which is displayed in the specified screen position (text screen only).

A second form of POINT has a capability similar to that of SCREEN. POINT (X,Y) will give the color of the pixel at graphics screen location (X,Y). This form of POINT is useful in programs which provide animation and in programs which provide menu selection using a light pen or joystick.

BSAVE AND BLOAD

The example programs that have been given so far do not require a lot of time to produce their images. Practical graphics programs may require a greater amount of time. Further, some of the program listings are lengthy. In these cases it may not be efficient to have an image created within the program which is to use it. Instead, the image can be created by one program, saved on a diskette by using the BSAVE command, and loaded again as needed by using the BLOAD command.

BSAVE will create a memory image file on diskette. Such files are denoted in the diskette directory by using an extension of .M. As the term indicates, the file is a copy of the data in a portion of the computer memory. The format of the command is

```
BSAVE filespec, offset, length
```

For *filespec*, choose any valid file name. *Offset* is the offset (within the current memory segment) to the beginning of the region of memory to be copied. The BSAVE command should be preceded by a DEF SEG statement to define the proper memory segment. *Length* refers to the number of bytes of memory to be saved in the diskette file.

There are various applications which depend on BSAVE and BLOAD, but the only one we will consider is the saving and loading of the graphics screens. To make a diskette file copy of the graphics page of memory (either medium or high resolution),

1. Define the current memory segment to begin at &HB8000 by using the statement **DEF SEG = &HB800.**
2. Copy the graphics screen with **BSAVE "PICTURE", 0, &H4000.**

> **NOTE:** The choice of DEF SEG = &HB800 means that the offset will be zero. Other segment/offset combinations can be used, but there is no advantage in doing so.

The BLOAD command will load an image from a diskette file and store it in the computer memory. The format is

```
BLOAD filespec[,offset]
```

To use BLOAD,

1. Define the current memory segment: DEF SEG = &HB800
2. Load the file: BLOAD "PICTURE",0

NOTES

1. Again, different segment/offset combinations are possible, but of no advantage.
2. Although the offset is optional when using BLOAD, it is good practice to include it. If no offset is specified, the file is loaded in the current memory segment, using the offset which was used when the file was saved.

GET AND PUT

A display on either of the graphics screens is really an interpretation of the data which is stored in the graphics page of the computer memory. The GET and PUT statements permit the transfer of data from the graphics page of memory to an array, or from an array to the graphics page.

The format of the GET statement is

```
GET (x1,y1) - (x2,y2),arrayname
```

where (x1,y1) and (x2,y2) identify the diagonal corners of a rectangle having its sides parallel to the screen boundaries. The image within this rectangle is determined by data in a portion of the graphics page of memory. GET stores this data in the numeric array specified by *arrayname*.

PUT has the format

```
PUT (x,y),arrayname [action]
```

where (x,y) is the point which is the top left corner of the rectangle which will receive the data stored in *arrayname*. This transfer can be effected in several ways; *action* identifies the method to be used.

For complete details on the use of GET and PUT, refer to the IBM PC BASIC reference manual. We will illustrate the use of these statements in the next example programs.

Program P1-10 used GET and PUT to move the image of a car across the screen. In order to discuss the use of the GET and PUT statements, that program is repeated here as Program P3-12.

Program P3-12: ANIMATED CAR

```
10 'PROGRAM P3-12  (ANIMATED CAR)
20 'Repeat of program P1-10
100 '===================================
110 PI = 3.141593
120 KEY OFF: SCREEN 1,0: COLOR 1,4: CLS
130 'Draw a car.
140 LINE (25,19) - (80,35),2,BF
150 LINE (25,5) - (50,20),2,BF
160 LINE (3,33) - (82,35),2,BF
170 LINE (32,7) - (48,18),,BF
180 CIRCLE (25,35),20,2,-PI/2,-PI
190 PAINT (22,32),2
```

```
200 CIRCLE (25,35),8
210 PAINT (25,35)
220 CIRCLE (70,35),8
230 PAINT (70,35)
240 'Store it.
250 DIM A(268)
260 GET (1,5)-(84,55),A
270 'Move it.
280 FOR I = 1 TO 200
290   PUT (I,5),A,PSET
300 NEXT I
```

Lines 140–230 draw the image, which is a collection of boxes, circles, and arcs. Line 260 stores the rectangular screen region having diagonal corners at (1,5) and (84,55) in the array A. In preparation for line 260, the array A is dimensioned in line 250.

There are three steps in determining the size of the array needed to store a given rectangular image:

1. Determine the number of pixels (X and Y) along the horizontal and vertical sides. In this case, X = 84 − 1 + 1 = 84, and Y = 55 − 5 + 1 = 51.
2. Calculate B = 4 + Y*INT((2*X + 7)/8). In this case B = 1075.
3. B is the number of bytes of storage needed. For a single precision array such as A, we require B/4 elements, so we should specify the dimension of A to be B/4 − 1 or larger. (Remember, A(0) is the first element of the array, unless you choose to use the **OPTION BASE** 1 statement.) That is why line 250 dimensions A as **DIM A(268).**

The calculation of array size will vary with the precision of the array and is also dependent on whether the rectangular image is taken from the medium-resolution screen or from the high-resolution screen. Consult the IBM PC BASIC reference manual for the details.

Note that the rectangular image saved in line 260 is slightly wider than the image of the car. This additional width is provided in order to enable effective animation. Line 290 places the stored image on the screen, with the upper left corner of the rectangle at the point (I,5). As I is increased the excess width of the rectangle serves to erase the previous image of the car.

The PSET option used by PUT in line 270 is one of five actions from which we can choose. PSET uses the stored rectangular image to replace a portion of the screen image. Another action that can be used is XOR, which is especially useful for animating an object across a background image. To see this option in use, replace the end of Program P3-12 with the following:

```
280 FOR X = 100 TO 160 STEP 15
290  C = C + 1
300  LINE (X,0) - X+14,199),C MOD 4, BF
310 NEXT X
320 FOR I = 2 TO 200
330  PUT (I-1,5),A,XOR
340  PUT (I,5),A,XOR
350 NEXT I
```

Within the FOR–NEXT loop of lines 320–350, the first use of PUT (line 330) erases the previous image, and the second use of PUT (line 340) displays the image in a new location. XOR, which is referred to as exclusive-or, is a complementary display action. Two successive complementary displays return the screen to its original condition.

To see the effect of all five of the placement actions, try Program P3-13, which modifies the last part of Program P3-12. The program produces 15 copies of the car image. The five basic actions are used to produce the images along the left side of the screen. Each of the other ten images results from using two of the actions in succession.

Program P3-13: MULTIPLE PUTS

```
10 'PROGRAM P3-13  (MULTIPLE PUT'S)
20 'Illustrates actions available for PUT
100 '=======================================
110 PI = 3.141593
120 SCREEN 1,1: COLOR 1,4: CLS: KEY OFF
130 'Draw a car.
140 LINE (25,19) - (80,35),2,BF
150 LINE (25,5) - (50,20),2,BF
160 LINE (3,33) - (82,35),2,BF
170 LINE (32,7) - (48,18),1,BF
180 CIRCLE (25,35),20,2,-PI/2,-PI
190 PAINT (22,32),2
```

```
200 CIRCLE (25,35),8
210 PAINT (25,35)
220 CIRCLE (70,35),8
230 PAINT (70,35)
240 '==========================================
250 'Store image in array A
260 DIM A(205)
270 GET (0,5)-(83,43),A
280 '==========================================
290 'Display assortment of colors on screen
300 CLS
310 FOR I = 0 TO 300 STEP 15
320 C = C+1
330 LINE (I,0) - (I+15,199),C MOD 4,BF
340 NEXT I
350 '==========================================
360 'Illustrate some options
370 PUT (0,0),A,PSET
380 PUT (0,40),A,PRESET
390 PUT (0,80),A,AND
400 PUT (0,120),A,OR
410 PUT (0,160),A,XOR
420 PUT (100,0),A,PSET: PUT (100,0),A,XOR
430 PUT (100,40),A,PRESET: PUT (100,40),A,AND
440 PUT (100,80),A,PRESET: PUT (100,80),A,OR
450 PUT (100,120),A,PRESET: PUT (100,120),A,XOR
460 PUT (100,160),A,OR: PUT (100,160),A,AND
470 PUT (200,0),A,AND: PUT (200,0),A,OR
480 PUT (200,40),A,AND: PUT (200,40),A,XOR
490 PUT (200,80),A,XOR: PUT (200,80),A,OR
500 PUT (200,120),A,XOR: PUT (200,120),A,AND
510 PUT (200,160),A,XOR: PUT (200,160),A,XOR
```

The example programs given in this chapter have been provided to illustrate the usage of the graphics language provided in IBM PC BASIC. The language has many more options than could be given in one chapter. Examples and text discussion are only the beginning of understanding of the language. The best (perhaps only) way to become proficient is to practice and experiment. If there is an aspect of the graphics language which is not clear to you, try it under a variety of situations. Develop examples to test the power and versatility of the statements. The time invested will be well spent.

Chapter 4

Application to Business Graphics

"A picture is worth a thousand words," so they say. A good visual representation can convey ideas far better than a verbal description. Graphics can have a very powerful impact when used to produce an orderly image which represents massive amounts of numerical data. While the use of graphics for this purpose is widespread, it is most commonly seen in business applications.

The examples given in this chapter make use of the graphics statements which were introduced earlier and illustrate ways to develop graphical representations of numerical information. Although the examples are brief, and the data used are limited, the techniques are appropriate for more extensive applications.

HISTOGRAM

Program P4-1 illustrates the display of organized data to form a histogram, or bar graph. The data is given in program lines 420–450 and is intended to represent monthly income figures (measured in thousands—or millions, if you prefer).

Program P4-1: HISTOGRAM

```
10 'PROGRAM P4-1  (HISTOGRAM)
20 'Example of data display
100 '===========================================
110 KEY OFF: SCREEN 1,0: CLS
120 COLOR 0,0: WINDOW (0,0) - (319,199)
130 '===========================================
```

```
140 'Identify maximum data value
150 FOR I = 1 TO 12
160  READ MONTH$, INCOME
170  IF MAX < INCOME THEN MAX = INCOME
180 NEXT I
190 RESTORE
200 '==============================================
210 'Draw and label histogram
220 FOR I= 1 TO 12
230  READ MONTH$, INCOME
240  FOR J = 1 TO 3
250   LOCATE 18+J,3*I-1: PRINT MID$(MONTH$,J,1)
260  NEXT J
270  HEIGHT = 120*INCOME/MAX
280  LEFT = 24*I-16: RIGHT = 24*I
290  LINE (LEFT,60+HEIGHT) - (RIGHT,60),1+I MOD 3,BF
300 NEXT I
310 IF INKEY$ = "" THEN 310
400 '==============================================
410 'Data for monthly income
420 DATA JAN,77, FEB,80, MAR,82
430 DATA APR,75, MAY,72, JUN,65
440 DATA JULY,60, AUGUST,64, SEPT,70
450 DATA OCT,78, NOV,85, DEC,88
```

The data are read twice within the program. Lines 150–180 read the data solely for the purpose of identifying the maximum value. MAX is used to scale the graph so that it fills, yet fits, the screen. Note that it is necessary to read the month name in order to get to the numerical data, even though the month name is not used at this time.

The data are read a second time by line 230. At this time the program will use the information in the preparation of a graphic display. Instead of reading the data twice this way, we could have read them only once, and stored them in two arrays, say MONTH$(I) and INCOME(I). Either method could be used in this example, with no real difference in effect. In programs which access large quantities of data, array storage may not be practical because it requires a large amount of memory. In such cases, of course, the data typically are not stored in DATA statements, but are accessed from a file.

As each month's name and income are read into MONTH$ and INCOME (line 230), MONTH$ is used by lines 240–260 to print the first three letters of the name as a label for the graph. The value of INCOME is used by line 270 to calculate HEIGHT, which identifies the size of the block used to represent that month's income.

Line 280 calculates the locations of the left and right sides of the monthly block, which is then drawn by line 290. Note that the color of the box is varied through all but the background color by 1 +I MOD 3.

With the histogram complete, line 310 keeps the cursor off the screen until a key is pressed.

The brevity of Program P4-1 may cause some to question the value of commercially available software which produce such images. Generally, the value of such software lies not just in a brief subroutine which produces a graphic image. The user interface, which allows a novice to enter data and obtain quality results, is not a trivial component. A quality software product is capable of receiving data by several means: from the keyboard, from a disk file, from another program, by telephone hookup, etc. Finally, a quality package will be capable of sending output not just to the screen, but also to a plotter, a printer-plotter, or to disk storage for later retrieval.

NOTES

1. Program P4-1 uses the WINDOW statement to place the (0,0) point at the lower left of the screen. Most people seem to be more at ease with this coordinate system. Throughout this book we will use both the standard coordinate system (no WINDOW statement) and systems which are developed using WINDOW.

2. If your version of BASIC is prior to version 2.0 you will not have the WINDOW statement available. Leave it out of line 120, and replace line 290 with

   ```
   290 LINE (LEFT,140-HEIGHT)-(RIGHT,140),1+I
   MOD 3,BF
   ```

   You will have to make similar adjustments to some later programs.

3. A graph is not complete until it is labelled. The intent of these example programs is to illustrate graphic techniques, and to do so with relatively short programs. So, labelling is limited. You could add a vertical scale of units to make the graph more meaningful.

ENHANCING THE HISTOGRAM

The intention of a bar graph is to present information graphically. Sometimes a more dramatic image can be more interesting to the viewer, and as a result can be more effective in conveying information. Program P4-2 draws a bar graph with a three-dimensional aspect.

Programs P4-1 and P4-2 are identical through lines 280. In Program P4-2, line 290 draws a rectangular box but does not fill it. Lines 300–340 specify points to draw the rest of the framework of a three-dimensional box. Lines 350–370 then PAINT the sides of the box.

Program P4-2: 3-D HISTOGRAM

```
10 'PROGRAM P4-2  (3-D HISTOGRAM)
20 'Imitates 3-D image
100 '==============================================
110 KEY OFF: SCREEN 1,0: CLS
120 COLOR 0,0: WINDOW (0,0) - (319,199)
130 '==============================================
140 'Identify maximum data value
150 FOR I = 1 TO 12
160  READ MONTH$, INCOME
170  IF MAX < INCOME THEN MAX = INCOME
180 NEXT I
190 RESTORE
200 '==============================================
210 'Draw and label histogram
220 FOR I= 1 TO 12
230 READ MONTH$, INCOME
240  FOR J = 1 TO 3
250   LOCATE 18+J,3*I-1: PRINT MID$(MONTH$,J,1)
260  NEXT J
270  HEIGHT = 120*INCOME/MAX
280  LEFT = 24*I-16: RIGHT = 24*I-4
290  LINE (LEFT,HEIGHT+60) - (RIGHT,60),3,B
300  LINE - (RIGHT+3,63)
310  LINE - (RIGHT+3,HEIGHT+63)
320  LINE - (LEFT+3,HEIGHT+63)
330  LINE - (LEFT,HEIGHT+60)
340  LINE (RIGHT+3,HEIGHT+63) - (RIGHT,HEIGHT+60)
350  PAINT (LEFT+5,HEIGHT+61),2,3
360  PAINT (LEFT+5,65),2,3
370  PAINT (RIGHT+1,65),2,3
```

```
380 NEXT I
390 IF INKEY$ = "" THEN 390
500 '=============================================
510 'Data for monthly income
520 DATA JAN,77, FEB,80, MAR,82
530 DATA APR,75, MAY,72, JUN,65
540 DATA JULY,60, AUGUST,64, SEPT,70
550 DATA OCT,78, NOV,85, DEC,88
```

> **NOTE:** Horizontal divisions on the boxes can make the graph easier to interpret. For efficiency when PAINTing, such divisions should be drawn *after* the box has been painted.

MULTIPLE HISTOGRAMS

Program P4-3 shows one way to display more than one set of data on a graph. This is a useful technique if the sets of data are related, as the INCOME/COST figures are here.

Program P4-3: INCOME/COST HISTOGRAM

```
10 'PROGRAM P4-3  (INCOME/COST HISTOGRAM)
20 'Two graphs; one display
100 '========================================
110 KEY OFF: SCREEN 1,0: CLS
120 COLOR 0,0: WINDOW (0,0) - (319,199)
130 '========================================
140 'Identify maximum data value
150 FOR I = 1 TO 24
160  READ MONTH$, INCOME
170  IF MAX < INCOME THEN MAX = INCOME
180 NEXT I
190 RESTORE
200 '========================================
210 A = 16: B = 0
220 FOR DAT = 1 TO 2
230 'Draw and label histogram
240  FOR I = 1 TO 12
250   READ MONTH$, INCOME
260   HEIGHT = 120*INCOME/MAX
270   LEFT = 24*I - A: RIGHT = 24*I - B
```

```
280     LINE (LEFT,60+HEIGHT) - (RIGHT,60),DAT,BF
290     IF DAT = 1 THEN GOSUB 430
300   NEXT I
310   A = 20: B = 4
320 NEXT DAT
330 '========================================
340 'Print heading for display
350 POKE &H4E,1: LOCATE 3,14: PRINT "INCOME";
360 POKE &H4E,3: PRINT "/";
370 POKE &H4E,2: PRINT "COST";
380 POKE &H4E,3
390 IF INKEY$ = "" THEN 390
400 LOCATE 23,1: END
410 '========================================
420 'Labelling subroutine
430 FOR J = 1 TO 3
440   LOCATE 18+J,3*I-1: PRINT MID$(MONTH$,J,1)
450 NEXT J
460 RETURN
470 '========================================
480 'Data for monthly income
490 DATA JAN,77, FEB,80, MAR,82
500 DATA APR,75, MAY,72, JUN,65
510 DATA JULY,60, AUGUST,64, SEPT,70
520 DATA OCT,78, NOV,85, DEC,88
530 '========================================
540 'Data for monthly costs
550 DATA JAN,70, FEB,72, MAR,72
560 DATA APR,73, MAY,70, JUN,60
570 DATA JULY,58, AUGUST,55, SEPT,65
580 DATA OCT,70, NOV,78, DEC,75
```

Two bars will be drawn for each month, one for income and one for cost, using different colors for contrast. Further, so that the one which is drawn second does not cover up the first, the second is drawn a little to the left of the first.

The blocks are all drawn by line 280. However, when DAT = 1 (reading income data) the value of LEFT is different (see lines 210, 270, and 310) than when DAT = 2. Note also that DAT controls the color of the box (line 280).

In order to print a color-coded title for the display, lines 350–380 change the color code which is stored in memory location &H4E of BASIC's Data Segment. Usually the number stored there is 3, causing characters to be printed in color number 3 of the current palette. By changing this code to 2 or 1, we can arrange that the title colors correspond to the colors used in the graph. Note that it was not necessary to use DEF SEG to identify the segment. Since no other DEF SEG statements have been used in this program, the default segment (BASIC's Data Segment) is active.

POLYGONAL GRAPHS

A bar chart is a popular way of representing data graphically. Polygon graphs are closely related. The magnitude of numbers is used to determine the height of bars for the histogram; when a polygon is drawn, these magnitudes determine the distance at which points are located above a base line. The points are connected to form the polygon (or ogive).

Program P4-4 uses the data of Program P4-1 to draw a polygon. Note the similarities between the two programs. The calculations are identical through line 270. Line 280 draws a left boundary for the polygon. As consecutive data entries are read, line 290 draws the line segments which make up the polygon. When the data have all been read, lines 310–330 provide a right side and a bottom to a polygonal region which line 340 paints.

Program P4-4: OGIVE–POLYGON GRAPH

```
10 'PROGRAM P4-4  (OGIVE - POLYGON GRAPH)
20 'Alternate to histogram
100 '========================================
110 KEY OFF: SCREEN 1,0: CLS
120 COLOR 0,0: WINDOW (0,0) - (319,199)
130 '========================================
140 'Read data and determine max
150 FOR I = 1 TO 12
160  READ MONTH$, INCOME
170  IF MAX < INCOME THEN MAX = INCOME
180 NEXT I
190 RESTORE
200 '========================================
210 'Read data, plot graph
```

```
220 FOR I = 1 TO 12
230  READ MONTH$, INCOME
240  FOR J = 1 TO 3
250   LOCATE 19+J,3*I: PRINT MID$(MONTH$,J,1)
260  NEXT J
270  HEIGHT = 120*INCOME/MAX
280  IF I = 1 THEN LINE (8,50) - (8,50+HEIGHT)
290  LINE - (24*I-4,50+HEIGHT),3
300 NEXT I
310 LINE - (296,50+HEIGHT)
320 LINE - (296,50)
330 LINE - (8,50)
340 PAINT (10,55),1,3
350 LOCATE 3,17: PRINT "INCOME"
360 IF INKEY$ = "" THEN 360
370 LOCATE 23,1: END
400 '========================================
410 'Data for monthly income
420 DATA JAN,77, FEB,80, MAR,82
430 DATA APR,75, MAY,72, JUN,65
440 DATA JULY,60, AUGUST,64, SEPT,70
450 DATA OCT,78, NOV,85, DEC,88
```

NOTE: We have used the first and last data entries to determine the heights of the sides of the polygonal region. Ideally, the lengths of the sides are influenced by the data for the adjacent months.

Program P4-5 draws a three-color polygon graph. The INCOME/COST data of Program P4-3 is used. In addition, the PROFIT (INCOME − COST) is calculated.

Program P4-5: INCOME/COSTS/PROFITS

```
10 'PROGRAM P4-5  (INCOME/COSTS/PROFITS)
20 'Displays three-color ogive
100 '==================================================
110 KEY OFF: SCREEN 1,0: CLS
120 COLOR 0,0: WINDOW (0,0) - (319,199)
130 OPTION BASE 1
140 DIM MONTH$(12), AMT(3,12)
150 'For AMT(N,I),
160 'N = 1: Income; N = 2: Costs; N = 3: Profits
```

```
170 '=====================================================
180 'Fill arrays
190 FOR I = 1 TO 12
200  READ MONTH$(I), AMT(1,I)
210  IF MAX < AMT(1,I) THEN MAX = AMT(1,I)
220 NEXT I
230 FOR I = 1 TO 12
240  READ MONTH$, AMT(2,I)
250  AMT(3,I) = AMT(1,I) - AMT(2,I)
260 NEXT I
270 '=====================================================
280 'Draw and paint graphs
290 FOR N = 1 TO 3
300  FOR I = 1 TO 12
310   IF N = 1 THEN GOSUB 520: 'Print label
320   HEIGHT = 120*AMT(N,I)/MAX
330   IF I = 1 THEN LINE (8,50) - (8,50+HEIGHT)
340   LINE - (24*I-12,50+HEIGHT),3
350  NEXT I
360  LINE - (24*I-16,50+HEIGHT)
370  LINE - (24*I-16,50)
380  LINE - (8,50)
390  PAINT (10,55),N,3
400 NEXT N
410 '=====================================================
420 'Print heading in coded colors
430 POKE &H4E,1: LOCATE 3,11: PRINT "INCOME";
440 POKE &H4E,3: PRINT "/";
450 POKE &H4E,2: PRINT "COST";
460 POKE &H4E,3: PRINT "/PROFIT"
470 LOCATE 23,1
480 IF INKEY$ = "" THEN 480
490 END
500 '=====================================================
510 'Monthly label subroutine
520 FOR J = 1 TO 3
530  LOCATE 19+J,3*I: PRINT MID$(MONTH$(I),J,1);
540 NEXT J
550 RETURN
600 '=====================================================
610 'Data for monthly income
620 DATA JAN,77, FEB,80, MAR,82
630 DATA APR,75, MAY,72, JUN,65
640 DATA JULY,60, AUGUST,64, SEPT,70
650 DATA OCT,78, NOV,85, DEC,88
660 'Data for monthly costs
670 DATA JAN,70, FEB,72, MAR,72
680 DATA APR,73, MAY,70, JUN,60
690 DATA JULY,58, AUGUST,55, SEPT,65
700 DATA OCT,70, NOV,78, DEC,75
```

The numerical data are placed in the array AMT(N,I) with N = 1, 2, 3 and I = 1–12. AMT(1,I) identifies the 12 income figures, AMT(2,I) receives the monthly costs, and AMT(3,I) receives the associated monthly profits. These arrays are filled in lines 190–260. Note that the MONTH$(I) array is filled twice. No harm is done by this, and the month names must be read from the data statements whether needed or not.

The heart of the program (lines 290–400) is little changed from the corresponding part of Program P4-4 (lines 220–300 there). Since the data have been stored in arrays, it is not necessary to read them as they are needed. In Program P4-5, AMT(N,I) (representing income, cost, and profit) serves the role of INCOME in Program P4-4, and three polygons are drawn as N progresses from 1 to 3. Since the labels (month names) need not be printed every time a new polygon is added, the labelling is done by a subroutine which is called only once (lines 310, 520–550). As each polygon is completed, its interior is painted (line 390).

With the polygons completed, lines 430–460 print a heading for the graph. The heading is printed in colors which are coded to the interpretation of the graph.

Note: As before, we have not included a vertical scale. You might add one on either the left or right screen boundaries.

PIE CHARTS

Pie charts are the last type of graph we will consider in this chapter. We will use the monthly income data from the previous examples, but will organize it differently. Rather than showing monthly income, Program P4-6 draws a pie chart which shows quarterly income.

Program P4-6: PIE CHART

```
10 'PROGRAM P4-6  (PIE CHART)
20 'Quarterly analysis of data
100 '==============================================
110 KEY OFF: SCREEN 1: CLS: COLOR 0,0
120 OPTION BASE 1
130 DIM Q(4): PI = 3.141593: START = .000001
140 '==============================================
150 'Read quarterly totals
160 FOR I = 1 TO 12
```

```
170  READ MONTH$, INCOME
180  Q(INT((I-1)/3)+1) = Q(INT((I-1)/3)+1) + INCOME
190  TOTAL = TOTAL + INCOME
200 NEXT I
210 '==================================================
220 'Draw sectors of circle
230 FOR I = 1 TO 4
240  EN = EN + 2*PI*Q(I) / TOTAL
250  CIRCLE (100,100),75,3,-START,-EN
260  XLAB = 50*COS((START+EN)/2) + 100
270  YLAB = 100 - 50*SIN((START+EN)/2)
280  PAINT (XLAB,YLAB),I MOD 4,3
290  YTAB = INT(YLAB/8)+1: XTAB = INT(XLAB/8)
300  LOCATE YTAB,XTAB: PRINT I
310  START = EN
320 NEXT I
330 '==================================================
340 'Place labels
350 N$(1) = "1st": N$(2) = "2nd"
360 N$(3) = "3rd": N$(4) = "4th"
370 FOR I = 1 TO 4
380  LOCATE 3*I,25
390  PRINT I;" ";N$(I);" "; "QUARTER"
400  LOCATE 3*I+1,30: PRINT Q(I)
410 NEXT I
420 IF INKEY$ = "" THEN 420
430 '==================================================
440 'Data for monthly income
450 DATA JAN,77, FEB,80, MAR,82
460 DATA APR,75, MAY,72, JUN,65
470 DATA JULY,60, AUGUST,64, SEPT,70
480 DATA OCT,78, NOV,85, DEC,88
```

A circular region (the pie) is divided into sectors whose areas are proportional to the corresponding quarterly income, and each sector is painted a different color. Program lines 160–200 read the income data, calculate the quarterly totals [Q(1), Q(2), Q(3), Q(4)], and the grand total. (MONTH$ is not used, but must be read.) Note how the quarter number (1, 2, 3, 4) is determined by the calculation INT((I − 1)/3) + 1.

The CIRCLE statement in line 250 draws the sector with starting and ending angles (START, EN) being determined by the fraction of income in each quarter. Note that it is necessary to specify START and EN with a minus sign prefix, so that the radial lines are drawn. Note also that the initial value of START cannot be exactly 0, since CIRCLE will not accept −0.

Lines 260 and 270 calculate the screen coordinates (XLAB,YLAB) of a point within each sector. The point is used by the PAINT statement which paints each sector, and is also used to calculate the text coordinates (XTAB,YTAB) which position a label in each sector. The method of calculating XLAB and YLAB may not be familiar; it is described in chapter 7, along with the discussion of circles.

Note that the WINDOW statement was not used in this program. As noted earlier, although WINDOW can provide a more convenient coordinate system, it is good to be able to work without special windows.

AN APPLICATION OF PUT AND GET

Much of Program P4-6 is repeated in Program P4-7. The changes are:

1. Four pie charts are drawn in lines 230–430. They differ because in each of the graphs the sector for one of the quarters is made to stand out from the rest of the pie.
2. The circular sectors are centered at (CX,CY) instead of at (100,100) as was the case in Program P4-6. For three of the four sectors of each pie, CX is equal to 100 and CY is equal to 100, but for the other one, (CX,CY) is calculated (line 300) to make the sector stand out. The calculation of CX and CY is similar to the calculation of XLAB, YLAB.
3. As each pie chart is completed, it is stored in an array by the GET statement of lines 390–420.
4. When the four pie charts have been completed, they may be recalled to the screen by pressing one of the keys 1, 2, 3, 4 (lines 550–610).

The ability to quickly change the image being displayed is very valuable. GET and PUT are used here to illustrate an effective way to do this. They are quite wasteful to memory capacity, however, and it may not always be possible to use them, especially with large programs which use many arrays and variables.

Program P4-7: MULTIPLE PIES

```
10 'PROGRAM P4-7  (MULTIPLE PIES)
20 'Uses GET and PUT to emphasize graph
100 '=======================================
110 KEY OFF: SCREEN 1: CLS: COLOR 0,0
```

```
120 OPTION BASE 1: DIM Q(4): PI = 3.141593
130 DIM A(1840), B(1840), C(1840), D(1840)
140 '=====================================================
150 'Read quarterly totals
160 FOR I = 1 TO 12
170  READ MONTH$, INCOME
180  Q(INT((I-1)/3)+1) = Q(INT((I-1)/3)+1) + INCOME
190  TOTAL = TOTAL + INCOME
200 NEXT I
210 '=====================================================
220 'Draw sectors of circle
230 FOR N = 1 TO 4
240  EN = 0 : START = .000001: CLS
250  FOR I = 1 TO 4
260   EN = EN + 2*PI*Q(I) / TOTAL
270   AN = (START + EN)/2
280   CX = 100: CY = 100
290   IF I <> N THEN 310
300    CX = 100 + 10*COS(AN): CY = 100 - 10*SIN(AN)
310   CIRCLE (CX,CY),75,3,-START,-EN
320   XLAB = CX + 50*COS(AN)
330   YLAB = CY - 50*SIN(AN)
340   PAINT (XLAB,YLAB),I MOD 4,3
350   YTAB = INT(YLAB/8)+1: XTAB = INT(XLAB/8)
360   LOCATE YTAB,XTAB: PRINT I
370   START = EN
380  NEXT I
390  IF N = 1 THEN GET (15,15) - (185,185),A
400  IF N = 2 THEN GET (15,15) - (185,185),B
410  IF N = 3 THEN GET (15,15) - (185,185),C
420  IF N = 4 THEN GET (15,15) - (185,185),D
430 NEXT N
440 '=====================================================
450 'Place labels
460 N$(1) = "1st": N$(2) = "2nd"
470 N$(3) = "3rd": N$(4) = "4th"
480 FOR I = 1 TO 4
490  LOCATE 3*I,25
500  PRINT I;" ";N$(I);" "; "QUARTER"
510  LOCATE 3*I+1,30: PRINT Q(I)
520 NEXT I
530 LOCATE 25,1: PRINT "Press 1,2,3,4 to view pies";
540 PRINT "; ESC to exit";
550 ST$ = INKEY$: IF LEN (ST$) = 0 THEN 550
560 IF ST$ = "1" THEN PUT (15,15),A,PSET
570 IF ST$ = "2" THEN PUT (15,15),B,PSET
580 IF ST$ = "3" THEN PUT (15,15),C,PSET
```

```
590 IF ST$ = "4" THEN PUT (15,15),D,PSET
600 IF ASC(ST$) = 27 THEN END
610 GOTO 550
700 '===============================================
710 'Data for monthly income
720 DATA JAN,77, FEB,80, MAR,82
730 DATA APR,75, MAY,72, JUN,65
740 DATA JULY,60, AUGUST,64, SEPT,70
750 DATA OCT,78, NOV,85, DEC,88
```

Chapter 5

Animation

In this chapter we will consider the animation techniques that are available when programming in BASIC. We will have the choice of displaying images on the text screen (SCREEN 0) or either of the two graphics screens. Since animated images are most interesting when color is available, we will use the text screen and the medium-resolution graphics screen in the example programs.

Program P1-2 used the high-resolution graphics screen to simulate the movement of a bouncing ball. Review that program and the accompanying discussion. Although the image used there (two dots) was a simple one, the methods used to animate it will be used here also.

In all of our animation we really will be displaying a sequence of still images that only simulate motion. Although there are several ways to simulate movement, the basic principle is always the same. We must draw an image, then remove it as it is replaced by its successor. The successor may be the same image, slightly displaced from its previous position; or it may be an image that differs slightly from the first in size or composition. In many instances, the animated image is a sequence of many individual images; the program cycles repeatedly through the sequence.

Most animation programs will have an erase cycle to remove an image from the display screen, and a draw cycle to provide a new image or the same image in a new position. The program repeatedly runs through the erase and draw cycles to animate images. If several images are to be animated, each may require its own erase-draw cycle. These cycles vary in length and technique since they are dependent on the way the graphics images are produced.

CHARACTER GRAPHICS FOR TEXT ANIMATION

We will first turn to the use of the text screen for the display of graphics images. Graphics on the text screen are frequently referred to as character graphics, since the only way to generate graphic images is to PRINT characters on the screen. The characters which are available are given in Appendix G of the IBM PC BASIC reference manual. By choosing from among these symbols it is possible to create some useful graphics images. Example programs P5-1, P5-2, P5-3, and P5-4 illustrate ways to use character graphics.

Program P5-1 requests an input string from the user, then scrolls the string inside a window on the screen in the manner of advertising message boards. The rectangular window is outlined by a pair of lines which are made up of the graphics characters numbered 186, 187, 188, 200, 201, and 202.

Line 110 sets the basic screen parameters. The selection of width is somewhat arbitrary; you may want to try width 80. If so, the later lines should be modified in order to have the image centered on the screen.

Lines 130–160 reconfigure the input string A$ to define a string S$ which will be sufficiently long to fill the window while scrolling.

Lines 190–230 define strings T$ and B$, which will provide the top and bottom borders of the window. These, along with the left and right borders, are printed by lines 290–320.

Finally, lines 380–430 print the modified input string within the border, continuing until a key is pressed.

Program P5-1: MESSAGE MOVER

```
10 'PROGRAM P5-1  (MESSAGE MOVER)
20 'Animated character graphics
100 '========================================
110 SCREEN 0,1: WIDTH 40: KEY OFF: CLS
120 INPUT "ENTER A MESSAGE: "; A$
130 A$ = A$ + " ... "
140 WHILE LEN(S$) < 20 + LEN(A$)
150  S$ = S$ + A$
160 WEND
170 '========================================
180 'Define the border strings
190 T$ = CHR$(201): B$ = CHR$(200)
200 WHILE LEN(T$) < 21
```

```
210  T$ = T$ + CHR$(205): B$ = B$ + CHR$(205)
220 WEND
230 T$ = T$ + CHR$(187): B$ = B$ + CHR$(188)
240 '==========================================
250 'Set foreground/background colors
260 COLOR 14,9: CLS
270 '==========================================
280 'Print the border
290 LOCATE 9,9: PRINT T$
300 LOCATE 10,9: PRINT CHR$(186)
310 LOCATE 10,30: PRINT CHR$(186)
320 LOCATE 11,9: PRINT B$
330 '==========================================
340 'Reset colors
350 COLOR 7,0
360 '==========================================
370 'Print the message until a key is pressed
380 WHILE LEN(INKEY$) = 0
390  LOCATE 10,10
400  N = N + 1: IF N = LEN(A$)+1 THEN N = 1
410  PRINT MID$(S$,N,20)
420  FOR I = 1 TO 75: NEXT I
430 WEND
440 CLS
```

Notice that the erase and draw cycles are not distinct in this example. The only active part of the display screen is the part which lies within the defined window. Each time the message is printed in this window it erases the previous image. As a result, the erase-draw cycle is reduced to a PRINT cycle (line 410).

> **NOTE:** The extended graphics characters (those with ASCII codes larger than 127) can be entered as part of the input string. To enter such a character, first depress the ALT key, then enter the number, then release the ALT key. You cannot use the number keys at the top of the keyboard when doing this, but must use the numeric keypad.

CHARACTER GRAPHICS FOR GAMES

Program P5-2 gives a second example of character graphics. This program provides an elementary graphics game. A total of 20 target blocks are placed in random locations on the screen. A "ball" bounces around the screen. If it hits a target block, the block is erased and four points are added to the score. If the ball touches the lower screen boundary, the player's score is decreased by one point. A paddle is positioned near the bottom of the screen. By pressing the keys "<," or ">." the player can move the paddle left or right to intercept the ball, thus preventing it from reaching the lower screen boundary. The player can also press the space bar to cause the paddle to remain stationary. Play continues until all target blocks are removed or until the player tires of the game and presses "ESC".

This game is clearly not strong competition for the current line of arcade-type games which are available for the PC, and it is not intended to be. Rather, its purpose is to further illustrate the techniques of character graphics and animation.

Program P5-2: CHARACTER GAME

```
10 'PROGRAM P5-2  (CHARACTER GAME)
20 'Keyboard controls character graphics
100 '==============================================
110 RANDOMIZE TIMER
120 KEY OFF: SCREEN 0,1,0: COLOR 4,1
130 WIDTH 40: CLS
140 'Define "ball"
150 A$ = CHR$(15): B$ = " "
160 '==============================================
170 'Define "paddle"
180 C$ = CHR$(220)+CHR$(220)+CHR$(220)+CHR$(220)
190 D$= "    ": 'Four spaces
200 '==============================================
210 'Draw targets
220 FOR I = 1 TO 20
230  VERT = 19*RND + 1: HORIZ = 39*RND + 1
240  LOCATE VERT,HORIZ,0
250  COLOR 2 + (I MOD 14): PRINT CHR$(178)
260 NEXT I
270 '==============================================
280 'Initialize positions and increments
290 X = 25: Y = 12: PAD = 25: TOT = 20
300 DX = 1 : DY = -1: DPAD = 2
310 OLDX = X: OLDY = Y: OLDPAD = PAD
320 '==============================================
330 'Main control loop
```

```
340 'Reposition moving dot
350 COLOR 4: SC = SCREEN(Y,X)
360 '============================================
370 'If hit paddle or target, bounce
380 IF SC = 178 THEN SCORE = SCORE+4: TOT = TOT-1
390 IF SC <> 32 THEN DY = - DY
400 LOCATE OLDY,OLDX: PRINT B$;
410 LOCATE Y,X: PRINT A$;
420 OLDX = X: OLDY = Y
430 LOCATE 25,1: PRINT "SCORE = "; SCORE;
440 IF TOT = 0 THEN END
450 '============================================
460 'If at screen boundary, bounce
470 IF X = 40 OR X = 1 THEN DX = -DX
480 IF Y = 23 THEN DY = -DY: SCORE = SCORE - 1
490 X = X + DX: Y = Y + DY
500 IF Y = 0 THEN DY = -DY:Y = Y + DY
510 '============================================
520 'Reposition paddle
530 COLOR 14
540 LOCATE 22,OLDPAD: PRINT D$;
550 LOCATE 22,PAD:PRINT C$;
560 OLDPAD = PAD
570 PAD = PAD + DPAD
580 'Change direction at edge of screen
590 IF PAD = 37 OR PAD = 1 THEN DPAD = -DPAD
600 '============================================
610 'Read key and interpret
620 K$ = INKEY$
630 IF LEN(K$) = 0 THEN K = 0 ELSE K = ASC(K$)
640 'If SPACE BAR then stop
650 IF K = 32 THEN DPAD = 0
660 'If < or , then move left
670 IF K = 44 AND PAD <> 1 THEN DPAD = -2
680 'If > or . then move right
690 IF K = 46 AND PAD <> 37 THEN DPAD = 2
700 'If ESC then end
710 IF K = 27 THEN COLOR 7,0: CLS: END
720 GOTO 350: 'Repeat
```

Line 150 identifies A$ as the ball (the character with ASCII code 15—see Appendix G of the IBM PC BASIC manual). At the same time B$ is defined as a single blank space. A$ and B$ will be used together to display the ball and then erase it in a sequence of locations thus causing it to appear to move. The actual animation takes place in lines 400 and 410. Line 400 erases the ball from its old position (OLDX, OLDY) and 410 displays it in a new location.

The paddle is defined as C$ in line 180. D$, which consists of four spaces, is used to erase the paddle as it moves horizontally. C$ and D$ are used to animate the paddle similar to the way that A$ and B$ animate the ball (lines 540, 550).

Lines 220–260 display 20 target blocks in randomly chosen screen locations. Lines 290–310 identify initial parameters.

The main control loop (lines 350–720) consists of two parts. Lines 350–500 move the ball (lines 400–410), test to see if it has hit a target block (lines 350, 380, and 390), or the screen baseline (lines 390, 480), or the paddle (line 390). The new position for the ball is calculated (lines 420, 490), and the score is updated (lines 380, 430, and 480).

The second part of the main control loop controls the movement of the paddle. The erasure and redisplay of the cursor is done in lines 540–570. Line 590 causes the cursor to bounce if it hits the edge of the screen. The remainder of the program (lines 620–710) is devoted to paddle control via keyboard input and interpretation. Four keys are recognized and interpreted. All other input is ignored.

The erase-draw cycle is obvious at two points of the program. Note that in both cases (lines 400, 410 and 540, and 550) the drawing of a new image is done immediately after the erasure of the old one. It is important to have this done with little time between the erasure and the draw. Otherwise the image will flicker more noticeably as it moves.

PAGE FLIPPING

Program P1-4 used character graphics to draw a gremlin which ran back and forth across the screen. The program draws and displays images on two text pages in order to provide smoother animation. The program is repeated here as Program P5-3 so that we can discuss the animation methods used.

Program P5-3: GREMLIN

```
10 'PROGRAM P5-3  (GREMLIN)
20 'Repeat of PROGRAM P1-4
100 '=====================================
```

```
110 KEY OFF: SCREEN 0,1,0: COLOR 4,1,14
120 WIDTH 40: LOCATE ,,0: CLS: SCREEN ,,1: CLS
130 S$ = CHR$(32) + CHR$(32)
140 A$ = CHR$(8) + CHR$(8)
150 B$ = CHR$(219) + CHR$(219)
160 C$(0) = CHR$(188) + CHR$(186)
170 D$(0) = CHR$(32) + CHR$(200)
180 C$(1) = CHR$(186) + CHR$(200)
190 D$(1) = CHR$(188)
200 A = 2: B = 34: C = 1
210 '=======================================
220 FOR I = A TO B STEP C
230  GOSUB 320
240  FOR K = 1 TO 50: NEXT K
250 NEXT I
260 FOR L = 1 TO 30
270  GOSUB 320
280 NEXT L
290 SWAP A,B: C = -C
300 GOTO 220
310 '=======================================
320 SCREEN ,,J,1-J
330 LOCATE 5,I: PRINT S$ + A$ + S$
340 LOCATE 6,I: PRINT S$ + B$ + S$
350 LOCATE 7,I: PRINT S$ + C$(J) + S$
360 LOCATE 8,I: PRINT S$ + D$(J) + S$
370 J = 1 - J
380 IF INKEY$ <> "" THEN SCREEN 0,1,0,0: END
390 RETURN
```

In order to animate the gremlin, the program must first draw the image and then erase it in successive screen positions. Watching the draw-erase cycle can be distracting, so the program is designed so that the drawing takes place on one text page while another is being displayed. As soon as an image is drawn, the text page containing it is displayed, and a new image is drawn on an undisplayed page.

When in 80-column text display, the PC provides four different text pages. In 40-column text display, eight pages are available. The animation process used in this program requires only two of the available pages.

There are actually two different gremlins, as shown in Figure 5.1.

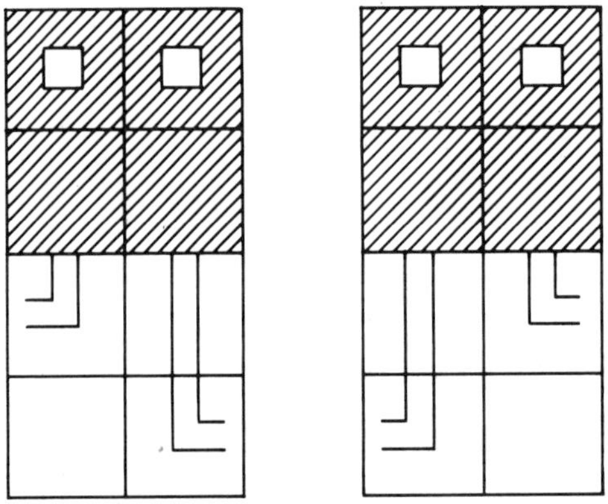

Image 1 Image 2

Figure 5.1

Image 0 displays the gremlin with its right foot up and left foot down. Image 1 shows the gremlin with feet in reversed positions. If the two images are displayed successively, the gremlin will appear to walk as the images are moved across the screen.

The body of the gremlin is the same in each of the two images; only the feet differ. Program lines 130 and 140 define A$ and B$ to be the body of the gremlin. C$(0) and D$(0) show the foot positions for image 0 while C$(1) and D$(1) show the foot positions for image 1. The string S$ consists of two spaces and is used in the erasure of images.

The draw-erase cycle of the program is contained in the subroutine which begins at line 320. In this line the active page (text page used for drawing) and visual page (page which is displayed) are set in the command SCREEN, , J,1 − J. The value of J varies, as controlled by line 370; but J is always either 0 or 1. Hence if the active page (J) is 0, the visual page (1 − J) is 1; if the active page is 1, the visual page is 0. As a result, the draw-erase cycle is *never* displayed.

As the value of J controls the active/visual pages, it also determines which of the gremlin images is displayed (lines 350, 360). In lines 330–360, the value of I, which is set in the loop 220–250, identifies the horizontal screen position at which the gremlin is displayed.

Notice that the draw-erase cycle is primarily a draw cycle (actually a PRINT cycle). The erasure is accomplished by the printing of two blank spaces (S$) on each side of the characters which define the gremlin. As a result the previous image is erased. Note the need for two spaces: Since consecutive images are drawn on different screens, the moving gremlin's horizontal position changes by two units between successive printings on a given screen.

The draw-erase subroutine (lines 320–390) is called by two different FOR/NEXT loops. The first (lines 220–250) moves the gremlin across the screen. The second (lines 260–280) causes the gremlin to dance in place at a screen edge. Line 290 then changes the values of variables A, B, and C so that the gremlin will move in the opposite direction during the next trip across the screen.

Note: You can make the gremlin more colorful, if you like. Use one color for the body, another for the legs. Or, change the background color for the body, to color the eyes. These color changes must be programmed carefully so that the spaces (S$) are drawn in the background color. Otherwise the erasure will not function properly.

CHARACTER GRAPHICS ON THE GRAPHICS SCREENS

The letter B can be displayed in the upper left corner of the SCREEN 0 display by storing its ASCII code in memory location &HB8000 (when using the Color/Graphics card). When in SCREEN 0 mode, the BASIC statement **LOCATE 1,1: PRINT "B"** will cause this to happen. When in SCREEN 1 or SCREEN 2 mode, this statement will still cause the letter B to appear in the upper left corner of the display screen, but the process used is different.

When the computer is in SCREEN 2 mode, the statement **LOCATE 1,1: PRINT "B"** will cause the computer to copy a sequence of dot patterns from a table and store the patterns in the bytes of memory that control the upper left of the screen. This is illustrated in Figure 5.2

If the computer is in SCREEN 1 mode, the statement **LOCATE 1,1: PRINT "B"** will cause the computer to access the *same* sequence of dot patterns. The dot patterns, together with the color to be used for PRINTing (usually color 3), determine the numbers that will be stored in the bytes of memory that control the upper left of the display screen. Two bits are required to control one pixel in medium-resolution graphics, so twice as many bytes of memory are needed to control the display of a single character.

Figure 5.3a shows how the bit pattern 11111100, together with color 3 (binary 11), are used when the bit pattern is accessed to display a part

Bit pattern	Address	Contents decimal	Contents binary
11111100	&HB8000	252	11111100
01100110	&HBA000	102	01100110
01100110	&HB8050	102	01100110
01111100	&HBA050	124	01111100
01100110	&HB80A0	102	01100110
01100110	&HBA0A0	102	01100110
11111100	&HB80F0	252	11111100
00000000	&HBA0F0	0	00000000

Screen Display

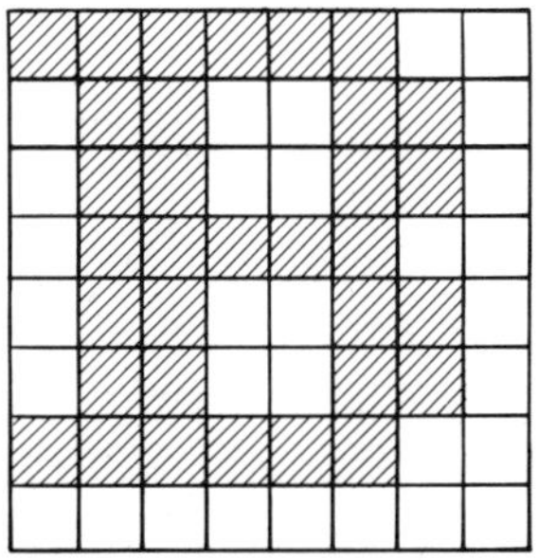

Figure 5.2 Text Display on Screen 2

of a character on the medium-resolution screen. Figure 5.3b shows the effect when the same bit pattern is used along with color 1 (binary 01). (It may be useful to refer back to the section Memory Usage by Graphics Screen 1, in Chapter 2). To print in color 1, **DEF SEG: POKE &H4E,1**.

Figure 5.4 shows how the bit pattern for the character B is used to store the color 3 code (11) in the memory locations which control the upper left grid of pixels on the medium-resolution graphics screen.

CUSTOM DESIGN OF CHARACTERS

The characters which are listed as having ASCII codes larger than 127 (Appendix G of the IBM PC BASIC manual) are not provided for use on the graphics screen. Rather, the programmer has the option of identifying

bit pattern	1	1	1	1	1	1	0	0
memory contents	1 1	1 1	1 1	1 1	1 1	1 1	0 0	0 0
screen display	← color 3 →						background	

Figure 5.3a

bit pattern	1	1	1	1	1	1	0	0
memory contents	0 1	0 1	0 1	0 1	0 1	0 1	0 0	0 0
screen display	← color 1 →						background	

Figure 5.3b

Bit pattern	Address	Contents decimal		Contents binary	
11111100	&HB8000–B8001	255	240	11111111	11110000
01100110	&HBA000–BA001	60	60	00111100	00111100
01100110	&HB8050–B8051	60	60	00111100	00111100
01111100	&HBA050–BA051	63	240	00111111	11110000
01100110	&HB80A0–B80A1	60	60	00111100	00111100
01100110	&HBA0A0–BA0A1	60	60	00111100	00111100
11111100	&HB80F0–B80F1	255	240	11111111	11110000
00000000	&HBA0F0–BA0F1	0	0	00000000	00000000

Screen Display

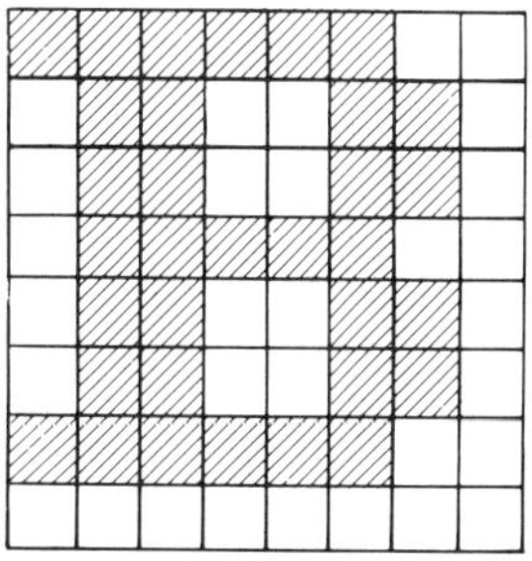

Figure 5.4 Text Display on SCREEN 1

characters to be associated with these ASCII codes and providing a table of bit patterns for these characters. This is both a disadvantage and a convenience. Although the text screen (SCREEN 0) can display all the ASCII characters shown in Appendix G of the IBM PC BASIC manual, the graphics screens can do so only after the programmer has entered the corresponding bit patterns for characters numbered 128–255. The characters available on the text screen are defined and inflexible; however, a person can define a new set of characters (with ASCII codes 128 through 255) for use on the graphics screens.

The next example illustrates the process of designing and using special characters. While the characters could be special symbols for math, chemistry, or a foreign language, in this example they will form the image of a butterfly.

The first task is to draw the butterfly on a dot matrix, as shown in Figure 5.5. The dot patterns are then converted to binary numbers, eight bits at a time. (If the dot pattern ends before the eighth bit, we fill in with 0s.) Next, the numbers are converted to decimal form. These numbers, in groups of eight, are then used to define the special characters. (Again we fill in with 0s as needed to obtain the full complement of eight.) In this way we define the eight special characters which will be assigned to ASCII codes 128–135.

Note that the dots that are *on* will correspond to the bits that are *on* in the bit pattern for each character and correspond to pixels that will be turned *on* to display the character. Further, when the character is PRINTed on the high-resolution graphics screen, the dot pattern (bit pattern) is copied directly into the memory locations that control the screen display. However, if the character is PRINTed on the medium-resolution

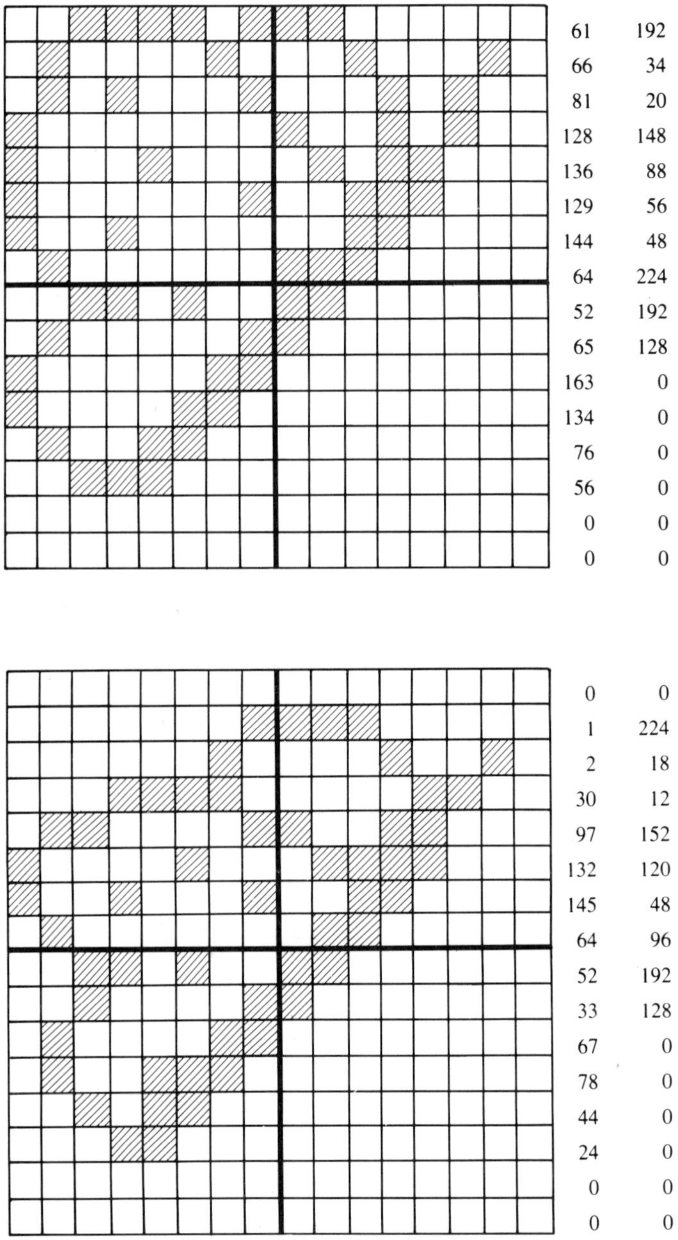
61 192
66 34
81 20
128 148
136 88
129 56
144 48
64 224
52 192
65 128
163 0
134 0
76 0
56 0
0 0
0 0
0 0
1 224
2 18
30 12
97 152
132 120
145 48
64 96
52 192
33 128
67 0
78 0
44 0
24 0
0 0
0 0

Figure 5.5

graphics screen, the dot pattern (bit pattern) is not copied directly into the display page memory locations but is used to determine where the PRINT color code is to be stored (see Figure 5.3).

In order to print these characters it is necessary to store their defining code numbers in a table and then identify the location of the table so that it can be accessed by BASIC. The location of the table is arbitrary; we may store it in any convenient part of memory. One way to do this is to use the CLEAR statement to reserve a section of memory at the upper reaches of BASIC's Data Segment, then store the table there. This is done in lines 130–160 of Program P5-4.

> **Note:** If this procedure is unclear, refer to Appendix 2 for a discussion of memory usage.

Program P5-4: BUTTERFLY

```
10 'PROGRAM P5-4  (BUTTERFLY)
20 'User-defined character set
100 '=====================================
110 KEY OFF: SCREEN 1,0: COLOR 1,0: CLS
120 'Store data in special character table
130 CLEAR, &HF000
140 FOR I = 0 TO 63
150  READ X: POKE &HF000+I,X
160 NEXT I
170 '=====================================
180 'Identify location of table
190 DEF SEG = 0
200 POKE &H7C,&H0
210 POKE &H7D,&HF0
220 POKE &H7E, PEEK(&H510)
230 POKE &H7F, PEEK(&H511)
240 DEF SEG
250 '=====================================
260 'Define strings for printing
270 A$ = "  " + CHR$(128) + CHR$(129)
280 B$ = "  " + CHR$(130) + CHR$(131)
290 C$ = "  " + CHR$(132) + CHR$(133)
```

```
300 D$ = " " + CHR$(134) + CHR$(135)
310 '====================================
320 'Fly the butterfly
330 FOR X = 1 TO 38 STEP 2
340  LOCATE 5,X: PRINT A$;
350  LOCATE 6,X: PRINT B$;
360  FOR T = 1 TO 100: NEXT T
370  LOCATE 5,X+1: PRINT C$;
380  LOCATE 6,X+1: PRINT D$;
390  FOR T = 1 TO 100: NEXT T
400 NEXT X
410 END
420 '====================================
430 'Data for table
440 DATA 61, 66, 81, 128, 136, 129, 144, 64
450 DATA 192, 34, 20, 148, 88, 56, 48, 224
460 DATA 52, 65, 163, 134, 76, 56, 0, 0
470 DATA 192, 128, 0, 0, 0, 0, 0, 0
480 DATA 0, 1, 2, 30, 97, 132, 145, 64
490 DATA 0, 224, 18, 12, 152, 120, 48, 96
500 DATA 52, 33, 67, 78, 44, 24, 0, 0
510 DATA 192, 128, 0, 0, 0, 0, 0, 0
```

When BASIC is required to print a special character on one of the graphics screens, it looks at memory locations 00:&H7C–&H7F to find the address of the beginning of the special character table. Locations &H7E and &H7F should contain the *segment* address; locations &H7C and &H7D should contain the *offset*. In the present case the table is stored beginning at offset &HF000 of BASIC's Data Segment. Lines 200–210 store the offset and lines 220 and 230 copy the segment address from 00:&H510, &H511. BASIC can then access the table.

Strings A$ and B$ identify the butterfly in the wings-raised position, and C$ and D$ identify the butterfly in the wings-lowered position. Note that each of A$–D$ begins with a space, so that as each character is printed to the right of the previous print location the previous character will be erased.

The loop in lines 330–400 prints the characters which form the butterfly, with a delay loop (lines 360, 390) between successive images. Variation in the length of the delay loop will control the speed of movement of the butterfly.

NOTES AND SUGGESTIONS

1. If you would rather have the butterfly in a color other than color number 3 of the current palette, here's how to do it. Add a line to the program, say line 115, to read as follows:

```
115 POKE &H4E, c
```

where **c** is the color you want to use. **c** can be any number from 0 to 3, identifying a color from the current palette. (This works for printing text characters in SCREEN 1 also). Programs P4-3 and P4-5 used this method to print colored labels for a graph.

2. Special characters can be defined to provide a script alphabet or any other special symbols.

3. It is possible to have several special character alphabets available in memory at any one time. The alphabets can be stored at any convenient location. As a particular character set is needed, its beginning address is POKEd into memory locations 00:&H7C–&H7F. BASIC then will reference this table when printing characters with ASCII codes larger than 127.

4. If an extensive character set is needed, it is best to write a program which stores the character bit patterns in memory and then BSAVEs the entire set on disk. The character set can then be BLOADed by programs which use it.

5. It is clear that the creation of special characters is a time-consuming task, consisting of monotonous calculations. Since computers are very good at such jobs, it would be reasonable to design a program to do this. You might want to write such a program. Several are commercially available.

ANIMATION USING LINE

The LINE statement is not generally useful for animation, except for very simple objects. More complicated images take too long to draw. There is no way to hide the draw-erase cycle from view, and the process of drawing and erasing images can be very distracting to watch. As a result, we will use LINE sparingly when animating images from BASIC.

Program P5-5 illustrates the use of draw and erase cycles with LINE. Program line 170 is the erase cycle: it draws a rectangle in the background color, thus erasing it. Similarly, program line 180 is the draw cycle. Note that the first time the erase cycle is used, there is nothing to erase. There is no harm in this, since the erasure has no visible effect. Note also that the draw cycle follows the erasure immediately. This keeps to a minimum the time a blank screen is displayed. All of the calculations needed between successive images are done after the draw, but before the next erase.

Program P5-5: ANIMATED SQUARES

```
10 'PROGRAM P5-5  (ANIMATED SQUARES)
20 'Simple animation using LINE
100 '==============================================================
110 KEY OFF: SCREEN 1,0: COLOR 0,0:CLS
120 A1 = 10: A2 = 60: ST = 2
130 C1 = 100:C2 = 100: C3 = 130: C4 = 30: C5 = 270: C6 = 170
140 FOR A = A1 TO A2 STEP ST
150  L2 = L1: T2 = T1: R2 = R1: B2 = B1
160  L1 = C1 - A: T1 = C2 - A: R1 = C1 + A: B1 = C2 + A
170  LINE (L2,T2) - (R2,B2),0,B
180  LINE (L1,T1) - (R1,B1),1,B
230 NEXT A
240 SWAP A1,A2: ST = -ST
250 IF LEN(INKEY$) = 0 THEN 140
```

Note that the animation is accompanied by flicker. This is caused by having the erase-draw cycles displayed as they occur and by having a blank screen displayed for a brief time between the erasure and the drawing of the next image. The flicker can be made less noticeable by holding the new drawing on the screen for a longer time before it is erased (add a FOR-NEXT delay loop). Unfortunately, this will also slow the animation.

Animation which uses the LINE statement is generally effective only for very simple images. Even slight increases in complexity result in significant changes in animation speed. To illustrate, insert the following lines into Program P5-5.

```
190 L4 = L3: T4 = T3: R4 = R3: B4 = B3
200 L3 = C3 + A: T3 = C4 + A: R3 = C5 - A:
B3 = C6 - A
210 LINE (L4,T4) - (R4,B4),0,B
220 LINE (L3,T3) - (R3,B3),2,B
```

An even greater reduction in speed will be noticed if the rectangles are drawn and erased by using LINE to draw each side of the rectangle instead of having the B option of LINE provide the sides. This is because of the time requirements of BASIC statements. The B option causes more to be done by the machine language subroutines which are accessed by the BASIC interpreter.

It should be clear that better animation will result from machine language programs than from BASIC programs. To obtain such programs you may either use a BASIC compiler or write them in assembly language. Although neither is a topic of discussion for this book, the processes we are describing are applicable in either case.

ANIMATION USING DRAW

Writing programs which animate images requires a considerable amount of preparation. Although the design of the object to be animated is the primary concern, it is also necessary to plan the pattern of movement and the sequence of images needed to produce the desired motion. In the previous example the image and its location changed, but the change in the image was a change of scale; the change in position was dictated by the change in scale. The next example extends the procedure, simulating motion by drawing a sequence of shapes.

Figure 5.6 shows a sequence of images intended to represent positions of a moving inchworm. Each image is coded as a string and can then be displayed by the DRAW statement.

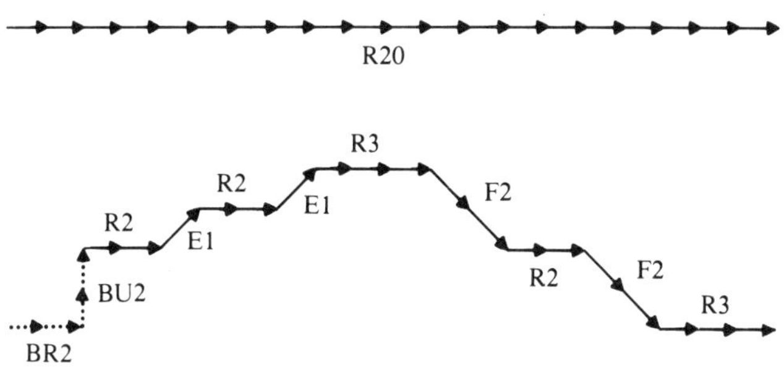

Figure 5.6

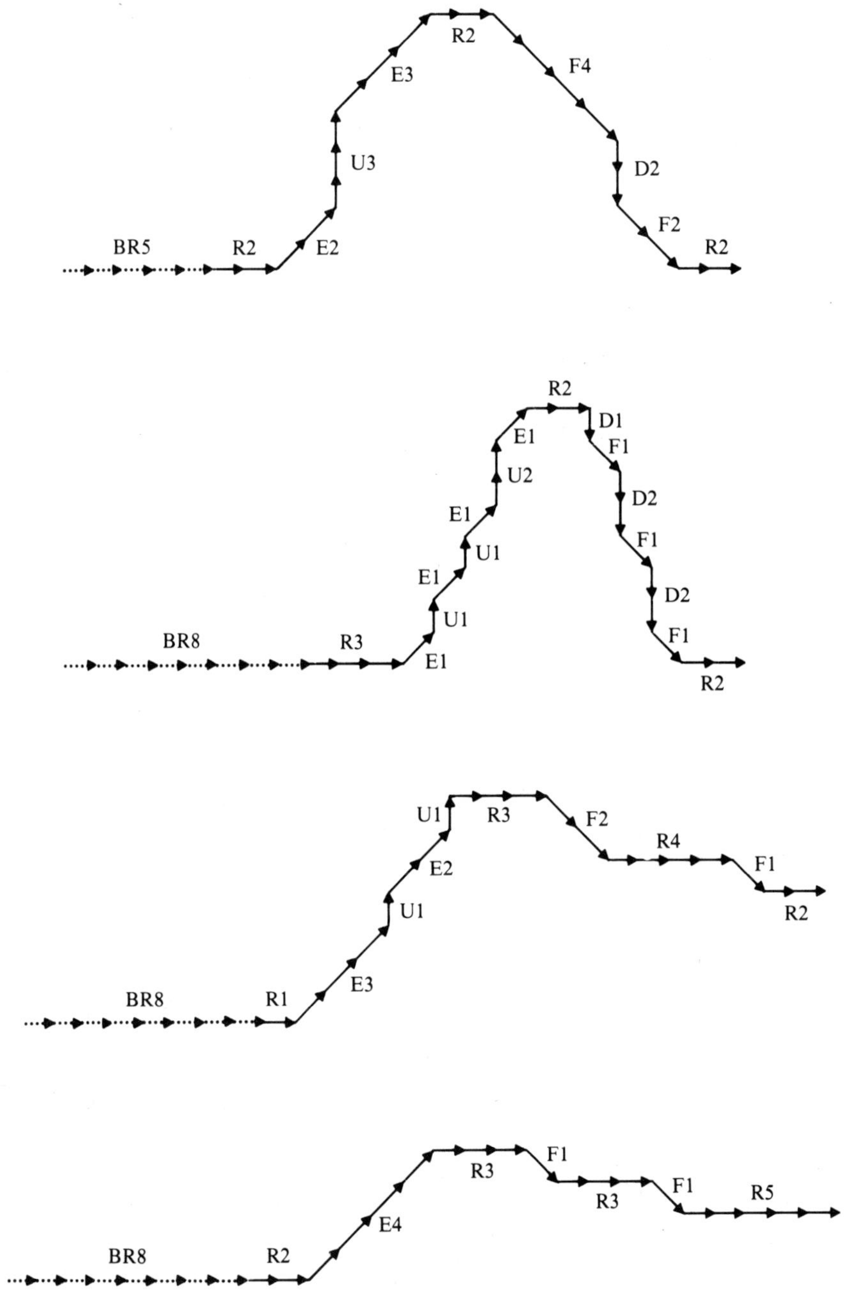

Figure 5.6 continued

Program P5-6 puts the inchworm in motion. Program lines 130–180 define the inchworm shapes as strings. Lines 200–260 use the DRAW statement to consecutively draw, then erase each of the six images. The delay loop in line 230 holds each image on the screen briefly before it is erased. Shorten the delay loop to speed up the animation.

Program P5-6: INCHWORM

```
10 'PROGRAM P5-6  (INCHWORM)
20 'DRAW graphics animation
100 '=========================================
110 KEY OFF: SCREEN 1,0: COLOR 0,0: CLS
120 Y = 25: OPTION BASE 1: DIM A$(6)
130 A$(1) = "R20"
140 A$(2) = "BR2 BU2 R2 E1 R2 E1 R3 F2 R2 F2 R3"
150 A$(3) = "BR5 R2 E2 U3 E3 R2 F4 D2 F2 R2"
160 A$(4) = "BR8 R3 E1 U1 E1 U1 E1 U2 E1 R2 D1 F1 D2 F1 D2 F1 R2"
170 A$(5) = "BR8 R1 E3 U1 E2 U1 R3 F2 R4 F1 R2"
180 A$(6) = "BR8 R2 E4 R3 F1 R3 F1 R5"
190 '=========================================
200 FOR X = 1 TO 200 STEP 8
210  FOR I = 1 TO 6
220   DRAW "BM=X;,=Y;C3;XA$(I);"
230    FOR K = 1 TO 60: NEXT K
240   DRAW "BM=X;,=Y;C0;XA$(I);"
250  NEXT I
260 NEXT X
```

NOTES AND SUGGESTIONS

1. Use LINE to display a rotating arrow (like the hand of a clock). Try the same with the DRAW statement (use the TA option).
2. The inchworm of program P5-6 shows the animation of a simple figure. Write a program that uses several such images to show a person walking. Use a stick figure person; design several images that present the person with various leg and arm positions. You might also try having a person ascend stairs.
3. For another example of animation using the DRAW statement, review program P1-3.

GET, PUT, LINE, AND CHARACTERS FOR ANIMATION

Program P5-7 is more elaborate than the preceding examples. It also illustrates several concepts and techniques which are central to animation. In brief, the program moves an aircraft across the top of the screen. Periodically it drops characters from a defined string and the characters streak downward, each stopping at the same level.

Program P5-7: NAME DROPPER

```
10 'PROGRAM P5-7  (NAME DROPPER)
20 'Illustrates GET, PUT, and animation
100 '=================================================
110 KEY OFF: SCREEN 1,0: COLOR 1,0: CLS
120 COUNT = 1: YP = 20: J = 1: A$ = "IBMPC"
130 CIRCLE (17,10),10,,,,.4
140 PAINT (17,10)
150 LINE (7,6) - (8,14),,BF
160 DIM A(14)
170 GET (4,6) - (27,14),A
180 '=================================================
190 FOR X = 6 TO 290 STEP 2
200  PUT (X,6),A,PSET
210  IF (X-18)*(X-66)*(X-114)*(X-210)*(X-260) = 0 THEN F = 1
220  IF F = 1 THEN GOSUB 260 ELSE GOSUB 440
230 NEXT X
240 LOCATE 23,1: END
250 '=================================================
260 IF FL = 0 THEN FL = 1: XP = X+10
270 ON COUNT GOSUB 310, 380
280 RETURN
290 '-------------------------
300 'Projectile
310 LINE (XP,YP) - (XP,YP+5),0
320 YP = YP + 10
330 LINE (XP,YP) - (XP,YP+5),1
340 IF YP = 120 THEN COUNT = COUNT + 1
350 RETURN
360 '-------------------------
370 'Print characters
380 LOCATE 17,XP/8
390 PRINT MID$(A$,J,1): J = J + 1
400 LINE (XP,YP) - (XP,YP+5),0
410 YP = 20: COUNT = 1: FL = 0: F= 0: RETURN
420 '--------------------------------------
430 'Timing loop
440 FOR I = 1 TO 25: NEXT I
450 RETURN
```

The aircraft is defined in program lines 130–150 and the image is collected in an array by line 170. The array is accessed by line 200, which places the image at horizontally incremented positions.

Notice that no overt erase cycle is present. This is because the drawing of the image also arranges for the erasure of the image from its previous position. When the aircraft was drawn, it was contained within a rectangle having diagonal corners (7,6) and (27,14). The rectangle saved in the array (by line 170) extended to the left of the image. When the PUT statement is used with the PSET option (line 200) the data in the array are used to replace a rectangular region of the screen. Since the rectangles are placed consecutively farther to the right, the extra width of the rectangle serves to erase the previous image by copying over it with a new image of the aircraft or with the background color.

The main control loop is in lines 190–230. After line 200 puts the image on the screen, line 210 uses the horizontal position of the aircraft to signal the release of a projectile. One is released whenever X is equal to one of the numbers 18, 66, 114, 210, or 260.

The value of F is used in line 220 to direct program flow to one of two subroutines. The subroutine beginning at line 260 draws the line segments which represent the falling missile or, if the missile has reached the desired level, prints the appropriate character. If no missile is falling, this subroutine is not called. Instead, the subroutine starting at line 440 is used. This is a timing loop and is intended as a counterbalance. If it were not called the aircraft would move more slowly when a missile was falling (because of the time required to draw the dropping missile). To see the effect of the timing loop, remove it; replace line 220 with

```
220 IF F = 1 THEN GOSUB 260
```

It was pointed out earlier that the LINE statement was effective in the animation of only simple images. The falling missile is such an image, represented by a short vertical line segment. It is drawn by line 330 and erased by line 310.

Program P1-10 also used GET and PUT to simulate animation. The program is not discussed in Chapter 1, but was repeated in Chapter 3 (see discussion on pages 51–52).

Chapter 6

Software Tools for Computer Graphics

The large station wagon my wife drives has an automatic transmission, power brakes, power steering, and air conditioning. The car I drive has none of these. I must change gears as I drive, crank down the windows in warm weather, and use more muscle to steer and to brake.

We face similar, though more dramatic, differences if we compare full-scale graphics computers with the graphics capabilities of a microcomputer. Some of the built-in gadgetry of the large system is not available in a microcomputer; other features are available only when provided by the programmer.

It is the intent of this chapter to provide a description of some of the tools of the trade of a microcomputer graphics programmer. Each tool is presented in a form which explains all the hows and whys, for those who are interested. Example programs illustrate the use of the techniques discussed.

SCALING THE SCREEN

It is fairly common to find differences between the horizontal and vertical scales on a microcomputer display screen. The IBM PC medium-resolution graphics screen provides a 320 × 200 matrix of pixels, which suggests that horizontal and vertical scales must differ. Likewise, the 640 × 200 resolution of the high-resolution screen makes it clear that an increase of one unit vertically is not equivalent to an increase of one unit horizontally.

There are occasions when it is important that the horizontal and vertical scales be equivalent—that a square appear to have sides of equal length, for example. We can meet this need by scaling points before plotting them.

When plotting points on the medium-resolution screen, it might appear that we could multiply all vertical distances by 200/320 (=5/8). However, that will not quite suffice. In addition to considering the differences in the numbers of pixels in the horizontal and vertical directions, we must also take note of what is referred to as the *aspect ratio* of the display screen.

The standard aspect ratio of a television or a display monitor is 4/3, meaning that the width of the screen is 4/3 of the height. (In addition to the aspect ratio, the adjustment of the display screen can distort the horizontal and vertical scales.)

When the pixel ratio of 5/8 and the aspect ratio of 4/3 are combined (multiplied), a scaling factor of 5/6 is established for the medium-resolution screen. The same type of calculation gives a scaling factor of 5/12 for the high-resolution screen.

Images of proper proportion will result if the appropriate scaling factor is introduced into a graphics program. Program P6-1 illustrates the usage. There SCALE is defined as 5/6, and vertical distances are multiplied by SCALE before points are plotted.

Program P6-1: SCALED SQUARE

```
10 'PROGRAM P6-1  (SCALED  SQUARE)
20 'Uses scaling factor to equate horizontal and vertical
scales
100 '==========================================
110 SCALE = 5/6         'For medium resolution screen
120 SIDE =100           'Length of side of square
130 VSIDE = SCALE*SIDE  'Length of vertical side
140 X1 = 20: Y1 = 50    'Top left corner of square
150 KEY OFF: SCREEN 1,0: CLS
160 LINE (X1,Y1) -STEP(SIDE,VSIDE),,B
```

The WINDOW statement can be used to rescale the graphics screen coordinate system. Note that a window which is established as **WINDOW (0,0)–(120,120)** does not provide equivalent horizontal and vertical scales. While such a window does equate the number of horizontal and vertical units, it does not consider the effect of the display screen aspect ratio.

Setting the display window by using statements such as **WINDOW (0,0)–(120,90)** or **WINDOW (0,0)–(160,120)** will properly scale the display screen coordinate system. We may then plot points without regard for scaling factors.

In many applications it is not important that the horizontal and vertical scales be equivalent. In most of the example programs in this book we will not be concerned with equivalence of scaling. It can easily be provided when needed.

CLIPPING

The statement **LINE (100,50)–(700,150)** identifies a line segment which has the endpoint (700,150) to the right of the screen boundary. When the statement is encountered in a program, it will result in drawing the part of the line segment which does lie on the screen.

Clipping refers to the process of displaying visible points and parts of line segments while clipping and discarding points and parts of line segments which are beyond the screen boundaries. Clipping individual points is a relatively easy process. The coordinates of a point can be compared with the coordinates of the screen boundaries. The only points plotted are those whose coordinates lie between the boundary coordinates. All others are discarded.

Clipping of line segments is more troublesome. If one or both of the endpoints of a line segment lie offscreen, it is necessary to determine the points of intersection of the line segment and the screen boundaries; then the points of intersection can be used to plot the visible portion of the line segment.

IBM PC BASIC handles all clipping automatically, although versions of BASIC prior to version 2.0 sometimes lose the last referenced point when lines are clipped. With version 2.0 that problem was corrected, and clipping with WINDOW and VIEW statements is fully operative.

Because clipping is a fundamental concept of computer graphics, we are including a discussion and an example program which illustrate a method of clipping line segments. Since the IBM PC handles clipping automatically, you may consider this topic to be optional, at least on an initial reading.

A STRATEGY FOR CLIPPING

A line clipping subroutine must systematically determine any points of intersection of the line segment and the screen boundaries (or boundaries of the portion of the screen which we wish to have active—the viewport). The segment is thus divided into smaller portions. Any portion of the line segment which lies on the screen may be plotted; other portions are discarded.

Program P6-2 provides an example of a clipping subroutine applied to the line segments which make up a rectangle. The program defines artificial screen boundaries (a viewport) in line 130. Program line 140 boxes this active region, to define the viewport more clearly.

Program P6-2: CLIPPING

```
10 'PROGRAM P6-2  (CLIPPING)
20 'Clipping routines are based on the Cohen- Sutherland algorithm
100 '=========================================================
110 KEY OFF: SCREEN 1,0: CLS
120 'Establish artificial boundaries
130 XL = 75: XR = 250: YT = 20: YB = 170
140 LINE (XL,YT) - (XR,YB),2,B
150 OPTION BASE 1: DEFINT L,R,T,B
160 DIM X(2),Y(2),L(2),R(2),T(2),B(2)
170 'Read line endpoints for rectangle
180 FOR J = 1 TO 4
190  FOR I = 1 TO 2
200   READ X(I),Y(I)
210  NEXT I
220  GOSUB 270 'To clipping and drawing subroutine
230 NEXT J
240 END
250 '=========================================================
260 'CLIPPING AND DRAWING SUBROUTINE
270 FOR I = 1 TO 2
280  GOSUB 480 'Classify the endpoints
290 NEXT I
300 '=========================================================
310 FOR I = 1 TO 2
320  DISCARD = L(1)*L(2) + R(1)*R(2) + T(1)*T(2) + B(1)*B(2)
330   IF DISCARD THEN I = 2: GOTO 360
340  CLIP = L(I) + R(I) + T(I) + B(I)
350   IF CLIP THEN GOSUB 420: GOTO 320
360 NEXT I
370 IF DISCARD THEN 390
380 LINE (X(1),Y(1)) - (X(2),Y(2))
390 RETURN
400 '=========================================================
410 'CLIP
420 IF L(I) = 1 THEN Y(I) = Y(1) + (Y(2) - Y(1)) *
(XL - X(1))/(X(2) - X(1)): X(I) = XL: GOTO 480
430 IF R(I) = 1 THEN Y(I) = Y(1) + (Y(2) - Y(1)) *
(XR - X(1))/(X(2) - X(1)): X(I) = XR: GOTO 480
440 IF T(I) = 1 THEN X(I) = X(1) + (X(2) - X(1)) *
(YT - Y(1))/(Y(2) - Y(1)): Y(I) = YT: GOTO 480
```

```
450 IF B(I) = 1 THEN X(I) = X(1) + (X(2) - X(1)) *
(YB - Y(1))/(Y(2) - Y(1)): Y(I) = YB: GOTO 480
460 '=====================================================
470 'CLASSIFY
480 L(I) = 0: R(I) = 0: T(I) = 0: B(I) = 0
490 IF X(I) < XL THEN L(I) = 1
500 IF X(I) > XR THEN R(I) = 1
510 IF Y(I) < YT THEN T(I) = 1
520 IF Y(I) > YB THEN B(I) = 1
530 RETURN
540 '=====================================================
550 DATA 100,10, 280,70
560 DATA 280,70, 240,190
570 DATA 240,190, 60,130
580 DATA 60,130, 100,10
```

The line endpoints are first read into arrays X(I) and Y(I) (lines 190–210) and control is passed to the clipping and drawing subroutine. There the endpoints are classified (lines 270–290). For endpoint X(1), Y(1) four variables are defined. The array values L(1), R(1), T(1), B(1) are individually set to 0 if the point X(1), Y(1) lies on the screen side of lines L, R, T, or B, respectively. If the point lies on the outside of the boundary lines, the corresponding array values are set to 1. In the same manner values for L(2), R(2), T(2), and B(2) are identified.

For example, for the points shown in Figure 6.1,

L(1) = 1	R(1) = 0	T(1) = 1	B(1) = 0
L(2) = 0	R(2) = 0	T(2) = 0	B(2) = 1

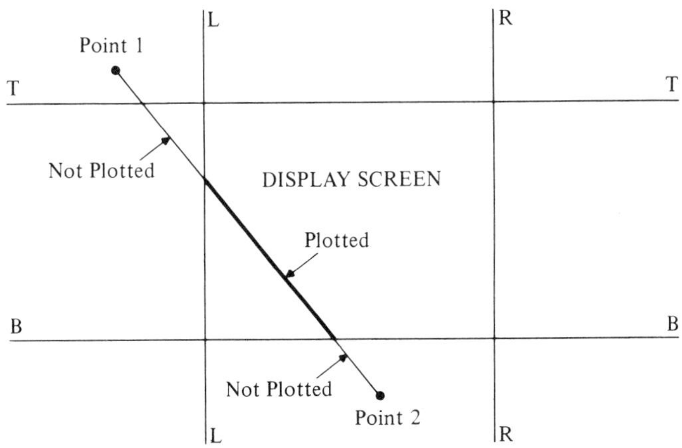

Figure 6.1

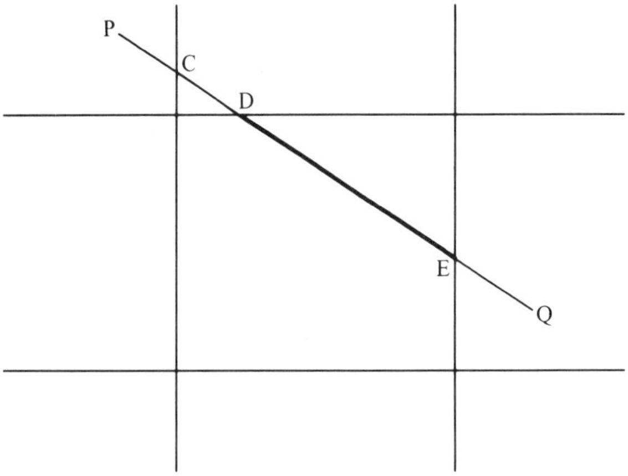

Figure 6.2

The clipping subroutine next determines whether the line segment can be discarded. If the endpoints both lie on the outside of any boundary line, then the corresponding product L(1)*L(2), R(1)*R(2), T(1)*T(2), or B(1)*B(2) will be 1. Otherwise, each of the products will be 0. Thus a line segment may be discarded if DISCARD = L(1)*L(2) + R(1)*R(2) + T(1)*T(2) + B(1)*B(2) is nonzero (lines 320 and 330).

If the line segment cannot be discarded, then it must be decided whether endpoint I (I = 1 or 2) lies on the screen. If it does, then each of L(I), R(I), T(I), and B(I) must be 0. If each of the endpoints lies on the screen, line 380 will plot the line.

The clipping is done within the subroutine in lines 420–450, where the point (X(I),Y(I)) is replaced with the point of intersection of the line segment and one of the screen boundaries. The newly identified (X(I),Y(I)) is then routed through the CLASSIFY routine and back to a new calculation of DISCARD.

The process continues until a segment is obtained which either has both endpoints in the viewport (the segment will then be plotted by line 380), or has both endpoints on the outside of one of the viewport boundaries (the segment is discarded by lines 320 and 330).

As an illustration, the line segment PQ shown in Figure 6.2 would be clipped to CQ, then to DQ, and finally to DE, which then would be plotted.

TRANSFORMATIONS

A 20 × 10 rectangle is drawn in the upper left-hand corner of the medium-resolution graphics screen by Program P6-3.

Program P6-3: RECTANGLE

```
10 'PROGRAM P6-3  (RECTANGLE)
20 'Plots a single rectangle
100 '===================================
110 KEY OFF: SCREEN 1,0: COLOR 1,0: CLS
120 READ X,Y: PSET (X,Y)
130 FOR I = 1 TO 4
140  READ X,Y: LINE - (X,Y)
150 NEXT I
160 LOCATE 23,1
170 DATA 0,0, 20,0, 20,10, 0,10, 0,0
```

Program P6-4 has a basic structure that is similar to that of Program P6-3, but it draws eight rectangles. Each is derived from a common set of DATA. In contrast to Program P6-3, which reads values of X and Y, then plots a point or line segment, Program P6-4 transforms the coordinates (X,Y) to obtain the screen coordinates (SX,SY) to be plotted. The size, shape, and locations of the rectangles are controlled through changes in the values of A, B, C, and D.

Two types of transformations are at work in Program P6-4:

Program P6-4: RECTANGLES

```
10 'PROGRAM P6-4  (RECTANGLES)
20 'Plots 8 rectangles from one set of data
100 '=======================================
110 KEY OFF: SCREEN 1,0: COLOR 1,0: CLS
120 A = 20: B = 0: C = 10: D = 0
130 FOR J = 1 TO 8
140  READ X,Y: SX = A*X + B: SY = C*Y + D
150  PSET (SX,SY)
160  FOR I = 1 TO 4
170   READ X,Y: SX = A*X + B: SY = C*Y + D
180   LINE - (SX,SY)
```

```
190    NEXT I
200    A = A + 15: B = B + 15
210    C = C + 10: D = D + 10
220    RESTORE
230 NEXT J
240 LOCATE 23,1
250 DATA 0,0, 1,0, 1,1, 0,1, 0,0
```

1. The magnitudes of coordinates are controlled by multiplication by A and C. This is referred to as *scaling* the image.

2. The location of the image is controlled by the values of B and D. This is referred to as *translating* the image.

To become more familiar with the scaling and translation transformations, try the following:

1. Write a program that will draw eight rectangles of varying size, each with a corner in the top left corner of the screen. (Use *scaling*, not *translation*.)

2. Write a program that will draw eight rectangles, all the same size, in different regions of the screen. (Use *translation*, not *scaling*.)

Transformations are valuable in generating graphics images. While some introductory work with transformations can be pursued in the manner of Program P6-4, greater power and versatility will result from first introducing some related topics: matrices, and homogeneous coordinate representation of points.

WHAT IS A MATRIX?

A matrix is a rectangular array of numbers, such as

$$A = \begin{pmatrix} 1 & 2 \\ 3 & 4 \end{pmatrix} \quad \text{or} \quad B = \begin{pmatrix} 0 & 2 \\ 5 & -3 \end{pmatrix}$$

We can add matrices:

$$A + B = \begin{pmatrix} 1 & 2 \\ 3 & 4 \end{pmatrix} + \begin{pmatrix} 0 & 2 \\ 5 & -3 \end{pmatrix} = \begin{pmatrix} 1 + 0 & 2 + 2 \\ 3 + 5 & 4 - 3 \end{pmatrix} = \begin{pmatrix} 1 & 4 \\ 8 & 1 \end{pmatrix}$$

and multiply matrices:

$$\begin{pmatrix}1 & 2\\3 & 4\end{pmatrix}\begin{pmatrix}0 & 2\\5 & -3\end{pmatrix} = \begin{pmatrix}(1)(0) + (2)(5) & (1)(2) + (2)(-3)\\(3)(0) + (4)(5) & (3)(2) + (4)(-3)\end{pmatrix}$$

$$= \begin{pmatrix}10 & -4\\20 & -6\end{pmatrix}$$

A summary of matrix notation and matrix calculation is given in Appendix 4.

MATRIX REPRESENTATION OF TRANSFORMATIONS

Transformations of points in a two-dimensional plane (the display screen) may be represented as products of points (1 × 2 matrices) with 2 × 2 matrices. For example, we may transform (move) a point (X,Y) to a new point (X′,Y′) as follows:

$$(X,Y)\begin{pmatrix}A & B\\C & D\end{pmatrix} = (AX + CY,BX + DY) = (X',Y')$$

Thus, for each point (X,Y), we identify a transformed point

$$(X,Y)' = (X',Y') = (AX + CY,BX + DY).$$

Clearly, the effect of a transformation is determined by the choice of values for A, B, C, and D. Program P6-5 accepts values for A, B, C, and D, then shows the effect of the transformation on the points of a square. We will use this program to illustrate several types of transformations.

Program P6-5: MATRIX

```
10 'PROGRAM P6-5  (MATRIX)
20 'Shows effect of a 2X2 transformation matrix
100 '================================================
110 KEY OFF: SCREEN 1,0: COLOR 0,0: CLS
120 WINDOW (-4,-3) - (4,3)
130 '================================================
140 'Input matrix
150 LOCATE 24,1: INPUT; "A =";A
```

```
160 LOCATE 24,15: INPUT; "B =";B
170 LOCATE 25,1: INPUT; "C =";C
180 LOCATE 25,15: INPUT; "D =";D
190 '================================================
200 'Draw axes
210 LINE (0,3) - (0,-3),2
220 LINE (3,0) - (-3,0),2
230 '================================================
240 'Draw rectangle
250 FOR LIN = 1 TO 4
260  READ X,Y
270  TX = A*X + C*Y: Y = B*X + D*Y: X = TX
280  PSET (X,Y)
290  READ X,Y
300  TX = A*X + C*Y: Y = B*X + D*Y: X = TX
310  LINE - (X,Y)
320 NEXT LIN
330 '================================================
340 RESTORE: LOCATE 23,1
350 INPUT "Press 'N' for new matrix; 'E' to end"; ST$
360 IF ST$ = "n" OR ST$ = "N" THEN CLS: GOTO 150
370 IF ST$ = "e" OR ST$ = "E" THEN CLS: END
380 GOTO 350
390 DATA 0,0, 1,0
400 DATA 1,0, 1,1
410 DATA 1,1, 0,1
420 DATA 0,1, 0,0
```

IDENTITY

The matrix

$$\begin{pmatrix} 1 & 0 \\ 0 & 1 \end{pmatrix}$$

represents the identity transformation. Since

$$(X,Y) \begin{pmatrix} 1 & 0 \\ 0 & 1 \end{pmatrix} = (X,Y)$$

the identity transformation leaves points unchanged.

Running Program P6-5 and identifying A = 1, B = 0, C = 0, and D = 1 will result in the display of a square, modified by the identity transformation (i.e., unmodified). (See Figure 6.3.)

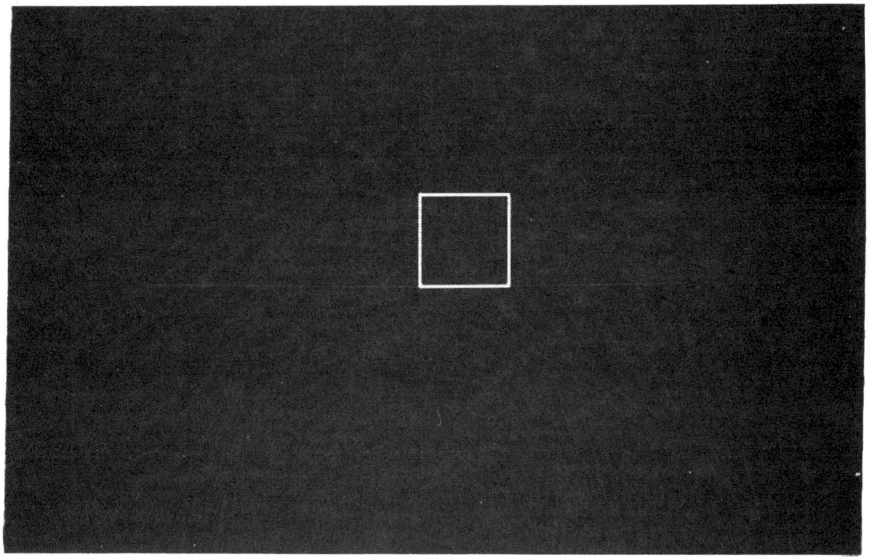

Figure 6.3

SCALING

Scaling may be controlled by a diagonal matrix. Note that

$$(X,Y)\begin{pmatrix} A & 0 \\ 0 & D \end{pmatrix} = (AX,DY).$$

The diagonal entries of the matrix thus may be used to provide independent scaling in the direction of each of the coordinate axes. For example, we may scale (stretch) points in the X direction by a factor of 2 through multiplication by

$$\begin{pmatrix} 2 & 0 \\ 0 & 1 \end{pmatrix}$$

(see Figure 6.4). To see this, run Program P6-5, identifying A = 2, B = 0, C = 0, and D = 1.

To scale (shrink) points in the direction of the Y axis by a factor of 1/5, multiply by

$$\begin{pmatrix} 1 & 0 \\ 0 & .2 \end{pmatrix}$$

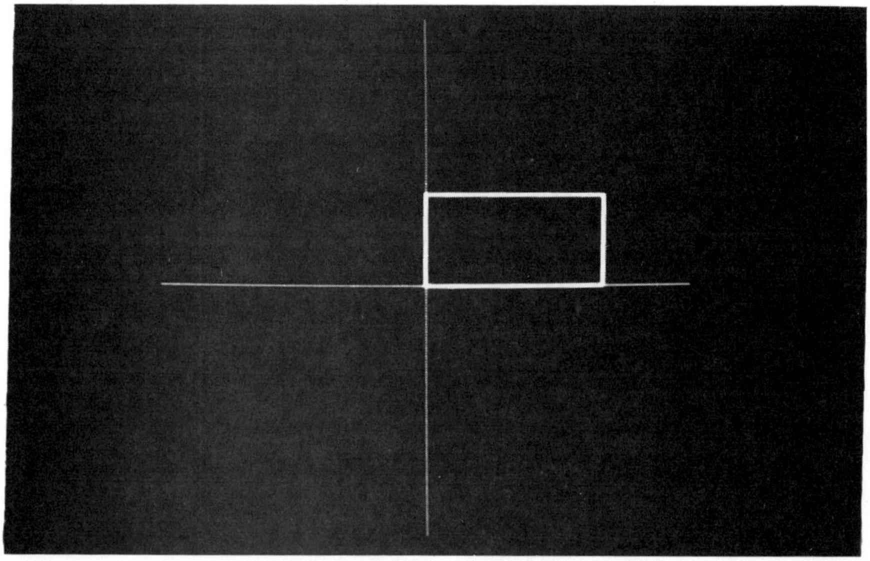

Figure 6.4

(see Figure 6.5). Overall scaling is provided by the matrix

$$\begin{pmatrix} K & 0 \\ 0 & K \end{pmatrix}$$

In Program P6-5, try a variety of values for A and D. Keep B = 0 and C = 0. This way, you are seeing only scaling transformations.

REFLECTION

Reflection of an object through the Y axis or X axis refers to the process of generating a mirror image of the object on the opposite side of the respective axis. A little thought will show that the matrices

$$\begin{pmatrix} -1 & 0 \\ 0 & 1 \end{pmatrix} \quad \text{and} \quad \begin{pmatrix} 1 & 0 \\ 0 & -1 \end{pmatrix}$$

represent reflections through the Y axis and X axis respectively. Reflection through the origin (0,0) is represented by the matrix

$$\begin{pmatrix} -1 & 0 \\ 0 & -1 \end{pmatrix}$$

Note that these reflections are essentially scalings for which the scale factor is negative.

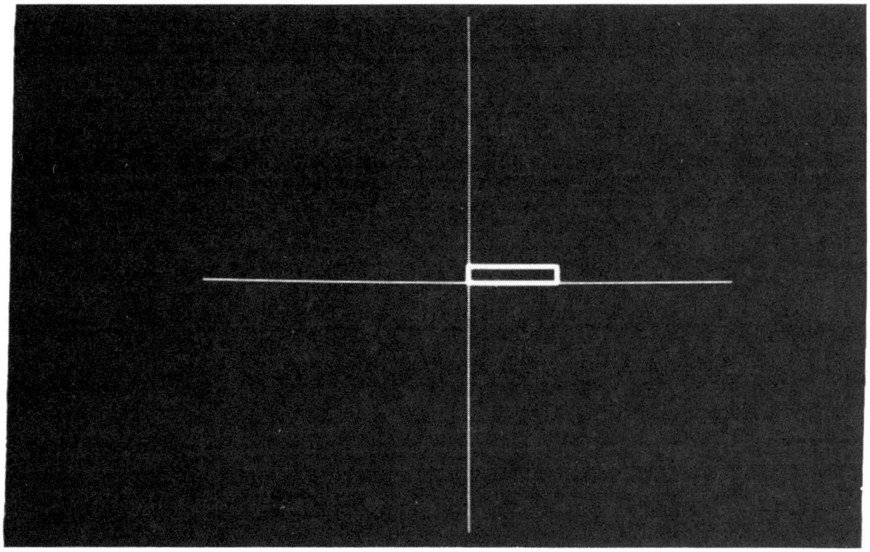

Figure 6.5

Reflection of images through other lines is possible, but the matrices, in general, are not so easy to identify. In order to do this it is necessary to combine transformations. The general process is described later, in the section Combinations of Transformations.

SHEAR

The effect of the matrix

$$\begin{pmatrix} 1 & 1.5 \\ 0 & 1 \end{pmatrix}$$

on the points of the square of Program P6-5 is shown in Figure 6.6. Algebraically,

$$(X',Y') = (X,Y)\begin{pmatrix} 1 & 1.5 \\ 0 & 1 \end{pmatrix} = (X, \quad 1.5X + Y)$$

The transformation is referred to as a Y shear (or shear in the direction of Y). An X shear is represented by matrices of the form

$$\begin{pmatrix} 1 & 0 \\ C & 1 \end{pmatrix}$$

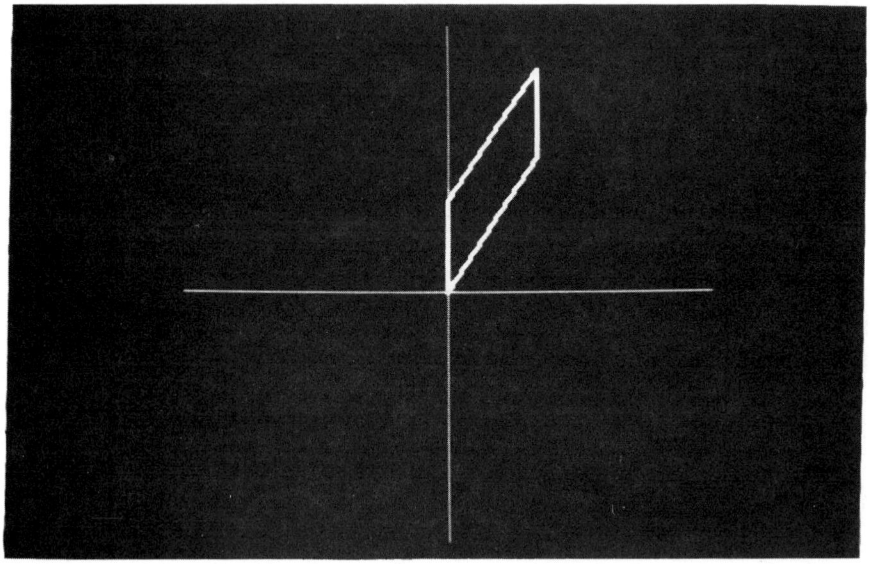

Figure 6.6

Run Program P6-5, identifying A, B, C, and D so as to define several shears.

ROTATION

The points of an image may be rotated counterclockwise by multiplying the points by the matrix

$$\begin{pmatrix} \text{COS}\theta & \text{SIN}\theta \\ -\text{SIN}\theta & \text{COS}\theta \end{pmatrix}$$

> **NOTE:** The symbol θ is the Greek letter **theta**. It is common to use such letters to represent angles, although we could just as well use English letters (e.g., SIN A). In BASIC, we'll use TH or THETA instead of θ. We'll also have to use parentheses, so SINθ will be written as SIN(TH).

The effect of the components of the matrices for scaling, reflection, and shear were fairly easy to identify. The components of the rotation matrix are less obvious. First note that

$$(A,B) = (1,0)\begin{pmatrix} A & B \\ C & D \end{pmatrix}$$

and

$$(C,D) = (0,1)\begin{pmatrix} A & B \\ C & D \end{pmatrix}$$

Thus, the first row of the matrix of a transformation shows the effect the transformation has on the point (1,0), and the second row of the matrix shows the effect the transformation has on the point (0,1). If we know the effect we want a transformation to have on the two points (1,0) and (0,1), we can now identify each of the components of the matrix.

From trigonometry we observe that the rotation of (1,0) through a counterclockwise angle θ yields the point (COSθ,SINθ), while rotation of (0,1) through the same angle yields (−SINθ,COSθ).

NOTE: The trigonometric functions SIN and COS may be used to represent ratios of sides of a right triangle. These right triangle relationships provide the justification for the above results.

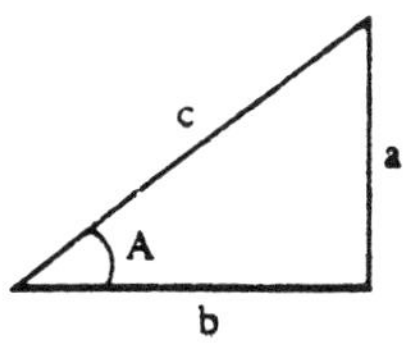

$$SIN(A) = \frac{a}{c}$$

$$COS(A) = \frac{b}{c}$$

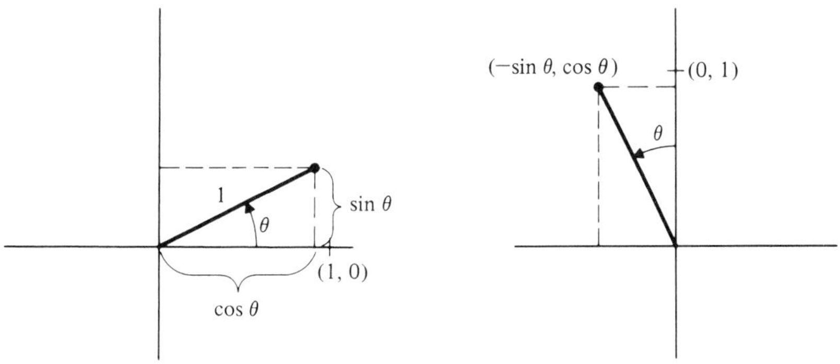

Figure 6.7

The matrix which represents the rotation is thus

$$\begin{pmatrix} \text{COS}\theta & \text{SIN}\theta \\ -\text{SIN}\theta & \text{COS}\theta \end{pmatrix}$$

Figure 6.8 shows the result of using Program P6-5 with A = COS(.5) = .878, B = SIN(.5) = .479, C = −SIN(.5) = −.479, and D = COS(.5) = .878.

> **NOTE:** In BASIC angles must be measured in *radians*. A radian is about 57.3 degrees. The exact relation is that 2π radians = 360°, so 1 radian = 360°/6.2832 = 57.2956°. A more complete description of radian measure is given in Appendix 5.

We now may use matrices to represent the following transformations: identity, scale, reflection, shear, and rotation. Still others may be derived, either through the process used to justify the rotation matrix, or by combining the existing transformation matrices.

Example: Define the transformation T to consist of rotating through a counterclockwise angle of θ = .4 radians followed by scaling the X component by a factor of 2.

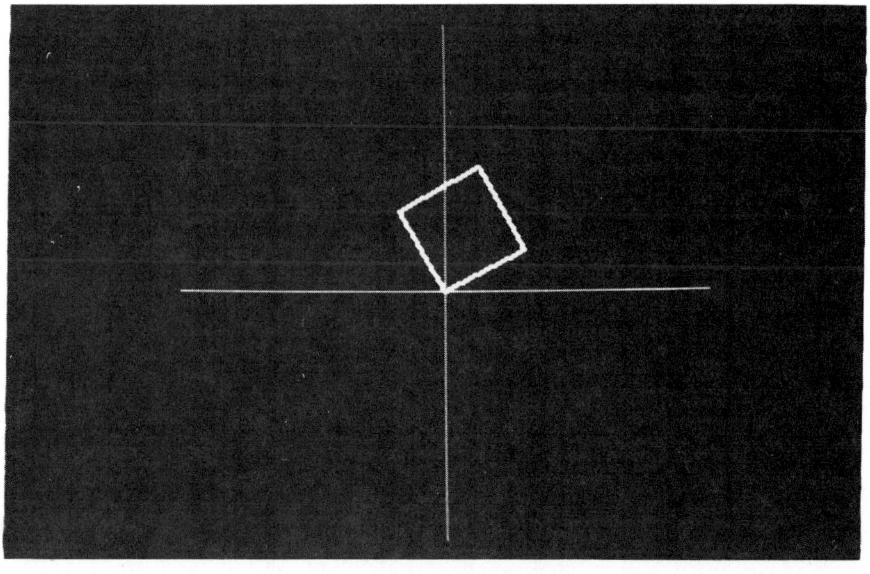

Figure 6.8

The rotation may be accomplished by

$$(X',Y') = (X,Y)\begin{pmatrix} COS(.4) & SIN(.4) \\ -SIN(.4) & COS(.4) \end{pmatrix}$$

and the scaling by

$$(X'',Y'') = (X',Y')\begin{pmatrix} 2 & 0 \\ 0 & 1 \end{pmatrix}$$

or, replacing (X′,Y′),

$$(X'',Y'') = \left[(X,Y)\begin{pmatrix} COS(.4) & SIN(.4) \\ -SIN(.4) & COS(.4) \end{pmatrix}\right]\begin{pmatrix} 2 & 0 \\ 0 & 1 \end{pmatrix}$$

$$(X'',Y'') = (X,Y)\left[\begin{pmatrix} COS(.4) & SIN(.4) \\ -SIN(.4) & COS(.4) \end{pmatrix}\begin{pmatrix} 2 & 0 \\ 0 & 1 \end{pmatrix}\right]$$

$$= (X,Y)\begin{pmatrix} 2COS(.4) & SIN(.4) \\ -2SIN(.4) & COS(.4) \end{pmatrix}$$

The matrix of the transformation is

$$\begin{pmatrix} 2COS(.4) & SIN(.4) \\ -2SIN(.4) & COS(.4) \end{pmatrix} = \begin{pmatrix} 1.842 & .389 \\ -.779 & .921 \end{pmatrix}$$

The matrix of a series of sequentially applied transformations is the product of the matrices of the transformations. When calculating the product, one must be careful to have the matrices in the proper order. In general, matrix products are not commutative (i.e., the statement AB = BA is not always true). Note that we get a transformation T* that is very different from T if we first scale the X component by a factor of 2, then rotate through a counterclockwise angle of $\theta = .4$.

Suggestion: Show that the matrix of the transformation T* described above is

$$\begin{pmatrix} 1.842 & .779 \\ -.389 & .921 \end{pmatrix}$$

One serious deficiency exists in our present ability to represent transformations by matrices: Each of the transformations we have considered is centered at (0,0). Stated differently, if each of the transformations is applied to (0,0), the result is (0,0); the point (0,0) is invariant under the transformations. In the long term this is not a healthy situation. Rotation through a counterclockwise angle θ is rotation about the point (0,0). Rotation about other points is not available. Similarly, reflections may be

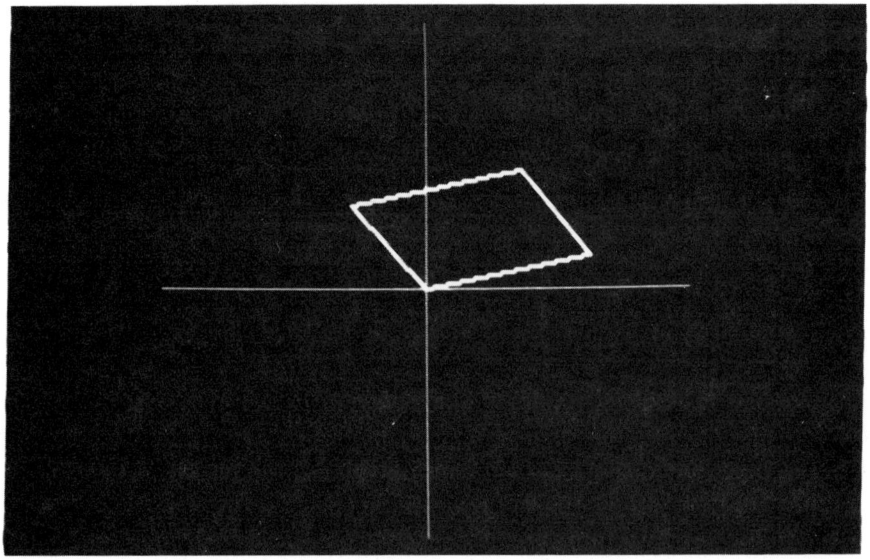

Figure 6.9a Effect of T on the square of Program P6-5

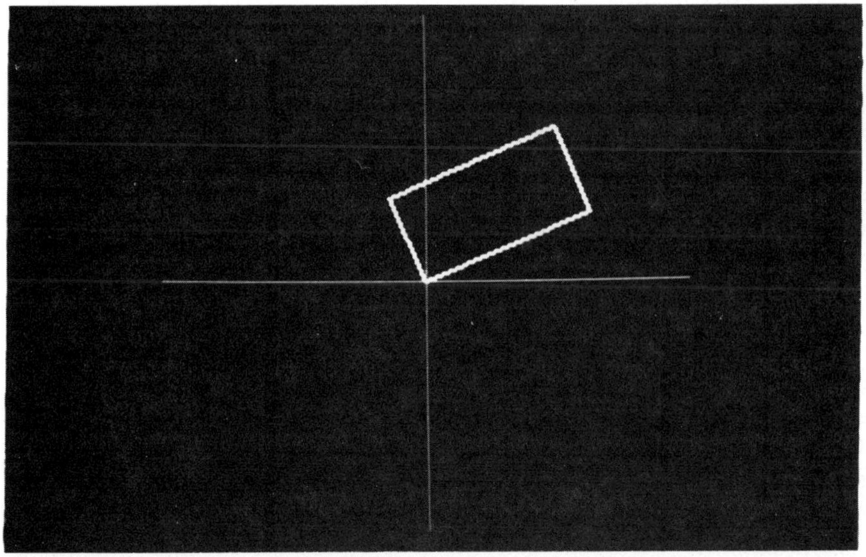

Figure 6.9b Effect of T* on the square of Program P6-5

through the X axis, the Y axis, or the origin, but not through other points or lines.

As a step in developing the ability to remove the zero-centered nature of transformations, we now will introduce homogeneous coordinates.

HOMOGENEOUS COORDINATES

The two-coordinate representation of points is a convenient and efficient reference system for points in a plane. A reference point (the origin) is established, and a pair of directed perpendicular lines intersecting at the origin is chosen as the coordinate axes. Each point in the plane is then associated with the ordered pair of its directed distances from the coordinate axes.

The homogeneous coordinate representation of points in a plane associates, with each point (A,B), an ordered triple (P,Q,R), with P, Q, and R chosen so that A = P/R and B = Q/R.

The homogeneous coordinate representation of a point is not unique. The point (2,5), for example, may be identified as (4, 10, 2), (−20, −50, −10), (2.1, 5.25, 1.05), or (2,5,1), among others. We will use the representation (2,5,1) and, in general, will refer to (A,B,1) as the *normalized* homogeneous coordinate representation of the point (A,B). As a result, the point with homogeneous coordinates (P,Q,R) has normalized form (P/R,Q/R,1) and Cartesian coordinates (P/R,Q/R).

When using the normalized homogeneous coordinates (A,B,1) of the point (A,B), we may consider the third coordinate to be an appendage. While unnecessary at times, homogeneous coordinates add to our ability to represent transformations as matrix products.

The most obvious effect of the introduction of homogeneous coordinates is that our previous matrix representations of transformations must be upgraded. This is easily done, since each of the earlier matrices

$$\begin{pmatrix} A & B \\ C & D \end{pmatrix} \quad \text{becomes} \quad \begin{pmatrix} A & B & 0 \\ C & D & 0 \\ 0 & 0 & 1 \end{pmatrix}$$

TRANSLATION

The problem which led to the introduction of homogeneous coordinates is easily addressed by adding *translation* to the list of transformations. By "translate through (H,K)" we intend that the points of an object be moved horizontally through H units and vertically through K units. While translations could not previously be represented by matrix multiplication, homogeneous coordinate representation of points adds the transformation matrix:

$$\begin{pmatrix} 1 & 0 & 0 \\ 0 & 1 & 0 \\ H & K & 1 \end{pmatrix}$$

Multiplying the point (X,Y,1) by this matrix yields (X + H,Y + K,1).

COMBINATIONS OF TRANSFORMATIONS

Many transformations that cannot be represented by one of the matrices described above are combinations of several. For example, the rotation transformation matrix represents a rotation about the origin through a counterclockwise angle θ. We will now obtain the matrix of a rotation about the point (2,1) through a counterclockwise angle of 30°.

The rotation transformation matrix represents a rotation which is centered at (0,0). A rotation centered at (2,1) may be effected by:

1. Translating (2,1) to the origin [translating the origin to (−2,−1)]. The matrix of this transformation is

$$T = \begin{pmatrix} 1 & 0 & 0 \\ 0 & 1 & 0 \\ -2 & -1 & 1 \end{pmatrix}$$

2. Rotation through 30°. The transformation matrix is

$$R = \begin{pmatrix} \text{COS } 30^\circ & \text{SIN } 30^\circ & 0 \\ -\text{SIN } 30^\circ & \text{COS } 30^\circ & 0 \\ 0 & 0 & 1 \end{pmatrix} = \begin{pmatrix} .866 & .5 & 0 \\ -.5 & .866 & 0 \\ 0 & 0 & 1 \end{pmatrix}$$

3. Translate (0,0) to (2,1) in order to restore the system to its original position:

$$T^* = \begin{pmatrix} 1 & 0 & 0 \\ 0 & 1 & 0 \\ 2 & 1 & 1 \end{pmatrix}$$

Thus a point (X,Y) may be rotated through 30° about the point (2,1) to a position (X′,Y′) by the sequence (X′,Y′,1) = (X,Y,1)TRT*.

Rather than multiplying (X,Y,1) by the three matrices, we might first multiply the matrices together to obtain M = TRT*. Then, (X′,Y′,1) = (X,Y,1)M. In this case,

$$M = \begin{pmatrix} .866 & .5 & 0 \\ -.5 & .866 & 0 \\ .768 & -.866 & 1 \end{pmatrix}$$

and (X′,Y′,1) = (.866X − .5Y + .768, .5X + .866Y − .866, 1).

Products of the transformation matrices for homogeneous coordinates will always be of the form

$$\begin{pmatrix} A & B & 0 \\ C & D & 0 \\ H & K & 1 \end{pmatrix}$$

and the effect of the transformation on a point (X,Y) may be described by

$$(X',Y',1) = (X,Y,1)\begin{pmatrix} A & B & 0 \\ C & D & 0 \\ H & K & 1 \end{pmatrix}$$

or X′ = AX + CY + H and Y′ = BX + DY + K.

To illustrate the effects of such transformations we may use Program P6-6, which is a modification of Program P6-5. Then, by providing values for A, B, C, D, H, and K, we will see the effect of the transformation of the example above. The rectangle (same one as before) is rotated through an angle of 30°, with the rotation centered at the point (2,1). (See Figure 6.10.)

Program P6-6: HOMOGENEOUS COORDINATE MATRIX

```
10 'PROGRAM P6-6  (HOMOGENEOUS COORDINATE MATRIX)
20 'Illustrates effects of 3X3 transformation matrix
100 '=================================================
110 KEY OFF: SCREEN 1,0: COLOR 0,0: CLS
120 WINDOW (-4,-3) - (4,3)
130 '=================================================
140 'Input matrix
150 LOCATE 23,1: INPUT; "A =";A
160 LOCATE 23,15: INPUT; "B =";B
170 LOCATE 24,1: INPUT; "C =";C
180 LOCATE 24,15: INPUT; "D =";D
```

```
190 LOCATE 25,1: INPUT; "H =";H
200 LOCATE 25,15: INPUT; "K =";K
210 '=====================================================
220 'Draw axes
230 LINE (0,3) - (0,-3),2
240 LINE (3,0) - (-3,0),2
250 '=====================================================
260 'Draw rectangle
270 FOR LIN = 1 TO 4
280  READ X,Y
290  TX = A*X + C*Y + H: Y = B*X + D*Y + K: X = TX
300  PSET (X,Y)
310  READ X,Y
320  TX = A*X + C*Y + H: Y = B*X + D*Y + K: X = TX
330  LINE - (X,Y)
340 NEXT LIN
350 '=====================================================
360 RESTORE: LOCATE 22,1
370 INPUT "Press 'N' for new matrix; 'E' to end"; ST$
380 IF ST$ = "n" OR ST$ = "N" THEN CLS: GOTO 150
390 IF ST$ = "e" OR ST$ = "E" THEN CLS: END
400 GOTO 370
410 DATA 0,0, 1,0
420 DATA 1,0, 1,1
430 DATA 1,1, 0,1
440 DATA 0,1, 0,0
```

As a second example of the use of transformation matrices, we will work through the development of a program which draws a sequence of nested hexagons to generate the image in Figure 6.12.

We will center the hexagon at the origin (0,0) and provide one of the six vertices. Since the consecutive vertices of a hexagon are separated by a central angle of 60°, the second vertex will be derived by rotating the first through 60°. The third when will be calculated by rotating the second vertex through 60°. In this manner we will obtain vertices 4, 5, and 6.

The matrix of the rotation transformation is

$$R = \begin{pmatrix} \mathrm{COS}\theta & \mathrm{SIN}\theta & 0 \\ -\mathrm{SIN}\theta & \mathrm{COS}\theta & 0 \\ 0 & 0 & 1 \end{pmatrix}$$

At each stage of calculation, we obtain the coordinates (XN,YN) of the next vertex from the coordinates of the current vertex by (XN,YN,1) =

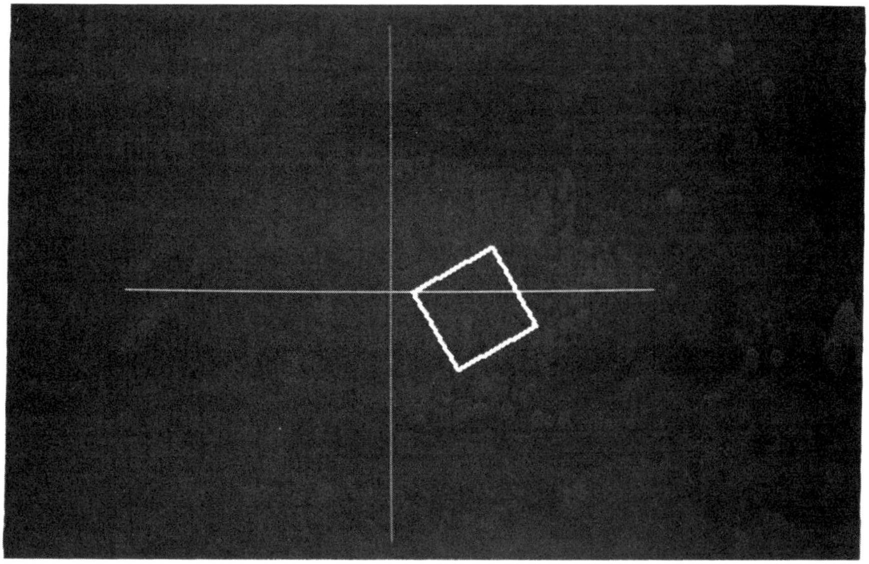

Figure 6.10

(X,Y,1)R, so that

$$XN = X*COS(TH) - Y*SIN(TH)$$

$$YN = X*SIN(TH) + Y*COS(TH)$$

Since the calculation of sine and cosine are time consuming, we will do this only once, identifying C = COS(60°) and S = SIN(60°). The calculation of (XN,YN) then becomes:

$$XN = X*C - Y*S$$

$$YN = X*S + Y*C.$$

Locating the hexagon's center at (0,0) is convenient for use of the rotation transformation, but inconvenient for use with the IBM PC display screen (we have not defined a WINDOW). Most of the hexagon will be offscreen, as indicated in Figure 6.11.

Before the points of the hexagon may be plotted, they must be translated to an onscreen location. Each point may be translated through (CX,CY) by multiplication by the matrix

$$\begin{pmatrix} 1 & 0 & 0 \\ 0 & 1 & 0 \\ CX & CY & 1 \end{pmatrix}$$

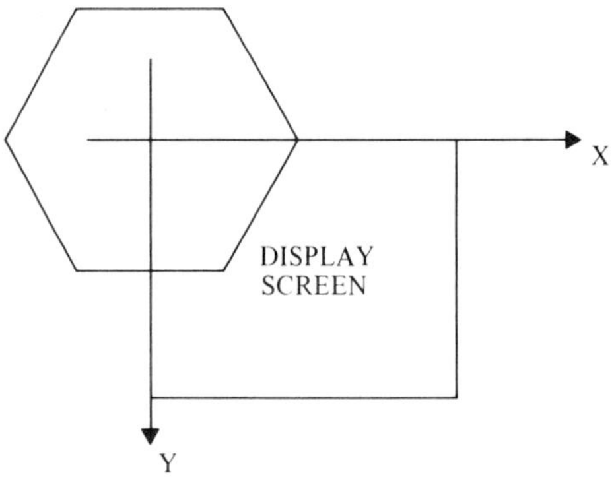

Figure 6.11

Note that this transformation could be avoided by using a WINDOW statement to rescale the screen. Of course, the transformation would still be performed, but we would not have to program it.

At this point we can draw a single hexagon using the following program:

Program P6-7: HEXAGON

```
10 'PROGRAM P6-7  (HEXAGON)
20 'Draws a single hexagon
100 '===============================================
110 'Initialize
120 PI = 3.14159: SC = 5/12
130 X = 250: Y = 0: CX = 320: CY = 100
140 C = COS(PI/3): S = SIN(PI/3)
160 KEY OFF: SCREEN 2: CLS
170 '===============================================
180 'Draw a hexagon
200  FOR I = 0 TO 6
210   SX = X + CX: SY = CY - Y*SC
220   IF I = 0 THEN PSET (SX,SY)
230   LINE - (SX,SY)
240   XN = X*C-Y*S: Y = X*S+Y*C: X = XN
250  NEXT I
```

We will add program lines to provide a sequence of hexagons nested within this one, each slightly smaller than the previous one, and each slightly rotated.

The size of the hexagons may be controlled by multiplication by the matrix

$$\begin{pmatrix} SF & 0 & 0 \\ 0 & SF & 0 \\ 0 & 0 & 1 \end{pmatrix}$$

where SF is a scale factor of our choice. To rotate each hexagon slightly, we again will use the rotation transformation matrix with a new value for θ.

The transition from one hexagon to the next (scaling, rotation) is effected by

$$(XN,YN,1) = (X,Y,1)\begin{pmatrix} SF & 0 & 0 \\ 0 & SF & 0 \\ 0 & 0 & 1 \end{pmatrix}\begin{pmatrix} COS\theta & SIN\theta & 0 \\ -SIN\theta & COS\theta & 0 \\ 0 & 0 & 1 \end{pmatrix}$$

or

$$XN = X*SF*COS(THETA) - Y*SF*SIN(THETA)$$

$$YN = X*SF*SIN(THETA) + Y*SF*COS(THETA)$$

Having identified one point of the next hexagon, we then use Program P6-7 to draw the hexagon. Program P6-8 combines the above calculations with Program P6-7 to draw the set of nested hexagons. The program uses a value of .95 for SF and a value of PI/36 for THETA.

Program P6-8: HEXAGON DESIGN

```
10 'PROGRAM P6-8  (HEXAGON DESIGN)
20 'Draws a sequence of spiralling hexagons
100 '=========================================
110 'Initialize
120 PI = 3.14159: SC = 5/12
130 X = 250: Y = 0: CX = 320: CY = 100: SF = .95
140 C = COS(PI/3): S = SIN(PI/3)
150 C1 = COS(PI/36): S1 = SIN(PI/36)
160 KEY OFF: SCREEN 2: CLS
170 '=========================================
180 'Draw hexagons
190 FOR J = 1 TO 40
200  FOR I = 0 TO 6
210   SX = X + CX: SY = CY - Y*SC
220   IF I = 0 THEN PSET (SX,SY)
```

```
230    LINE - (SX,SY)
240    XN = X*C-Y*S: Y = X*S+Y*C: X = XN
250   NEXT I
260   XN = SF*(X*C1-Y*S1): Y = SF*(X*S1+Y*C1): X = XN
270 NEXT J
```

NOTES AND SUGGESTIONS

1. Adapt Program P6-7 so that it will draw a pentagon or an octagon. Modify it again to ask for N, the number of sides, and then draw an N-sided polygon.

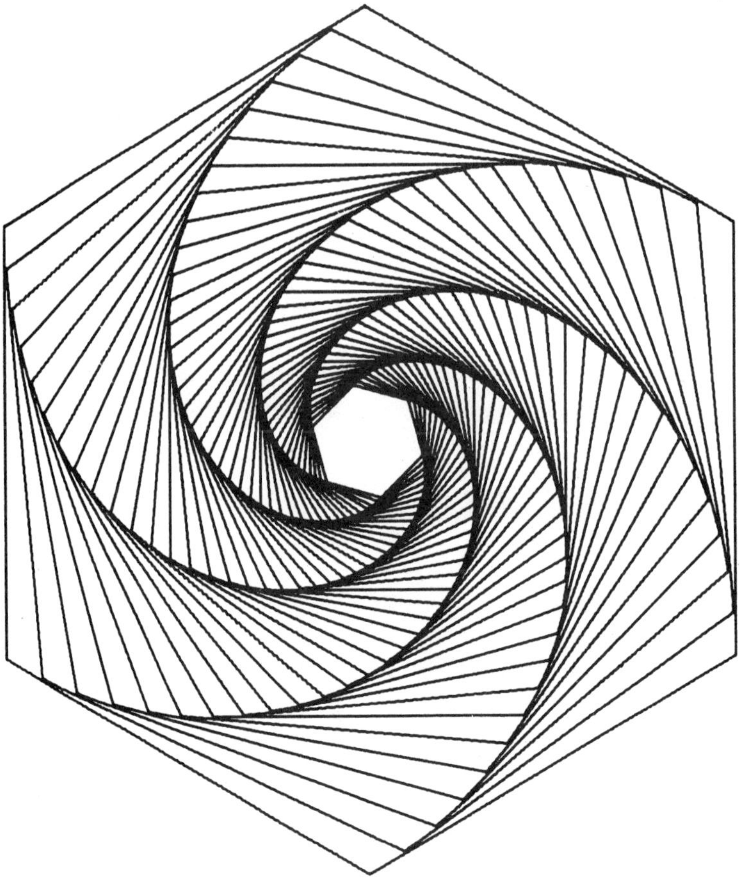

Figure 6.12

2. Figure 6.12 was drawn by a digital plotter, using a program which is a slight modification of the one above. The modifications needed are dependent on the plotter used. In its most elementary form, the information sent to the plotter identifies the pen status (UP or DOWN) and its position on the paper (these are the coordinates at which the pen is located). A sequence of instructions such as

```
UP
100,120
DOWN
UP
```

will result in raising the pen, moving it to location (100,120), pressing the pen to the paper, then raising it again. To draw a line from location (100,120) to (200,10), a sequence such as the following would be used:

```
UP
100,120
200,10
UP
```

3. Write a program to draw your initials on one of the graphics screens. Then, by using appropriate transformations, have the initials drawn:

(a) at three locations on the screen (use translation);
(b) rotated through 45° (use rotation);
(c) upside down (use reflection);
(d) in three sizes (use scaling).

Chapter 7
Analytic Geometry and Computer Graphics

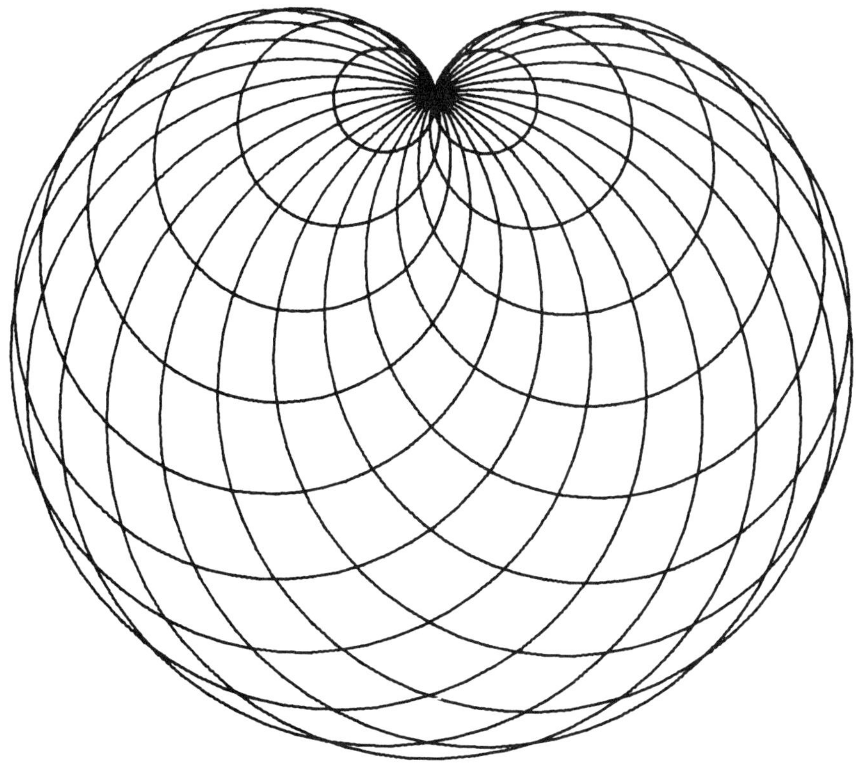

Figure 7.1

One of the topics of high-school mathematics is the sketching of graphs. It is part of analytic geometry, the study of processes for stating mathematical relationships both algebraically (or analytically) and graphically.

The pages ahead will mimic portions of a course in analytic geometry, but will leave the calculation and plotting to the computer while we focus on the design. The intent is to develop methods for obtaining useful and pleasing curves.

COORDINATE AXES

Analytic geometry is sometimes called coordinate geometry because of its reliance on a coordinate axis system. Students in analytic geometry begin by drawing a pair of directed perpendicular lines intersecting in the middle of the page, as suggested in Figure 7.2.

A coordinate axis system is provided on the IBM PC graphics screens, but its location and orientation differ somewhat from that which is shown above. The IBM PC coordinate system is shown in Figure 7.3.

We can reorient and relocate points so that they may be identified relative to a centrally located, Y-upward, X-rightward coordinate system.

For the high-resolution screen, first provide the lines for the coordinate axes:

```
LINE (320,0) - (320,199): LINE (0,100) -
(639,100)
```

Next identify the center of the coordinate system:

```
CX = 320: CY = 100
```

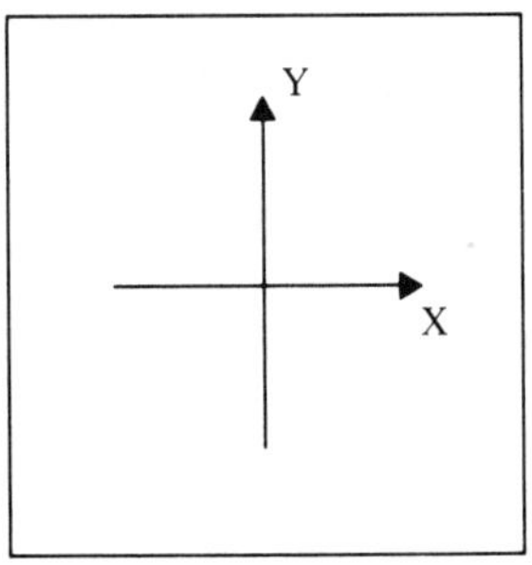

Figure 7.2

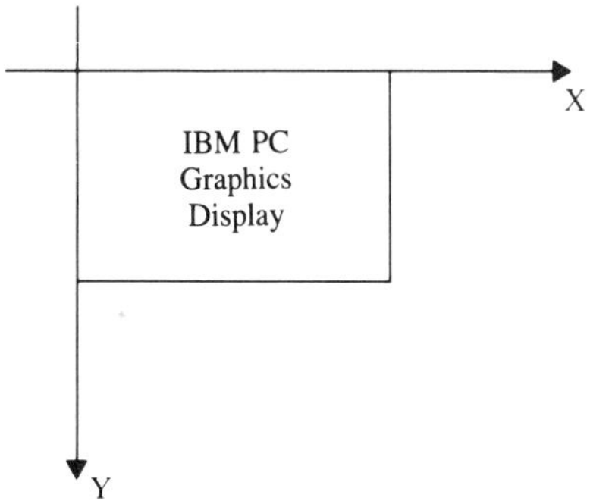

Figure 7.3

Then replace **PSET (X,Y)** with **PSET (X + CX,CY − Y)** and replace **LINE–(X,Y)** with **LINE–(X + CX,CY − Y)** for all future plotting.

Note that by replacing (X,Y) with (X + CX,CY − Y) for plotting purposes, we have effected a transformation: reflection through the X axis, followed by translation through (CX,CY). The matrix of the reflection is

$$\begin{pmatrix} 1 & 0 & 0 \\ 0 & -1 & 0 \\ 0 & 0 & 1 \end{pmatrix}$$

and the matrix of the translation is

$$\begin{pmatrix} 1 & 0 & 0 \\ 0 & 1 & 0 \\ CX & CY & 1 \end{pmatrix}$$

The product of the matrices is

$$\begin{pmatrix} 1 & 0 & 0 \\ 0 & -1 & 0 \\ CX & CY & 1 \end{pmatrix}$$

and

$$(X,Y,1) \begin{pmatrix} 1 & 0 & 0 \\ 0 & -1 & 0 \\ CX & CY & 1 \end{pmatrix} = (X + CX, CY - Y, 1)$$

For specified values of X and Y, we may identify the screen coordinates (SX,SY) relative to the centered coordinate system by calculating

SX = X + CX and SY = CY − Y or, if a scaling factor is needed to equate the horizontal and vertical units, SX = X + CX and SY = CY − SC*Y.

There is a far simpler method of arranging for the above transformation of points. That is to use the WINDOW statement to rescale the screen. The statement **WINDOW (−320, −99)–(319,100)** will have the same effect as the transformations outlined above. We will not have to transform the points to be plotted; the WINDOW statement causes the transformation to be applied without any further efforts on our part.

In most of the programs in this chapter, we will use a WINDOW statement to establish a coordinate system. Further, we will typically choose a WINDOW that will cause horizontal and vertical units of measurement to be equivalent. However, we will occasionally revert to the standard screen coordinates for plotting, to keep the transformations firmly in mind.

LINES

Aside from the point, the simplest geometric object is the line, algebraically represented by Y = MX + B. M is the slope of the line, providing a measure of its steepness; B is the value of Y at the point of intersection of the line and the Y axis. The following brief program (Program P7-1) will sketch the graph of Y = .5X + 2 on a WINDOWed screen.

Program P7-1: LINE

```
10 'PROGRAM P7-1  (LINE)
20 'Line Y = MX + B
100 '========================
110 KEY OFF: SCREEN 2: CLS
120 'Set WINDOW and draw axes
130 WINDOW (-6,-4) - (6,5)
140 LINE (0,-4) - (0,5)
150 LINE (-6,0) - (6,0)
160 'Define line and draw it
170 DEF FN Y(X) = .5*X + 2
180 X = - 6: Y = FN Y(X)
190 PSET (X,Y)
200 X = 6: Y = FN Y(X)
210 LINE - (X,Y)
```

If the term *slope* is not familiar to you, or if you have not used it lately, try the above program with several choices for the slope (M). Then replace the second parameter (B) with some other values, to get a better feel for the role of each of M and B in the linear function Y(X) = MX + B (line 170).

Further consideration of lines may not seem necessary. The algebraic representation of a line as Y = MX + B, together with the LINE statement, provide means of identifying and drawing lines quickly and easily. However, there are times when it is preferable to draw a line slowly, or to have an object move along a linear path, or to identify a point which is a fraction of the way between the ends of a line segment. In such cases it is necessary to have a way of identifying intermediate points of a line. Program P7-2 illustrates how this can be done.

Program P7-2: LINE–PARAMETRICALLY

```
10 'PROGRAM P7-2  (LINE - PARAMETRICALLY)
20 'Draws a line slowly
100 '===================================
105 KEY OFF: SCREEN 2: CLS
110 XL = 10: Y1 = 150: X2 = 300: Y2 = 10
120 DX = X2 - X1: DY = Y2 - Y1
130 PSET (X1,Y1)
140 FOR T = 0 TO 1 STEP .001
150  LINE - (X1 + T*DX,Y1 + T*DY)
160 NEXT T
```

In drawing from (X1,Y1) to (X2,Y2) it is necessary for X to change by an amount DX = X2 − X1, and for Y to change by an amount DY = Y2 − Y1. Rather than have the changes occur all at once [as in **LINE (X1,Y1)–(X2,Y2)**], the loop in lines 140–160 takes the changes in 1000 small increments. Control of the step size in this loop provides control of the rate of movement along the line.

The points of the line are identified by the parametric equations

$$X = X1 + T*DX$$
$$Y = Y1 + T*DY$$

and T is referred to as the *parameter*. If T = 0, then (X,Y) = (X1,Y1). If T = 1, then (X,Y) = (X2,Y2). It is the variation in T which identifies the intermediate points of the line. We will find parametric equations to be useful in describing other curves later in this chapter.

CIRCLES

A circle is described as the set of points (X,Y) at a fixed distance R from the center (H,K). Algebraically, we have

$$(X - H)^2 + (Y - K)^2 = R^2$$

For a circle with its center at (0,0), the equation becomes

$$X^2 + Y^2 = R^2$$

BASIC has a rather powerful CIRCLE statement which serves most needs when circles are to be drawn. There are occasions when it is necessary to identify points on a circle or a point within a circular sector (for example, to PAINT the sector), or to provide motion on a circular path. For these types of applications the CIRCLE statement is inadequate. It will also be inadequate for defining a circular arc which is part of a three-dimensional image (see Chapters 8, 9).

RECTANGULAR COORDINATE METHOD

The relation $X^2 + Y^2 = R^2$ may be decomposed into the two functions $YP = \sqrt{R^2 - X^2}$ and $YN = -\sqrt{R^2 - X^2}$. The following program (P7-3) will generate a sketch of the circle $X^2 + Y^2 = 16$, using the above two functions.

Program P7-3: CIRCLE 1

```
10 'PROGRAM P7-3  (CIRCLE 1)
20 'Rectangular coordinate circle
100 '===============================
110 KEY OFF: SCREEN 2: CLS
120 'Set WINDOW and draw axes
130 WINDOW (-6,-4) - (6,5)
140 LINE (0,-4) - (0,5)
150 LINE (-6,0) - (6,0)
160 'Define functions for semicircles
170 RAD = 4
180 DEF FN YP(X) = SQR(RAD^2 - X^2)
190 DEF FN YN(X) = -SQR(RAD^2 - X^2)
```

```
200 '================================
210 'Draw upper semicircle
220 X = RAD: Y = FN YP(X)
230 PSET (X,Y)
240 FOR X = RAD TO -RAD STEP -1
250 Y = FN YP(X)
260  LINE - (X,Y)
270 NEXT X
280 '================================
290 'Draw lower semicircle
300 FOR X = -RAD TO RAD
310 Y = FN YN(X)
320  LINE - (X,Y)
330 NEXT X
```

Note the angularity of the image. The program draws an upper semicircle (lines 220–270) and a lower semicircle (lines 300–330). The ends of each of these semicircles have an angular appearance. One cure for the problem is to choose a smaller step size for the point-generating loop, thus having a larger number of points calculated. This will result in a smoother circle. It will still not be uniformly smooth, however.

The fault for the angularity lies with the point-generating loops, which space points at equal distances as measured by increments in X-coordinates, rather than at equal distances around the arc of the circle. To see more clearly the lack of uniform spacing, remove lines 140, 150 and replace lines 260 and 320 with

```
260 PSET (X,Y)
320 PSET (X,Y)
```

POINT GENERATION BY ANGULAR INCREMENTS

The angularity in the image generated by the above program resulted from calculating points which were not evenly spaced around the arc of the circle. We consider next a technique which provides for equally spaced points.

From trigonometry we have, for a point (X,Y) on the circle $X^2 + Y^2 = R^2$,

$$X = RCOS(\theta)$$
$$Y = RSIN(\theta)$$

with θ measured as indicated in Figure 7.4.

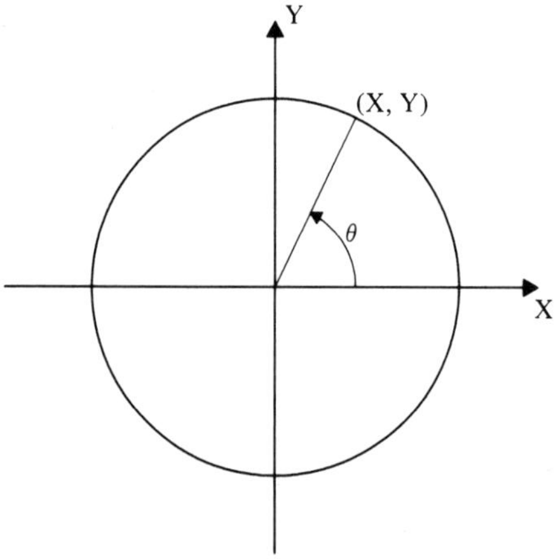

Figure 7.4

Program P7-4 makes use of these formulas to sketch a circle using points that are evenly spaced around the arc of the circle. The even spacing is a result of the equal angular increments provided by the step size of the FOR statement of line 190.

Program P7-4: CIRCLE 2

```
10 'PROGRAM P7-4  (CIRCLE 2)
20 'Draws a circle using angular increments
100 '================================
110 KEY OFF: SCREEN 2: CLS
120 'Set WINDOW and draw axes
130 WINDOW (-6,-4) - (6,5)
140 LINE (0,-4) - (0,5)
150 LINE (-6,0) - (6,0)
160 '================================
170 'Draw circle
180 RAD = 4
190 FOR T = 0 TO 6.4 STEP .2
200  X = RAD*COS(T): Y = RAD*SIN(T)
210  IF T = 0 THEN PSET (X,Y)
220  LINE - (X,Y)
230 NEXT T
```

The formulas used here to identify points of a circle are also useful for identifying points within a sector of a circle, for PAINTing the sector, and for placing labels within a sector or around the arc of a circle. This is the method used for calculating the XLAB, YLAB, and CX, CY values used in Program P4-6. There the point (XLAB, YLAB) was positioned using an angle which is halfway through the arc of the sector and 50 units from the center.

CIRCLE WITHOUT WINDOW

The WINDOW statement relieves us from much of the tedium associated with positioning and scaling an image. However, it is not difficult to handle this detail ourselves. Program P7-5 draws a circle on the high-resolution graphics screen, using the method of calculation presented for Program P7-4 but without defining a WINDOW.

Program P7-5: CIRCLE 3

```
10 'PROGRAM P7-5  (CIRCLE 3)
20 'Circle without WINDOW
100 '================================
110 KEY OFF: SCREEN 2: CLS: SC = 5/12
120 RAD = 200: CX = 320: CY = 100
130 LINE (CX,0) - (CX,199)
140 LINE (0,CY) - (640,CY)
150 '================================
160 'Draw circle
170 FOR T = 0 TO 6.4 STEP .2
180  X = RAD*COS(T): Y = RAD*SIN(T)
190  SX = X + CX: SY = CY - SC*Y
200  IF T = 0 THEN PSET (SX,SY)
210  LINE - (SX,SY)
220 NEXT T
```

Since Program P7-5 does not use the WINDOW statement, the screen has its default scale (horizontal 0–639; vertical 0–199). To obtain a circle which is centered on the screen and has proper horizontal and vertical scale, we define CX, CY (coordinates of the center of the screen), and SC (vertical scaling factor) to have values appropriate to the high-resolution graphics screen. As points (X,Y) are calculated they are transformed (line 190) before plotting. Note that the radius has a value appropriate to the screen scale.

RECURSIVE GENERATION OF POINTS

Program P1-9 sketched a spiral band by drawing concentric circles. The process used is derived from the one just described. It requires the calculation of the sine and cosine of only one angle. Each consecutive point around the circle will be obtained from the previous one.

We could number the points generated for use in sketching an image. In Program P7-4, 33 points are calculated. They would be numbered as (X_1,Y_1), (X_2,Y_2), (X_3,Y_3), . . . , (X_{33},Y_{33}). Two consecutive points (X_n,Y_n) and (X_{n+1},Y_{n+1}) are identified by

$$\begin{aligned} X_n &= R\text{COS}(\theta) \\ Y_n &= R\text{SIN}(\theta) \\ X_{n+1} &= R\text{COS}(\theta + D\theta) \\ Y_{n+1} &= R\text{SIN}(\theta + D\theta) \end{aligned}$$

where Dθ is the value of the step size for the point-generating loop.

From trigonometry, we get

$$\begin{aligned} X_{n+1} = R\text{COS}(\theta + D\theta) &= R\text{COS}(\theta)\text{COS}(D\theta) - R\text{SIN}(\theta)\text{SIN}(D\theta) \\ &= X_n\ \text{COS}(D\theta) - Y_n\ \text{SIN}(D\theta) \end{aligned}$$

and

$$\begin{aligned} Y_{n+1} = R\text{SIN}(\theta + D\theta) &= R\text{SIN}(\theta)\text{COS}(D\theta) + R\text{COS}(\theta)\text{SIN}(D\theta) \\ &= Y_n\ \text{COS}(D\theta) + X_n\ \text{SIN}(D\theta) \end{aligned}$$

By calculating COS(Dθ) and SIN(Dθ) only once and providing initial values for X_1 and Y_1, we can use the above formulas to calculate successive values for X_n and Y_n. To incorporate the formulas into a program we write [using DT for Dθ, C for COS(DT), and S for SIN(DT)],

```
TEMP = X*C - Y*S: Y = Y*C+ X*S: X = TEMP
```

Note that it is necessary to use the variable TEMP as a temporary stand-in for X until a new value for Y is calculated. Program P7-6 illustrates the process.

Program P7-6: CIRCLE 4

```
10 'PROGRAM P7-6  (CIRCLE 4)
20 'Recursively calculates points on a circle
```

```
100 '==================================
110 KEY OFF: SCREEN 2: CLS
120 'Set WINDOW and draw axes
130 WINDOW (-6,-4) - (6,5)
140 LINE (0,-4) - (0,5)
150 LINE (-6,0) - (6,0)
160 '==================================
170 'Draw circle
180 RAD = 4: X = RAD: Y = 0
190 DT = .1: N = 6.3/DT
200 C = COS(DT): S = SIN(DT)
210 PSET (X,Y)
220 FOR I = 1 TO N
230  TEMP = X*C - Y*S: Y = Y*C + S*X: X = TEMP
240  LINE - (X,Y)
250 NEXT I
```

Each of the circle-generating programs has centered the circle at the origin (0,0). We can generate a circle having center at point (H,K) by translating each of the points to be plotted. Each point (X,Y) can be translated to (X + H, Y + K) by the matrix product

$$(X,Y,1)\begin{pmatrix} 1 & 0 & 0 \\ 0 & 1 & 0 \\ H & K & 1 \end{pmatrix} = (X + H, Y + K, 1).$$

We can include the translation in Program P7-6 by changing lines 210 and 240 to read

```
210 PSET (X + H,Y + K)
240 LINE – (X + H,Y + K)
```

and adding a line to define the values of H and K. For example,

```
115 H = 1: K = 1
```

ELLIPSES

Elementary school students are sometimes taught (in art or math class) that they can draw an ellipse by using a pencil, two thumbtacks, and a length of string. The procedure is as follows:

1. Using the thumbtacks, fasten the ends of the string to a piece of pa-

Figure 7.5

per or cardboard (but not to the dining room table). The thumbtacks must be positioned so that some slack remains in the string.

2. Place a pencil point against the string, pulling it taut.
3. Keeping the pencil erect and the string taut, draw a curve on the paper through all points that the pencil can reach. The resulting curve is an ellipse.

The shape of the ellipse is dependent on the location of the thumbtacks and the length of the string. (The ratio of the length of the string to the distance between the thumbtacks is an item of value to students of analytic geometry.)

We describe the relationship between the thumbtacks, the length of string, and the associated ellipse by stating that:

> An ellipse is the set of points for which the sum of the distances from two fixed points (the thumbtacks) is constant (the length of the string). Each of the fixed points (thumbtacks) is called a focus (plural: foci) of the ellipse.

Our interest in ellipses is related to a desire to obtain images of pleasing and useful curves. We will want to be able to identify ellipses by specifying a size, shape, and location.

In the ellipse shown in Figure 7.8, it is conventional to identify the coordinates of point C (the center) as (H,K); the distance AC (=BC) is

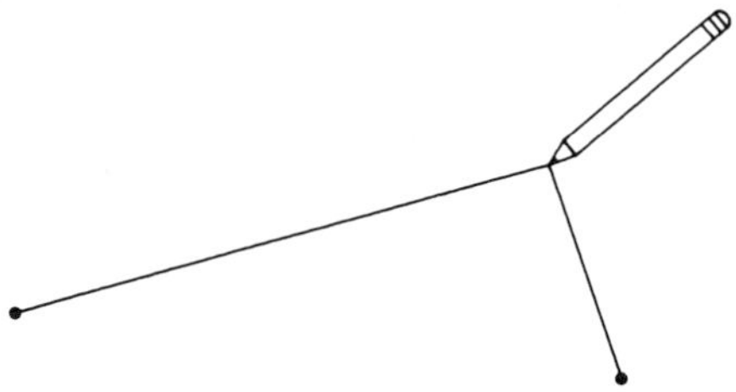

Figure 7.6

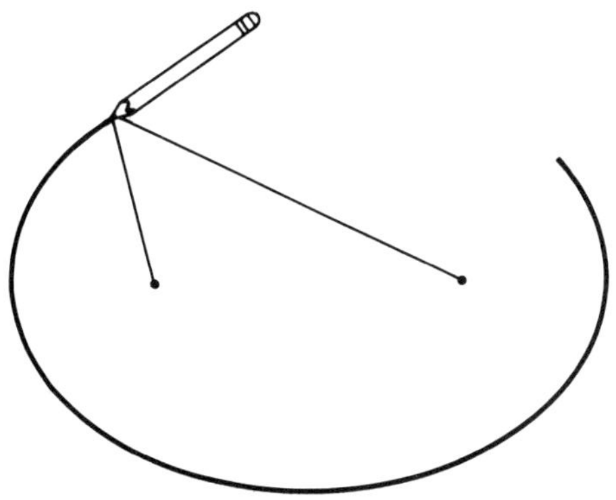

Figure 7.7

usually designated by A; and the distance EC (=CD) is usually identified as B. AB is called the *major* axis of the ellipse, and DE is called the *minor* axis. (In case you are interested, the foci (thumbtacks) are located on the line segment AB at a distance $\sqrt{A^2 - B^2}$ from the center. The length of the string is 2A.) With this notation, the ellipse is represented algebraically by

$$\frac{(X - H)^2}{A^2} + \frac{(Y - K)^2}{B^2} = 1$$

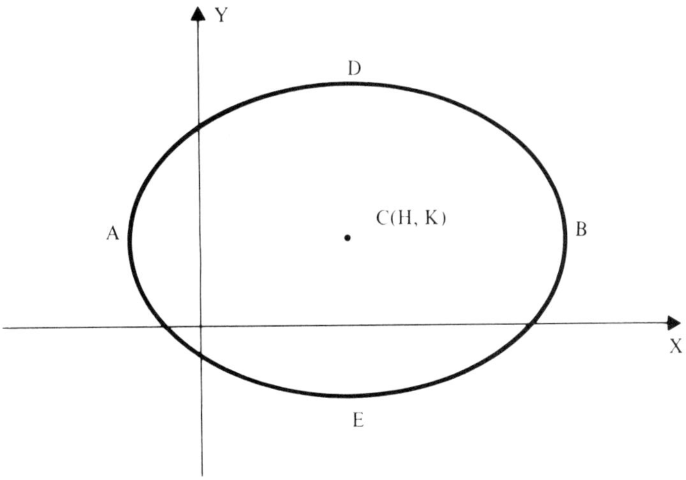

Figure 7.8

Although this equation for an ellipse is the form most commonly seen and represents the points of an ellipse accurately, other means are available that are more effective for our purposes.

When calculating the points on an ellipse it is best to change the relation

$$\frac{(X - H)^2}{A^2} + \frac{(Y - K)^2}{B^2} = 1$$

into a more convenient form. The following is algebraically equivalent and will be easier to use.

$$X = A\cos(\theta) + H$$
$$Y = B\sin(\theta) + K.$$

These equations are readily used in a program, as shown in Program P7-7.

Program P7-7: ELLIPSE 1

```
10 'PROGRAM P7-7  (ELLIPSE 1)
20 'Draws an ellipse centered on the screen
100 '================================
110 KEY OFF: SCREEN 2: CLS
120 'Set WINDOW and draw axes
130 WINDOW (-6,-4) - (6,5)
140 LINE (0,-4) - (0,5)
150 LINE (-6,0) - (6,0)
160 '================================
170 'Draw ellipse
180 A = 4: B = 2
190 FOR T = 0 TO 6.4 STEP .2
200  X = A*COS(T): Y = B*SIN(T)
210  IF T = 0 THEN PSET (X,Y)
220  LINE - (X,Y)
230 NEXT T
```

Note the similarities between this program and Program P7-4, which drew a circle. The resemblance should not be surprising. In fact, the CIRCLE statement can be used to draw ellipses.

ELLIPSE FROM CIRCLE

In a program which does not use a WINDOW, we can draw the ellipse which is defined by

$$\frac{(X - H)^2}{A^2} + \frac{(Y - K)^2}{B^2} = 1$$

with the statement

```
CIRCLE (H,K),r, , , , aspect
```

where *aspect* = SC*B/A, with SC = 5/12 in high-resolution graphics mode and SC = 5/6 in low-resolution graphics mode. If *aspect* < 1 then r = A; if *aspect* > 1 then r = B*SC. Program P7-8 illustrates this calculation.

First, an ellipse is drawn by calculating points on the ellipse. When the graph is complete, the same ellipse is drawn by the CIRCLE statement (line 280). You should be able to see the ellipse being redrawn, but it will clearly be superimposed on the earlier image. Experiment with different values of A and B to confirm the equivalence of the two methods of generating ellipses.

Program P7-8: ELLIPSE 2

```
10 'PROGRAM P7-8  (ELLIPSE 2)
20 'Ellipse via CIRCLE
100 '================================
110 KEY OFF: SCREEN 2: CLS: SC = 5/12
120 CX = 320: CY = 100
130 A = 280: B = 130
140 LINE (CX,0) - (CX,199)
150 LINE (0,CY) - (640,CY)
160 '================================
170 'Draw ellipse
180 FOR T = 0 TO 6.4 STEP .2
190  X = A*COS(T): Y = B*SIN(T)
200  SX = X + CX: SY = CY - SC*Y
210  IF T = 0 THEN PSET (SX,SY)
220  LINE - (SX,SY)
230 NEXT T
240 '================================
```

```
250 'Draw ellipse again
260 ASP = SC*B/A
270 R = A: IF ASP > 1 THEN R = B*SC
280 CIRCLE (CX,CY),R,,,,ASP
```

ROTATION AND TRANSLATION

Drawing an ellipse by using the CIRCLE statement is certainly faster and easier than calculating points on the ellipse. The advantage of calculating the points of the ellipse is that we can have greater control over the final image. If the ellipse is to be drawn by a digital plotter it may be necessary to have the individual points calculated (depending on the sophistication of the plotter).

If an ellipse whose major and minor axes are not parallel to the sides of the screen is to be drawn, then it is necessary to abandon the CIRCLE statement. Instead, the points of the ellipse must be calculated and a rotation transformation must be applied before the points are plotted.

Program P7-9 illustrates the process. The ellipse

$$\frac{X^2}{A^2} + \frac{Y^2}{B^2} = 1$$

is first rotated through an angle, (TH), and then translated through (H,K).

Program P7-9: ELLIPSE 3

```
10 'PROGRAM P7-9  (ELLIPSE 3)
20 'Rotation, translation of an ellipse
100 '==================================
110 KEY OFF: SCREEN 2: CLS
120 'Set WINDOW and draw axes
130 WINDOW (-6,-4) - (6,5)
140 LINE (0,-4) - (0,5)
150 LINE (-6,0) - (6,0)
160 '================================
170 'Draw ellipse
180 A = 4: B = 2
190 TH = .3: S1 = SIN(TH): C1 = COS(TH)
200 H = 1: K = 2
210 FOR T = 0 TO 6.4 STEP .2
220  X = A*COS(T): Y = B*SIN(T)
```

```
230    X1 = X*C1 - Y*S1 + H
240    Y1 = X*S1 + Y*C1 + K
250   IF T = 0 THEN PSET (X1,Y1)
260   LINE - (X1,Y1)
270 NEXT T
```

The rotation of points through an angle of measure TH is represented by the transformation matrix

$$\begin{pmatrix} \text{COS(TH)} & \text{SIN(TH)} & 0 \\ -\text{SIN(TH)} & \text{COS(TH)} & 0 \\ 0 & 0 & 1 \end{pmatrix}$$

The matrix of translation through (K,H) is

$$\begin{pmatrix} 1 & 0 & 0 \\ 0 & 1 & 0 \\ \text{H} & \text{K} & 1 \end{pmatrix}$$

The rotation of an image through an angle of measure TH, followed by the translation of the result through (H,K), is represented by

$$\begin{pmatrix} \text{COS(TH)} & \text{SIN(TH)} & 0 \\ -\text{SIN(TH)} & \text{COS(TH)} & 0 \\ 0 & 0 & 1 \end{pmatrix}\begin{pmatrix} 1 & 0 & 0 \\ 0 & 1 & 0 \\ \text{H} & \text{K} & 1 \end{pmatrix} = \begin{pmatrix} \text{COS(TH)} & \text{SIN(TH)} & 0 \\ -\text{SIN(TH)} & \text{COS(TH)} & 0 \\ \text{H} & \text{K} & 1 \end{pmatrix}$$

The transformation of a point (X,Y) results in

$$(\text{X},\text{Y},1)\begin{pmatrix} \text{COS(TH)} & \text{SIN(TH)} & 0 \\ -\text{SIN(TH)} & \text{COS(TH)} & 0 \\ \text{H} & \text{K} & 1 \end{pmatrix} =$$

$$(\text{XCOS(TH)} - \text{YSIN(TH)} + \text{H}, \text{XSIN(TH)} + \text{YCOS(TH)} + \text{K}, 1)$$

Adding this transformation to Program P7-7 yields Program P7-9.

MORE TRANSFORMATIONS

The fact that ellipses may be drawn by using the CIRCLE statement suggests that ellipses are really transformed circles. That is so. By scaling (stretching) a circle in the direction of the X or Y axis, we can change the circle into an ellipse. For example, a circle of radius 1 ($X^2 + Y^2 = 1$) may be changed into the ellipse

$$\frac{X^2}{A^2} + \frac{Y^2}{B^2} = 1$$

by scaling the X components by A and the Y components by B (compare line 220 of Program P7-9 with line 200 of Program P7-4). The matrix of such a scaling is

$$\begin{pmatrix} A & 0 & 0 \\ 0 & B & 0 \\ 0 & 0 & 1 \end{pmatrix}$$

By scaling, rotating, and translating the points of a circle, we obtain an ellipse, as shown by the following program (Program 7-10). To gain full use and control of the transformations involved, we have also dispensed with the WINDOW statement.

Program P7-10: ELLIPSE 4

```
10 'PROGRAM P7-10  (ELLIPSE 4)
20 'Ellipse as a transformed circle
30 'No use of WINDOW
100 '=================================
110 KEY OFF: SCREEN 2: CLS
120 CX = 320: CY = 100: SC = 5/12
130 TH = .3: S1 = SIN(TH): C1 = COS(TH)
140 DT = .1: S = SIN(DT): C = COS(DT)
150 N = 6.4/DT: H = 20: K = -50
160 '=================================
170 'Draw ellipse
180 A = 140: B = 90: X = 1: Y = 0
190 FOR I = 1 TO N
200  TEMP = X*C - Y*S: Y = Y*C + X*S: X = TEMP
210  X1 = X*A*C1 - Y*B*S1 + H
220  Y1 = X*A*S1 + Y*B*C1 + K
230  SX = X1 + CX: SY = CY - SC*Y1
240  IF I = 1 THEN PSET (SX,SY)
250  LINE - (SX,SY)
260 NEXT I
```

PARAMETRIC EQUATIONS

Equations such as

$$\begin{cases} X = T^2 + 10 \\ Y = T^2 - 5T \end{cases}$$

are called parametric equations. They make use of a parameter, T, to calculate values of X and Y. Parametric equations have been used in several of the programs in this chapter.

Applications of mathematics to science, engineering, and business frequently use parametric equations because the parameter and the values of X and Y are important to the application. We have used parametrically defined relations between X and Y because they enabled us to obtain smooth curves while reducing calculation time. They also will permit us to sketch some pleasing and exotic curves.

Program P7-11 sketches the graph defined by the equations

$$\begin{cases} X = 2 \text{ SIN}[2(T - \pi/13)] \\ Y = -3 \text{ COS}(T) \end{cases}$$

Program P7-11: PARAMETRIC

```
10 'PROGRAM P7-11  (PARAMETRIC)
20 'Draws Lissajous figures
100 '================================
110 KEY OFF: SCREEN 2: CLS
120 WINDOW (-6,-4) - (6,5)
130 PI = 3.141593
140 DEF FN X(T) = 2*SIN(2*(T-PI/13))
150 DEF FN Y(T) = -3*COS(T)
160 FOR T = 0 TO 6.3 STEP .1
170  X = FN X(T): Y = FNY(T)
180  IF T = 0 THEN PSET (X,Y)
190  LINE - (X,Y)
200 NEXT T
```

This pair of equations is a special case of the more general equations

$$\begin{cases} X = A \text{ SIN}(B(T - \pi/C)) \\ Y = D \text{ COS}(T) \end{cases}$$

for which we have chosen A = 2, B = 2, C = 13, and D = −3. Try a few other selections for A, B, C, and D.

Some other parametric equations which may interest you:

$$\begin{cases} X = 2\,T^2 \\ Y = 2\,T^3, \qquad -1.5 \le T \le 1.5 \end{cases}$$

$$\begin{cases} X = 2T - 3\ \text{SIN}\ T \\ Y = 2 - \text{COS}\ T, \qquad -4 \le T \le 4 \end{cases}$$

$$\begin{cases} X = 2(\text{COS}\ T + T\ \text{SIN}\ T) \\ Y = 2(\text{SIN}\ T - T\ \text{COS}\ T), \qquad 0 \le T \le 3 \end{cases}$$

The sections ahead will provide further examples of curves defined parametrically.

PARABOLAS

The parabola is a curve which has many physical applications. For example, if a stone or baseball is tossed upward, the path it follows (if wind resistance is ignored) is a parabola. Parabolic reflectors are useful because they concentrate reflected light at a single point, the focus. Comets follow parabolic orbits as they pass the sun, which is the focus of the parabola.

The equation $Y = X^2/4P$ identifies points of the parabola shown in Figure 7.9. The origin (0,0) is the vertex of the parabola; the focus is at the point (0,P). The line containing the focus and the vertex is referred to as the axis of the parabola. The value of P determines the relative posi-

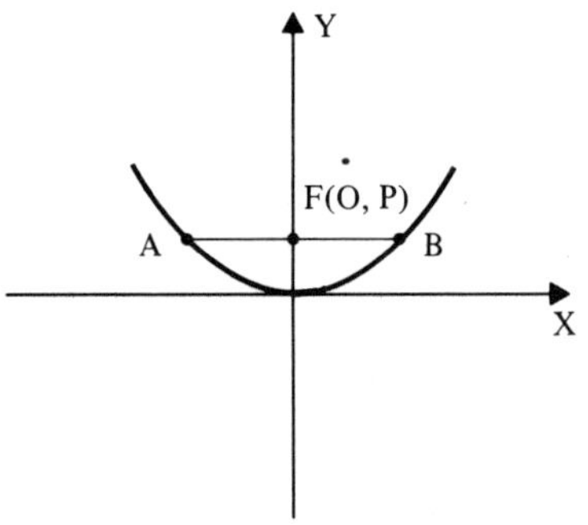

Figure 7.9

tion of the focus and the vertex, and also the shape of the parabola. The line segment AB, which contains the focus and is perpendicular to the axis of the parabola, has length $4|P|$. In a sense, the value of $4|P|$ provides a measure of the width of the parabola.

While the equation $Y = X^2/4P$ will identify the points of a parabola, a more useful formulation is the set of parametric equations

$$\begin{cases} X = 2PT \\ Y = PT^2 \end{cases}$$

When these equations are provided in a program, we may quickly identify parabolas of varied shapes by changing the value of P. Try several choices of P in Program P7-12. For example, try P = .2, .5, −2, or 3.

Program P7-12: PARABOLA

```
10 'PROGRAM P7-12  (PARABOLA)
20 'Parametric equations for a parabola
100 '==================================
110 KEY OFF: SCREEN 2: CLS
120 WINDOW (-6,-4) - (6,5)
130 P = 1
140 FOR T = -5 TO 5 STEP .2
150  X = 2*P*T: Y = P*T*T
160  IF T = -5 THEN PSET (X,Y)
170  LINE - (X,Y)
180 NEXT T
```

The process of passing to parabolas of arbitrary location and orientation by now should be obvious: We must transform the points of the parabola by rotation and translation. This is done in Program P7-13.

Program P7-13: ROTATED PARABOLA

```
10 'PROGRAM P7-13  (ROTATED PARABOLA)
20 'Draws a translated, rotated parabola
100 '=======================================
110 KEY OFF: SCREEN 2: CLS
120 WINDOW (-6,-4) - (6,5)
130 LINE (0,-4) - (0,5)
140 LINE (-6,0) - (6,0)
150 H = 2: K = -1
```

```
160 TH = .3: S1 = SIN(TH): C1 = COS(TH)
170 P = 1
180 FOR T = -5 TO 5 STEP .2
190   X = 2*P*T: Y = P*T*T
200   X1 = X*C1 - Y*S1 + H: Y1 = Y*C1 + X*S1 + K
210   IF T = -5 THEN PSET (X1,Y1)
220   LINE - (X1,Y1)
230 NEXT T
```

HYPERBOLAS

The circle, ellipse, and parabola are called *conic sections* because they are curves formed by the intersection of a cone and a plane. The hyperbola is another of the conic sections. We will consider the hyperbola briefly, as we leave the conics.

The hyperbola (Figure 7.10) is represented by the equation

$$\frac{X^2}{A^2} - \frac{Y^2}{B^2} = 1$$

The shape of the hyperbola obviously is controlled by the choice of values for A and B. The parametric equations

$$X = A \text{ SEC } T$$
$$Y = B \text{ TAN } T$$

also represent the hyperbola, and are more useful in writing a program to sketch the graph (see Program 7-14).

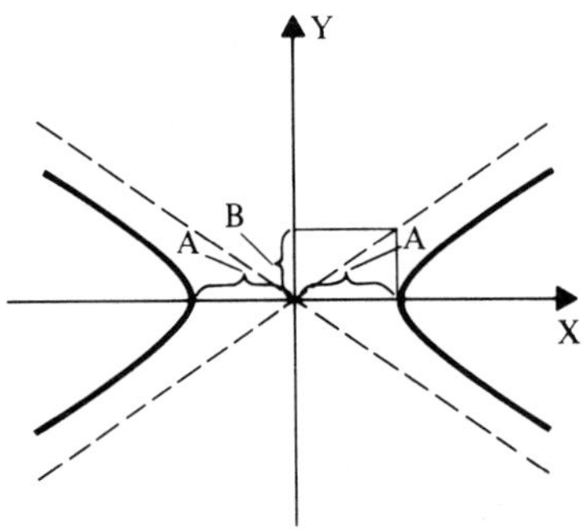

Figure 7.10

Program P7-14: HYPERBOLA

```
10 'PROGRAM P7-14   (HYPERBOLA)
20 'Parametric equations for a hyperbola
100 '====================================
110 KEY OFF: SCREEN 2: CLS
120 WINDOW (-6,-4) - (6,5)
130 FOR T = -1.6 TO 4.5 STEP .2
140  X = 3/COS(T): Y = 2*TAN(T)
150  IF T = -1.6 THEN PSET (X,Y)
160  LINE - (X,Y)
170 NEXT T
```

POLAR COORDINATE CURVES

Program P7-4 identified the graph of a circle by use of the parametric equations

$$X = RAD*COS(T)$$
$$Y = RAD*SIN(T)$$

RAD represented the radius of the circle. If we replace RAD with R and allow R to vary, instead of remaining constant, we obtain some very interesting and pleasing curves. We will define R as a function of T, and thus associate the variation in R with changes in T (see Program 7-15).

Program P7-15: POLAR

```
10 'PROGRAM P7-15   (POLAR)
20 'Draws a rose
100 '==================================
110 KEY OFF: SCREEN 2: CLS
120 WINDOW (-6,-4) - (6,5)
130 FOR T = 0 TO 6.3 STEP .1
140  R = 4*COS(2*T)
150  X = R*COS(T): Y = R*SIN(T)
160  IF FL = 0 THEN PSET (X,Y): FL = 1
170  LINE - (X,Y)
180 NEXT T
```

The association between the shape of a curve and the relationship between R and T is, at first, somewhat obscure. Some experimentation is recommended. Try the following.

R = 4*COS(3*T) Try $0 \le T \le 3.2$ with STEP .1
R = 4*COS(4*T) Try $0 \le T \le 6.3$ with STEP .1
R = 2*(COS(T) − 1)
R = 2*(2*COS(T) − 1)
R = .25*T with $-20 \le T \le 20$ STEP .2

CURVES OF THE FORM Y = F(X)

Graphs of points (X,Y) which satisfy functions Y = F(X) may be graphed using the processes discussed in previous sections. Program P7-16 illustrates one approach. Changes in the function (line 160) typically will require changes in the domain and the step size. It may be necessary to scale some functions to keep the image on the screen (set a new WINDOW).

Program P7-16: WAVE

```
10 'PROGRAM P7-16  (WAVE)
20 'Draws a sine curve
100 '==================================
110 KEY OFF: SCREEN 2: CLS
120 WINDOW (-6,-4) - (6,5)
130 LINE (0,-4) - (0,5)
140 LINE (-6,0) - (6,0)
150 FOR X = -6 TO 6.3 STEP .1
160  Y = SIN(X)
170  IF FL = 0 THEN PSET (X,Y): FL = 1
180  LINE - (X,Y)
190 NEXT X
```

Program P3-11 provides another graph of this type. If you would like to have a scale of units provided on the horizontal and vertical axes, you could use the method of Program P3-9.

A lot can be learned about curve sketching by experimenting. For example, try replacing program line 160 with each of the following:

1. Y = COS(3*X)
2. Y = SIN(X) + 2*COS(3*X)

3. Y = SIN(2*X) + 2*COS(3*X)

4. Y = 2*ATN(X)

5. Y = .1*(X^3 + X^2 − 12*X)

6. Y = .1*(X^4 + X^3 − 14*X^2 − 15*X + 36)

7. Y = 2/(1 + X^2)

Chapter 8

Basics of Three-dimensional Graphics

The computer screen is a two-dimensional display device. However, just as an artist can create the impression of a three-dimensional scene on a canvas, so we can display three-dimensional images on our graphics computer.

> **WARNING: READ SLOWLY—MATHEMATICS AHEAD**
>
> The process of displaying three-dimensional images requires additional mathematics. As is usual when travelling in rough terrain, we will progress more rapidly if we move slowly and carefully.

In order to be able to generate images of three-dimensional objects, it is necessary to establish a convention through which points in three-dimensional space can be identified. Two coordinate systems are described below.

COORDINATE SYSTEMS

The rectangular (or Cartesian) coordinate system requires three mutually perpendicular axes. The X and Y axes used in the two-dimensional system are augmented by a Z axis through the origin, perpendicular to the XY plane. Two possible orientations are possible for the Z axis. The orientation shown in Figure 8.1 identifies a right-hand system, so called because a right hand with first and second fingers pointing in the direction of the X and Y axes, as shown, will have the thumb pointing in the direction of the Z axis.

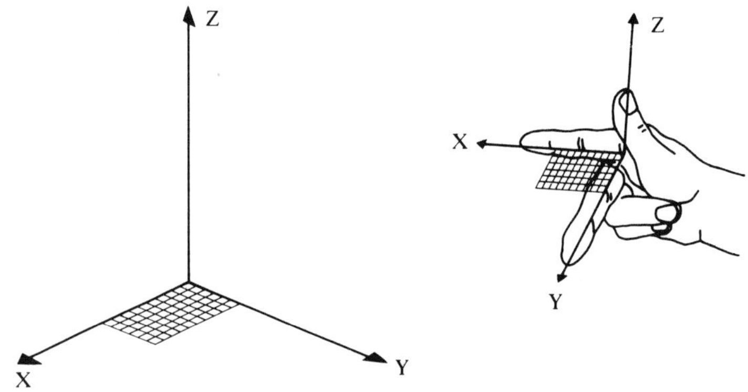

Figure 8.1

A left-hand system differs only in that the direction of the Z axis is reversed.

When viewing the two-dimensional XY plane the right-hand system will have the Z axis perpendicular to the plane, pointing toward the viewer's eye, as in Figure 8.2a. The left-hand system will have the Z axis pointing away from the viewer, as shown in Figure 8.2b.

The selection of a right-hand or left-hand system is somewhat arbitrary, since the calculations of interest to us could be completed with either coordinate system. As a matter of convenience, we will establish the right-hand system as standard.

Any pair of coordinate axes defines a plane, referred to as a coordinate plane. The three coordinate planes are identified as the XY plane, the YZ plane, and the XZ plane. Points are identified by ordered triples

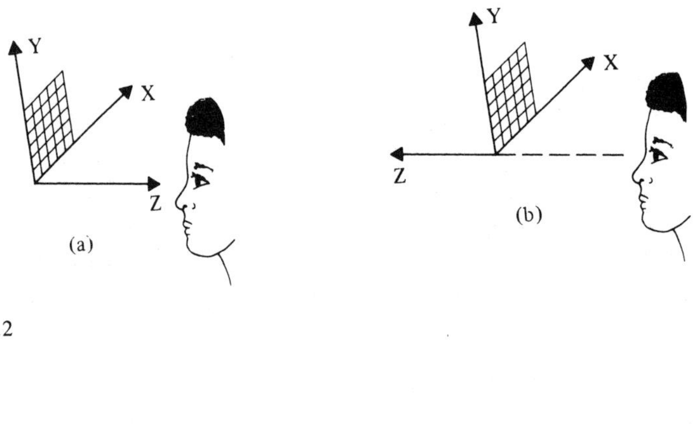

Figure 8.2

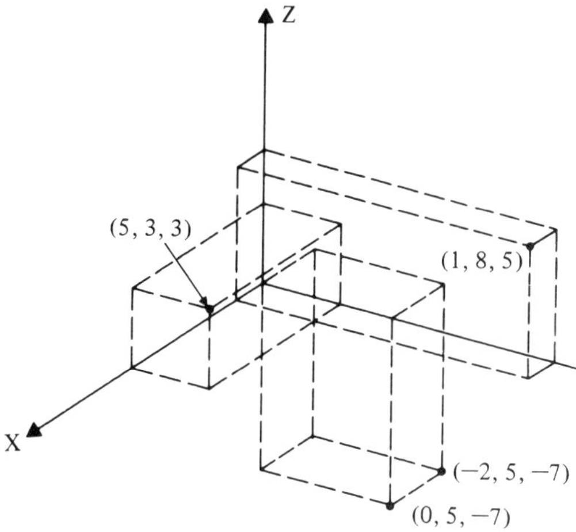

Figure 8.3

(A,B,C) of numbers, with A, B, and C providing the directed distance from the YZ, the XZ, and the XY planes, respectively.

Figure 8.3 shows the plotting of points (1,8,5), (5,3,3), (0,5,−7), and (−2,5,−7).

The second coordinate system we will use is the spherical coordinate system (see Figure 8.4). In this system, each point P is represented by an ordered triple (ρ,θ,ϕ) of numbers. The distance from the point to the origin is ρ. The angle between OP and the positive direction of the Z axis is ϕ. The angle between the positive direction of the X axis and the projection of OP onto the XY plane is θ, and is measured in a counterclockwise direction as viewed from a point on the positive Z axis.

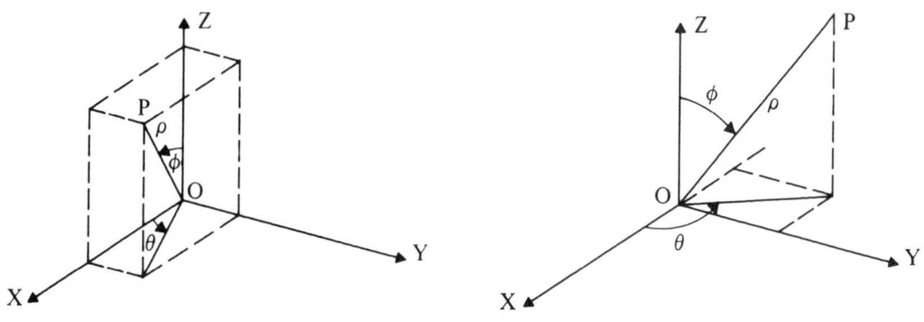

Figure 8.4

> **More Greek:** In the tradition of mathematics books, we're using the Greek letters ρ (rho), θ (theta), and ϕ (phi) for spherical coordinates. In BASIC we'll call these RHO, THETA, and PHI.

Since a point may be identified in terms of rectangular (X,Y,Z) or spherical (ρ,θ,ϕ) coordinates, it is necessary to have a means of conversion between the two systems. We will use the following formulas, which are based on right triangle trigonometry:

$$X = \rho \text{SIN}\phi \ \text{COS}\theta$$

$$Y = \rho \text{SIN}\phi \ \text{SIN}\theta$$

$$Z = \rho \text{COS}\phi$$

$$\rho = \sqrt{X^2 + Y^2 + Z^2}$$

In order to obtain an image of a three-dimensional object on a two-dimensional graphics display screen, it is necessary to associate a pair of screen coordinates (SX,SY) with each triple of rectangular coordinates (X,Y,Z) or spherical coordinates (ρ,θ,ϕ). The process used to obtain the screen coordinates is illustrated in Figure 8.5.

The position of the viewer is represented by point P. The display screen is a plane onto which an object is to be projected. This projection

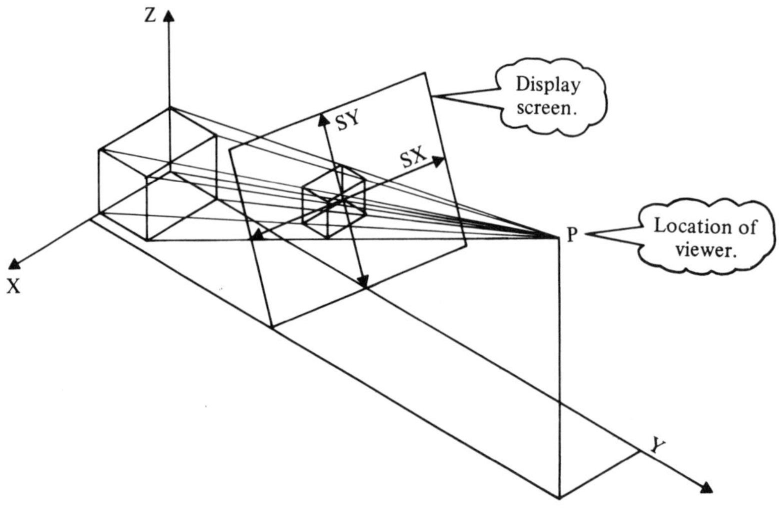

Figure 8.5

plane is assumed to be perpendicular to the line OP, and at a fixed distance D from point P. As the points of the object are projected onto the projection plane, we obtain screen coordinates (SX,SY) for each point (X,Y,Z). (See Figure 8.6.)

We will adopt the practice of identifying the viewpoint (location of the viewer's eye) in terms of its spherical coordinates. This will permit easy control over the location of the viewpoint:

- ρ (rho) will represent the distance from the viewpoint to the point (0,0,0). Increasing ρ will move the viewer away from the object being viewed. This will cause the object to appear as a smaller image. It will also affect the perspective view of the object.
- θ (theta) and ϕ (phi) identify the direction from which the viewer will see an object.

Figure 8.6 suggests that the projection plane (display screen) is located between the viewer and the object. It is not necessary that this be the case. Figure 8.7 positions the display screen on the opposite side of

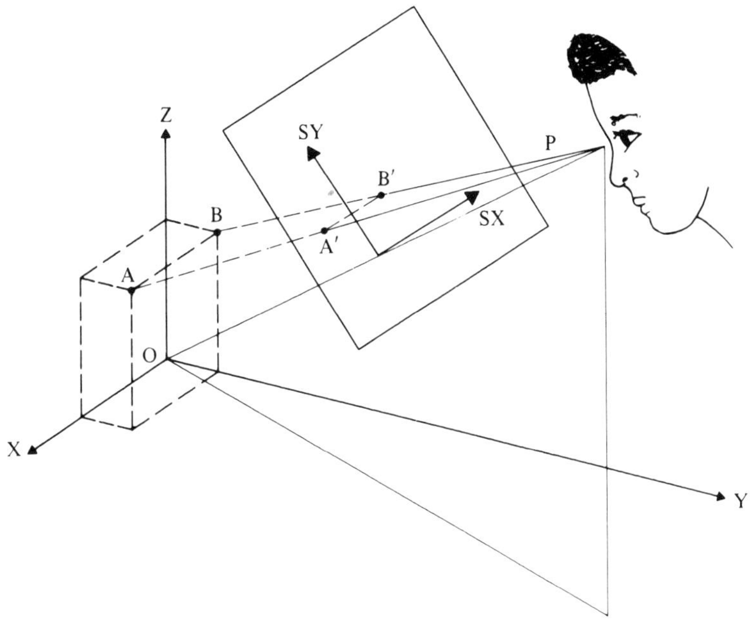

Figure 8.6

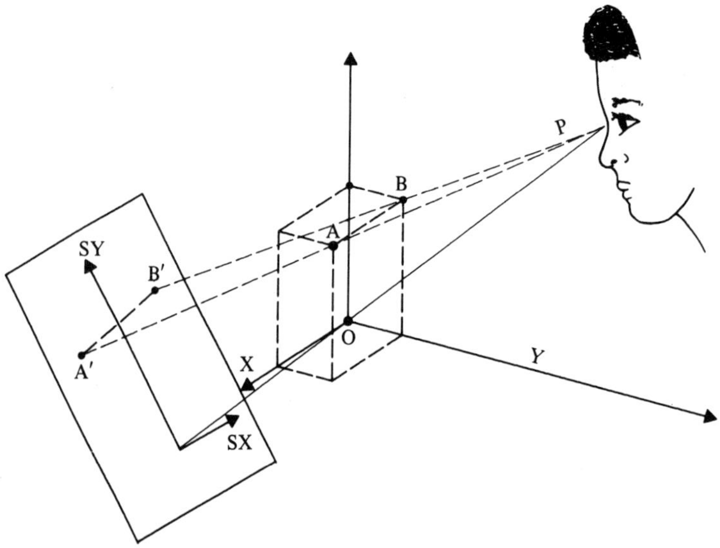

Figure 8.7

the object from the viewer. This results in a larger screen image. It is worth noting that

- moving the display screen closer to the viewer will result in a smaller projected image;
- moving the display screen farther from the viewer will result in a larger projected image.

Control over the viewing parameters ρ,θ,ϕ, and D provides control over the location and the direction of view and the size of the image. More on this later; first we must acquire some tools for manipulating three-dimensional objects.

TRANSFORMATIONS

Again we will use homogeneous coordinates to represent points. A point whose rectangular coordinates are given by (X,Y,Z) will have homogeneous coordinates (X,Y,Z,1). Linear transformations then may be represented by 4×4 matrices. We will not consider all of the transformations available to us but will focus on those which are most valuable.

SCALING

Diagonal matrices represent scaling transformations. Since

$$(X,Y,Z,1)\begin{pmatrix} A & 0 & 0 & 0 \\ 0 & B & 0 & 0 \\ 0 & 0 & C & 0 \\ 0 & 0 & 0 & 1 \end{pmatrix} = (AX,BY,CZ,1)$$

we may scale each of the coordinates individually to control scale in the direction of the coordinate axes. Overall scaling then may be provided as follows:

$$(X,Y,Z,1)\begin{pmatrix} K & 0 & 0 & 0 \\ 0 & K & 0 & 0 \\ 0 & 0 & K & 0 \\ 0 & 0 & 0 & 1 \end{pmatrix} = (KX,KY,KZ,1)$$

Since (X,Y,Z,D), when normalized, becomes (X/D,Y/D,Z/D,1), overall scaling also may be accomplished through multiplication by the matrix

$$\begin{pmatrix} 1 & 0 & 0 & 0 \\ 0 & 1 & 0 & 0 \\ 0 & 0 & 1 & 0 \\ 0 & 0 & 0 & 1/K \end{pmatrix}$$

ROTATION

It will be sufficient for us to be able to rotate an object about each of the coordinate axes. This ability is within easy reach. In Chapter 7, when considering a rotation about the origin, we use the transformation matrix

$$R = \begin{pmatrix} COS\theta & SIN\theta & 0 \\ -SIN\theta & COS\theta & 0 \\ 0 & 0 & 1 \end{pmatrix}$$

Multiplication of vector (X,Y,1) by R had the effect of rotating it about the origin through a counterclockwise angle θ. If we picture the Z axis pointing toward us from the XY plane, the action is described as a rotation about the Z axis. In applying the rotation to a three-dimensional vector we use the matrix

$$R_Z = \begin{pmatrix} \text{COS}\theta & \text{SIN}\theta & 0 & 0 \\ -\text{SIN}\theta & \text{COS}\theta & 0 & 0 \\ 0 & 0 & 1 & 0 \\ 0 & 0 & 0 & 1 \end{pmatrix}$$

The transformation matrices which effect rotations about the X axis and Y axis are

$$R_X = \begin{pmatrix} 1 & 0 & 0 & 0 \\ 0 & \text{COS}\theta & \text{SIN}\theta & 0 \\ 0 & -\text{SIN}\theta & \text{COS}\theta & 0 \\ 0 & 0 & 0 & 1 \end{pmatrix}$$

$$R_Y = \begin{pmatrix} \text{COS}\theta & 0 & -\text{SIN}\theta & 0 \\ 0 & 1 & 0 & 0 \\ \text{SIN}\theta & 0 & \text{COS}\theta & 0 \\ 0 & 0 & 0 & 1 \end{pmatrix}$$

In each case the rotation is through a counterclockwise angle, θ, as viewed from a point along the positive axis, facing the origin.

TRANSLATION

If it were not for our need for translation capability, we might not have elected to use homogeneous coordinates. It will prove convenient to represent a translation by means of a matrix transformation:

$$(X,Y,Z,1) \begin{pmatrix} 1 & 0 & 0 & 0 \\ 0 & 1 & 0 & 0 \\ 0 & 0 & 1 & 0 \\ H & K & L & 1 \end{pmatrix} = (X + H,\ Y + K,\ Z + L,\ 1)$$

To move a point or collection of points by displacing the coordinates a distance specified by the vector (H,K,L), we multiply by the transformation matrix, as shown above. Alternatively, we may consider that the effect of the transformation is to move the origin to the point $(-H, -K, -L)$.

REFLECTION

The reflection of an object through a plane refers to generating a mirror image of the object on the opposite side of the plane. Thus the reflection of points through the XY plane has the effect of changing the sign of the Z coordinates of each of the points. The transformation matrix for this reflection is

$$M_{XY} = \begin{pmatrix} 1 & 0 & 0 & 0 \\ 0 & 1 & 0 & 0 \\ 0 & 0 & -1 & 0 \\ 0 & 0 & 0 & 1 \end{pmatrix}$$

Transformation matrices which represent reflections through the XZ plane and the YZ plane are

$$M_{XZ} = \begin{pmatrix} 1 & 0 & 0 & 0 \\ 0 & -1 & 0 & 0 \\ 0 & 0 & 1 & 0 \\ 0 & 0 & 0 & 1 \end{pmatrix}$$

$$M_{YZ} = \begin{pmatrix} -1 & 0 & 0 & 0 \\ 0 & 1 & 0 & 0 \\ 0 & 0 & 1 & 0 \\ 0 & 0 & 0 & 1 \end{pmatrix}$$

SEQUENTIAL TRANSFORMATIONS

The effect of a sequence of transformations may be represented by a single matrix, which is the product of the matrices of the individual transformations. For example, we may create the effect of rotation through 30° about the ray PQ [P = (0,2,3), Q = (1,2,3)] by

1. Translation

$$T = \begin{pmatrix} 1 & 0 & 0 & 0 \\ 0 & 1 & 0 & 0 \\ 0 & 0 & 1 & 0 \\ 0 & -2 & -3 & 1 \end{pmatrix}$$

followed by

2. Rotation

$$R = \begin{pmatrix} 1 & 0 & 0 & 0 \\ 0 & \mathrm{COS30°} & \mathrm{SIN30°} & 0 \\ 0 & -\mathrm{SIN30°} & \mathrm{COS30°} & 0 \\ 0 & 0 & 0 & 1 \end{pmatrix}$$

followed by

3. Translation

$$T^* = \begin{pmatrix} 1 & 0 & 0 & 0 \\ 0 & 1 & 0 & 0 \\ 0 & 0 & 1 & 0 \\ 0 & 2 & 3 & 1 \end{pmatrix}$$

The same effect is available from the matrix

$$M = TRT^* = \begin{pmatrix} 1 & 0 & 0 & 0 \\ 0 & \text{COS}30^\circ & \text{SIN}30^\circ & 0 \\ 0 & -\text{SIN}30^\circ & \text{COS}30^\circ & 0 \\ 0 & -2\text{COS}30^\circ + 3\text{SIN}30^\circ + 2 & -2\text{SIN}30^\circ - 3\text{COS}30^\circ + 3 & 1 \end{pmatrix}$$

$$= \begin{pmatrix} 1 & 0 & 0 & 0 \\ 0 & .866 & .5 & 0 \\ 0 & -.5 & .866 & 0 \\ 0 & 1.768 & -.598 & 1 \end{pmatrix}$$

The ordering of a sequence of transformations is quite important. In general, changes in the order of transformations will change the effect of the sequence. For example, a rotation followed by a translation has a different effect than the same translation followed by the rotation.

INVERSES OF MATRICES

In the last example, the matrices T and T* had opposite effects. Multiplication by matrix T causes a translation through $(0, -2, -3)$, while T* represents a translation through (0,2,3). Successive multiplication by T and T* would place a point in its original location, since

$$TT^* = \begin{pmatrix} 1 & 0 & 0 & 0 \\ 0 & 1 & 0 & 0 \\ 0 & 0 & 0 & 1 \\ 0 & -2 & -3 & 1 \end{pmatrix} \begin{pmatrix} 1 & 0 & 0 & 0 \\ 0 & 1 & 0 & 0 \\ 0 & 0 & 1 & 0 \\ 0 & 2 & 3 & 1 \end{pmatrix} = \begin{pmatrix} 1 & 0 & 0 & 0 \\ 0 & 1 & 0 & 0 \\ 0 & 0 & 1 & 0 \\ 0 & 0 & 0 & 1 \end{pmatrix} = I$$

Pairs of matrices whose product is I are referred to as *inverses*. The inverse of a matrix M is frequently denoted by M^{-1}. While some matrices do not have inverses, many of the ones that are useful in computer graphics do have inverses. For example, the matrix

$$R = \begin{pmatrix} 1 & 0 & 0 & 0 \\ 0 & \mathrm{COS}30^\circ & \mathrm{SIN}30^\circ & 0 \\ 0 & -\mathrm{SIN}30^\circ & \mathrm{COS}30^\circ & 0 \\ 0 & 0 & 0 & 1 \end{pmatrix} = \begin{pmatrix} 1 & 0 & 0 & 0 \\ 0 & .866 & .5 & 0 \\ 0 & -.5 & .866 & 0 \\ 0 & 0 & 0 & 1 \end{pmatrix}$$

which represents a rotation of 30° about the X axis, has an inverse R^{-1} which represents a rotation of $-30°$ about the X axis:

$$R^{-1} = \begin{pmatrix} 1 & 0 & 0 & 0 \\ 0 & .866 & -.5 & 0 \\ 0 & .5 & .866 & 0 \\ 0 & 0 & 0 & 1 \end{pmatrix}$$

TRANSFORMING A COORDINATE SYSTEM

We have referred to transforming a point, or a set of points, within a coordinate system. It is also frequently useful to establish a new coordinate system through transformation of the axes. For example, we might move the origin to a new location, or rotate the axis system about one of the axes.

In such cases it is necessary to identify points in terms of the original, or standard, coordinates, and also in terms of coordinates relative to the new axis system. We will identify coordinates relative to a second axis system by affixing a prime ('). Thus the coordinates (2,1,3) are assumed to identify a point relative to the standard axis system, while (2,1,3)' identifies a (different) point relative to a second axis system.

As an example, a rotation about the Z axis through a counterclockwise angle of 30° can be represented by the transformation matrix

$$M = \begin{pmatrix} \mathrm{COS}30^\circ & \mathrm{SIN}30^\circ & 0 & 0 \\ -\mathrm{SIN}30^\circ & \mathrm{COS}30^\circ & 0 & 0 \\ 0 & 0 & 1 & 0 \\ 0 & 0 & 0 & 1 \end{pmatrix} = \begin{pmatrix} .866 & .5 & 0 & 0 \\ -.5 & .866 & 0 & 0 \\ 0 & 0 & 1 & 0 \\ 0 & 0 & 0 & 1 \end{pmatrix}$$

When applying this transformation matrix to points or sets of points, multiplication of the coordinate vector of the point by M will yield the coordinate of the rotated point.

For example, the point (2,4,1) rotates to the position $(-.268,4.464,1)$, since

$$(2,4,1,1)\begin{pmatrix} .866 & .5 & 0 & 0 \\ -.5 & .866 & 0 & 0 \\ 0 & 0 & 1 & 0 \\ 0 & 0 & 0 & 1 \end{pmatrix} = (-.268,4.464,1,1)$$

The point P′ results from rotation of point P through a counterclockwise angle of 30° about the Z axis. Consider the effect of rotating the coordinate system through a clockwise angle of 30° about the Z axis. The resulting coordinate system X′, Y′, Z′, will provide another means of referencing point P. The position of the rotated point P′ relative to the X, Y, Z coordinate system is the same as the position of point P relative to the rotated coordinate system X′, Y′, Z′.

Thus the matrix M above may be used to:

1. Determine the coordinates of points following rotation of the points through a counterclockwise angle of 30°; or
2. Determine the coordinates of points following a rotation of the coordinate axes through a clockwise angle of 30°.

The example above is not an isolated case, but represents a general principle which we will find valuable: The matrix required to represent the transformation of an axis system is the inverse of that needed to transform points within an axis system.

PROJECTION

We know how to manipulate three-dimensional figures, but we're not yet ready to show them on a computer graphics screen. The reason, of course, is that a graphics screen is a two-dimensional surface. To obtain a two-dimensional (screen) representation of a three-dimensional object we'll next develop a method for projecting each point of the object onto a plane.

TWO-DIMENSIONAL IMAGES OF THREE-DIMENSIONAL OBJECTS

Refer back to Figure 8.6. The location of the eye (point P) is identified as having rectangular coordinates (H,K,L) and spherical coordinates

(ρ,θ,ϕ). We position the projection plane (display screen) at a distance D from the viewer's eye, placed so that it is perpendicular to the line connecting the viewer's eye with the origin. A second rectangular axis system is located at point P. This is the eye coordinate system. Points then may be identified by giving eye coordinates (Xe,Ye,Ze) or standard coordinates (X,Y,Z).

The eye coordinate system is shown in Figure 8.8. It orients the axes so that, when the viewer's line of sight is directed toward the origin of the X,Y,Z axis system, the Ze axis points in the direction of the line of sight, the Xe axis points to the right, and the Ye axis points upward. (Note that the eye coordinate system is a *left-hand system.*)

The task we face has two stages:

1. The identification of eye coordinates (Xe,Ye,Ze) associated with a point having standard coordinates (X,Y,Z);
2. The identification of screen coordinates (SX,SY) associated with a specific set of eye coordinates (Xe,Ye,Ze).

The second of these calculations is the easier. With the eye coordinate system in place, we position the display screen at a distance D from the

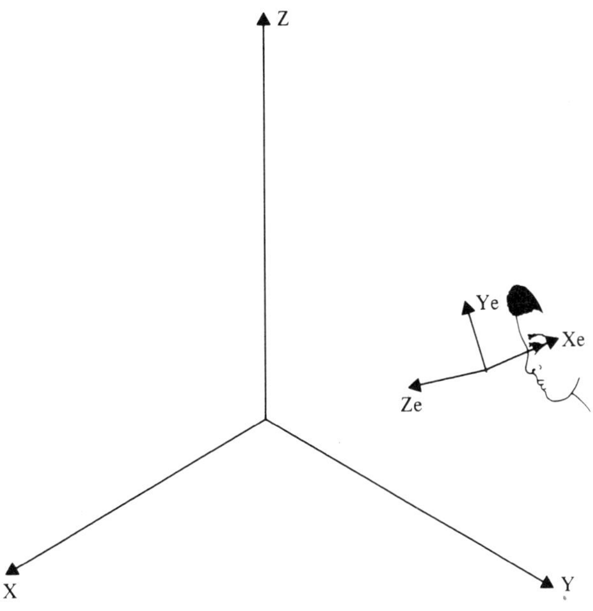

Figure 8.8

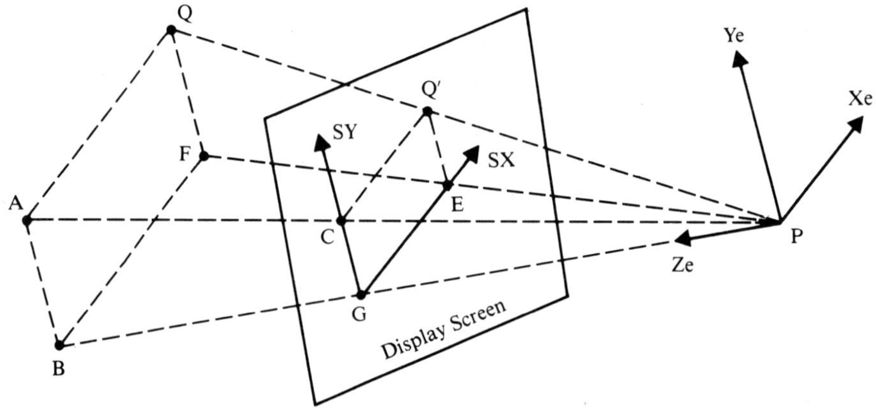

Figure 8.9

origin of this system (Figure 8.9) Point Q is given eye coordinates (Xe,Ye,Ze). To obtain the screen coordinates (SX,SY), note the right triangles PBA and PGC (Figures 8.9 and 8.10). These are similar triangles with

$$\frac{GC}{PG} = \frac{BA}{PB}$$

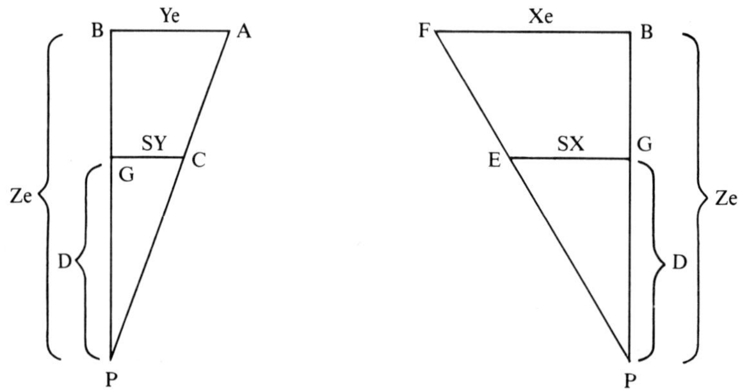

Figure 8.10

Thus,

$$\frac{SY}{D} = \frac{Ye}{Ze}$$

so that SY = D(Ye/Ze).

In the same fashion, from similar triangles PBF and PGE, we have

$$\frac{GE}{PG} = \frac{BF}{PB} \quad \text{and} \quad \frac{SX}{D} = \frac{Xe}{Ze}$$

Thus SX = D(Xe/Ze).

We now turn to the first task, establishing the association between the standard coordinates and the eye coordinates. This is done through a sequence of four transformations, each of which will partially transform the X, Y, Z axis system to the Xe, Ye, Ze axis system. The four transformations, along with pictorial representations of their effects, are given on pages 160–162. There, and in our notation, the intermediate axis systems are referred to as X′, Y′, Z′, with the final X′, Y′, Z′ axis system being the eye coordinate system Xe, Ye, Ze. (Compare Figure 8.14 with Figure 8.5.)

The effect of the transformations will be viewed as the establishment of a sequence of new coordinate systems, with the eye coordinate system as the final result.

For the purpose of these transformations, the point, P, at the viewer's eye is identified by rectangular coordinates (H,K,L) or by spherical coordinates (ρ,θ,ϕ), measured relative to the standard coordinate axes. Recall that $H = \rho\sin\phi\cos\theta$, $K = \rho\sin\phi\sin\theta$, and $L = \rho\cos\phi$.

In brief,

1. Step I establishes a coordinate system at the viewer's eye, retaining the orientation and directions of the original axis system.

2. Steps II and III rotate the axis system in order that the Z′ axis points toward the origin of the standard axis system, with the Y′ axis directed so that it intersects the positive Z axis. From the viewer's position, the Y′ axis points upward and the X′ axis points to the left.

3. Step IV converts to a left-hand system, inverting the X axis so that it points to the right. This provides a more conventional orientation for the viewer.

Since the transformations are best represented as matrices, we will consider each step separately, establishing the matrix of the transformations.

STEP I. Establish the origin at (H,K,L) = ($\rho\sin\phi\cos\theta$, $\rho\sin\phi\sin\theta$, $\rho\cos\phi$). The transformation matrix that has this effect is:

$$A = \begin{pmatrix} 1 & 0 & 0 & 0 \\ 0 & 1 & 0 & 0 \\ 0 & 0 & 1 & 0 \\ -H & -K & -L & 1 \end{pmatrix}$$

or

$$A = \begin{pmatrix} 1 & 0 & 0 & 0 \\ 0 & 1 & 0 & 0 \\ 0 & 0 & 1 & 0 \\ -\rho\sin\phi\cos\theta & -\rho\sin\phi\sin\theta & -\rho\cos\phi & 1 \end{pmatrix}$$

The spherical coordinate representation of (H,K,L) may appear to be less convenient, but it will simplify calculation.

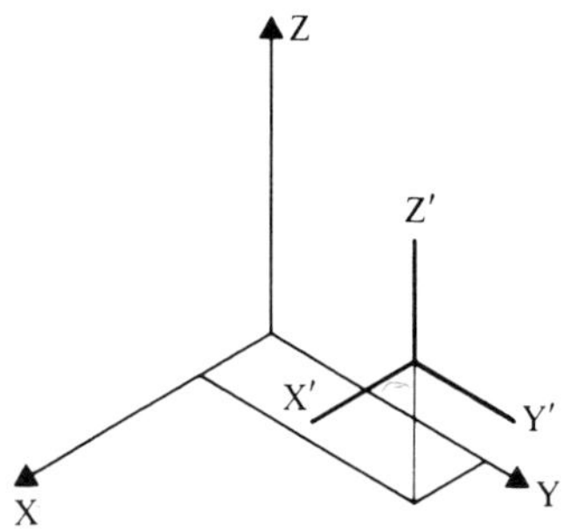

Figure 8.11

STEP II. Rotate the axis system about the Z′ axis through the clockwise angle (90° − θ). As a result of this rotation, the negative Y′ axis should intersect the Z axis. The transformation matrix which accomplishes this is:

$$B = \begin{pmatrix} \sin\theta & \cos\theta & 0 & 0 \\ -\cos\theta & \sin\theta & 0 & 0 \\ 0 & 0 & 1 & 0 \\ 0 & 0 & 0 & 1 \end{pmatrix}$$

(Remember, the transformation matrix required to transform an axis system is the inverse of that needed to transform points within an axis system.)

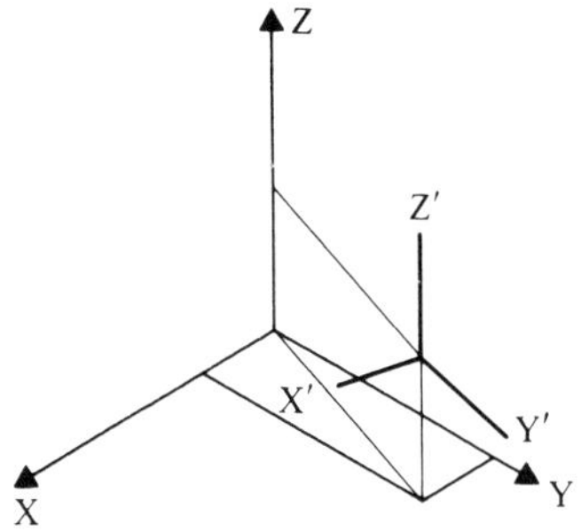

Figure 8.12

STEP III. Rotate the axis system about the X′ axis through the counterclockwise angle (180° − φ). As a result of this rotation, the Z′ axis should be directed toward the origin of the X, Y, Z axis system. The required matrix is

$$C = \begin{pmatrix} 1 & 0 & 0 & 0 \\ 0 & -\cos\phi & -\sin\phi & 0 \\ 0 & \sin\phi & -\cos\phi & 0 \\ 0 & 0 & 0 & 1 \end{pmatrix}$$

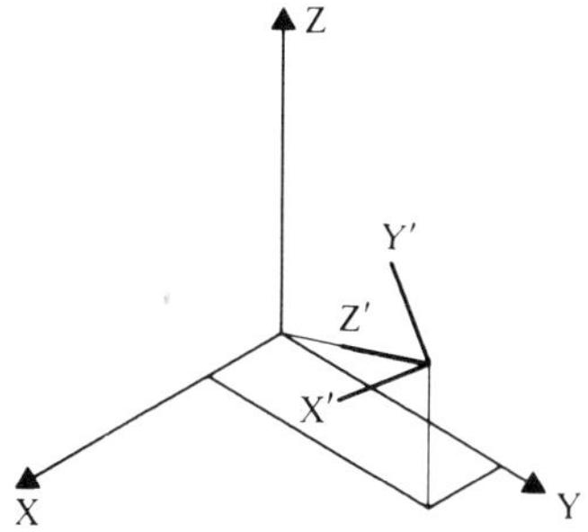

Figure 8.13

STEP IV. Change to a left-hand coordinate system, inverting the X′ axis using the matrix

$$D = \begin{pmatrix} -1 & 0 & 0 & 0 \\ 0 & 1 & 0 & 0 \\ 0 & 0 & 1 & 0 \\ 0 & 0 & 0 & 1 \end{pmatrix}$$

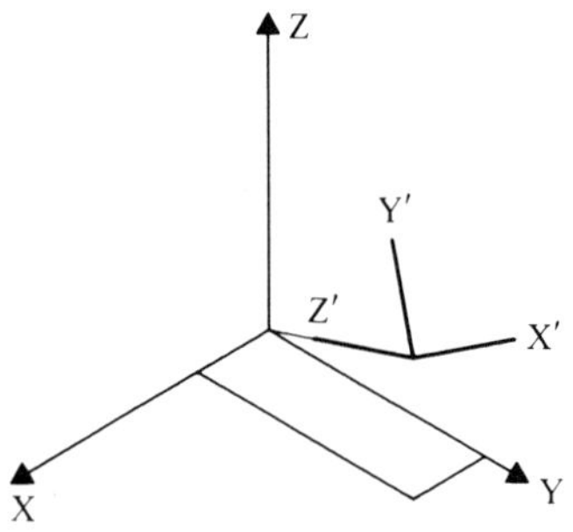

Figure 8.14

If the standard coordinates (X,Y,Z) of a point are known, the eye coordinates (Xe,Ye,Ze) may be obtained as (Xe,Ye,Ze) = (X,Y,Z)ABCD. Simplicity in calculation is obtained through the use of the single matrix T = ABCD. Thus

$$(Xe,Ye,Ze,1) = (X,Y,Z,1)\begin{pmatrix} -\sin\theta & -\cos\theta\cos\phi & -\cos\theta\sin\phi & 0 \\ \cos\theta & -\sin\theta\cos\phi & -\sin\theta\sin\phi & 0 \\ 0 & \sin\phi & -\cos\phi & 0 \\ 0 & 0 & \rho & 0 \end{pmatrix}$$

The multiplication of ABCD is outlined on page 164.

I. TRANSLATE ORIGIN TO (H,K,L):

$$A = \begin{pmatrix} 1 & 0 & 0 & 0 \\ 0 & 1 & 0 & 0 \\ 0 & 0 & 1 & 0 \\ -\rho\sin\phi\cos\theta & -\rho\sin\theta\sin\theta & -\rho\cos\phi & 1 \end{pmatrix}$$

II. ROTATE THROUGH (90° − θ) CLOCKWISE ABOUT Z′ AXIS:

$$B = \begin{pmatrix} \sin\theta & \cos\theta & 0 & 0 \\ -\cos\theta & \sin\theta & 0 & 0 \\ 0 & 0 & 1 & 0 \\ 0 & 0 & 0 & 1 \end{pmatrix}$$

III. ROTATE THROUGH (180° − ϕ) COUNTERCLOCKWISE ABOUT X′ AXIS:

$$C = \begin{pmatrix} 1 & 0 & 0 & 0 \\ 0 & -\cos\phi & -\sin\phi & 0 \\ 0 & \sin & -\cos\phi & 0 \\ 0 & 0 & 0 & 1 \end{pmatrix}$$

IV. CONVERT TO LEFT-HAND SYSTEM:

$$D = \begin{pmatrix} -1 & 0 & 0 & 0 \\ 0 & 1 & 0 & 0 \\ 0 & 0 & 1 & 0 \\ 0 & 0 & 0 & 1 \end{pmatrix}$$

PROGRAMMING

While matrices provide a convenient form for establishing relationships between standard and eye coordinates of a point, languages available for microcomputers frequently do not provide for matrix arithmetic. To include the above matrix product in a BASIC program, write

```
270 XE = -X*S1 + Y*C1
280 YE = -X*C1*C2 - Y*S1*C2 + Z*S2
290 ZE = -X*S2*C1 - Y*S1*S2 - Z*C2 + RHO
```

(Here we use S1, C1, S2, and C2 to represent SIN(THETA), COS(THETA), SIN(PHI), and COS(PHI), respectively.)
Screen coordinates are then provided by

```
300 SX = D*XE/ZE
310 SY = D*YE/ZE
```

Program P8-1 shows one way of using the formulas above to generate an image of a three-dimensional object. Viewing parameters are identified in lines 140–160. Note that we have chosen D larger than RHO, placing the object between the viewer and the projection plane. The coordinates of the visible vertices of a cube are given in lines 340–360. Lines 180–230 read the coordinates from the DATA statements and pass them to the subroutine in lines 270–320. On return from the subroutine, the projected points are plotted.

$$T = A\ B\ C\ D$$

$$= \begin{pmatrix} 1 & 0 & 0 & 0 \\ 0 & 1 & 0 & 0 \\ 0 & 0 & 1 & 0 \\ -\rho\cos\theta\ \sin\phi & -\rho\sin\theta\ \sin\phi & -\rho\cos\phi & 1 \end{pmatrix} \begin{pmatrix} \sin\theta & \cos\theta & 0 & 0 \\ -\cos\theta & \sin\theta & 0 & 0 \\ 0 & 0 & 1 & 0 \\ 0 & 0 & 0 & 1 \end{pmatrix} \begin{pmatrix} 1 & 0 & 0 & 0 \\ 0 & -\cos\phi & -\sin\phi & 0 \\ 0 & \sin\phi & -\cos\phi & 0 \\ 0 & 0 & 0 & 1 \end{pmatrix} \begin{pmatrix} -1 & 0 & 0 & 0 \\ 0 & 1 & 0 & 0 \\ 0 & 0 & 1 & 0 \\ 0 & 0 & 0 & 1 \end{pmatrix}$$

$$= \begin{pmatrix} \sin\theta & \cos\theta & 0 & 0 \\ -\cos\theta & \sin\theta & 0 & 0 \\ 0 & 0 & 1 & 0 \\ 0 & -\rho\sin\phi & -\rho\cos\phi & 1 \end{pmatrix} \begin{pmatrix} 1 & 0 & 0 & 0 \\ 0 & -\cos\phi & -\sin\phi & 0 \\ 0 & \sin\phi & -\cos\phi & 0 \\ 0 & 0 & 0 & 1 \end{pmatrix} \begin{pmatrix} -1 & 0 & 0 & 0 \\ 0 & 1 & 0 & 0 \\ 0 & 0 & 1 & 0 \\ 0 & 0 & 0 & 1 \end{pmatrix}$$

$$= \begin{pmatrix} \sin\theta & -\cos\theta\ \cos\phi & -\cos\theta\ \sin\phi & 0 \\ -\cos\theta & -\sin\theta\ \cos\phi & -\sin\theta\ \sin\phi & 0 \\ 0 & \sin\phi & -\cos\phi & 0 \\ 0 & 0 & \rho & 1 \end{pmatrix} \begin{pmatrix} -1 & 0 & 0 & 0 \\ 0 & 1 & 0 & 0 \\ 0 & 0 & 1 & 0 \\ 0 & 0 & 0 & 1 \end{pmatrix}$$

$$= \begin{pmatrix} -\sin\theta & -\cos\theta\ \cos\phi & -\cos\theta\ \sin\phi & 0 \\ \cos\theta & -\sin\theta\ \cos\phi & -\sin\theta\ \sin\phi & 0 \\ 0 & \sin\phi & -\cos\phi & 0 \\ 0 & 0 & \rho & 1 \end{pmatrix}$$

Figure 8.15

Program P8-1: CUBE

```
10 'PROGRAM P8-1   (CUBE)
20 'Draws the visible parts of a cube
100 '=========================================
110 KEY OFF: SCREEN 2: CLS
120 WINDOW (-4,-3) - (4,3)
130 'Establish viewpoint and viewing parameters
140 RHO = 10: D = 20
150 THETA = .7: S1 = SIN(THETA): C1 = COS(THETA)
160 PHI = 1.3: S2 = SIN(PHI): C2 = COS(PHI)
170 'Read data and draw the cube
180 READ X,Y,Z: GOSUB 270: PSET (SX,SY)
190 FOR I = 1 TO 8
200  READ X,Y,Z: GOSUB 270: LINE - (SX,SY)
210 NEXT I
220 READ X,Y,Z: GOSUB 270: PSET (SX,SY)
230 READ X,Y,Z: GOSUB 270: LINE - (SX,SY)
240 END
250 '=========================================
260 'Perspective projection subroutine
270 XE = -X*S1 + Y*C1
280 YE = -X*C1*C2 - Y*S1*C2 + Z*S2
290 ZE = -X*S2*C1 - Y*S1*S2 - Z*C2 + RHO
300 SX = D*XE/ZE
310 SY = D*YE/ZE
320 RETURN
330 '=========================================
340 DATA 1,1,0, 1,1,1, 0,1,1, 0,1,0
350 DATA 1,1,0, 1,0,0, 1,0,1, 0,0,1
360 DATA 0,1,1, 1,0,1, 1,1,1
```

VIEWPOINT AND PERSPECTIVE

It is worthwhile noting how each of RHO, THETA, PHI, and D affect the image generated on the display screen.

Changing the values of THETA and PHI will permit us to view an object from different directions. Changing the value of RHO (the distance from the viewer to the origin) permits us to move the viewer closer to, or farther from, the object. This will change the perceived size of the object.

There is a second way to control the size of the screen image: change

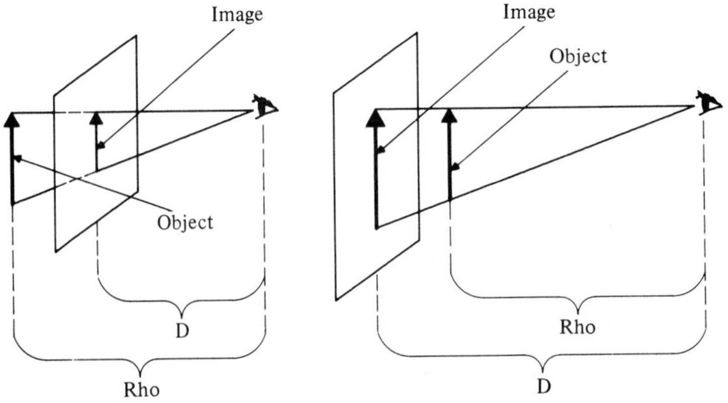

Figure 8.16

the value of D. When a viewpoint (ρ,θ,ϕ) is specified, changes in D will affect the size of the image on the projection plane. Increasing D will increase the size of the image. Figure 8.16 illustrates the consequences of variations in the relative values of RHO and D.

Since RHO and D both affect the size of the image, it is important to understand the relationship between them. If the effect of each is to control size, why provide control over both? The answer to this lies in *perspective*: an object close to the viewer appears larger than when it is farther away because it occupies a larger proportion of the field of view. Thus, for example, a perspective view of a cube will cause the edges close to the viewer to appear larger than edges farther away. To decrease the apparent effect of perspective, increase the value of RHO. This will decrease the perceived size of the image. To compensate, increase D. (What happens if the ratio RHO/D is maintained?). As a result the edges of the cube will appear to be of nearly the same size.

Program P8-2: VIEWPOINT

```
10 'PROGRAM P8-2   (VIEWPOINT)
20 'Illustrates effect of changing viewpoint parameters
100 '=================================================
110 KEY OFF: SCREEN 2: CLS
120 WINDOW (-4,-3) - (4,3)
130 'Establish viewpoint and viewing parameters
140 RHO = 10: D = 20: THETA = .7: PHI = 1.3
150 GOSUB 490 ' Draw the cube from current viewpoint
160 LOCATE 24,1: PRINT"RHO ="; RHO;
```

```
170 LOCATE 24,20: PRINT"D ="; D;
180 LOCATE 25,1: PRINT"THETA ="; THETA;
190 LOCATE 25,20: PRINT"PHI ="; PHI;
200 LOCATE 1,1: PRINT "To exit program, press 'E'"
210 PRINT "To change viewing parameters, press 'C'"
220 INPUT A$
230 IF A$ = "E" OR A$ = "e" THEN CLS: END
240 IF A$ <> "C" AND A$ <> "c" THEN 200
250 '==================================================
260 'Get new viewing parameters
270 CLS
280 PRINT "RHO ="; RHO
290 PRINT "THETA ="; THETA
300 PRINT "PHI ="; PHI
310 PRINT "D ="; D
320 PRINT: PRINT "To accept a value, press 'RETURN'"
330 LOCATE 1,10: INPUT;A$
340  IF LEN(A$) <> 0 THEN RHO = VAL(A$)
350  LOCATE 1,6: PRINT RHO; "        "
360 LOCATE 2,12: INPUT;A$
370  IF LEN(A$) <> 0 THEN THETA = VAL(A$)
380  LOCATE 2,8: PRINT THETA; "        "
390 LOCATE 3,10: INPUT;A$
400  IF LEN(A$) <> 0 THEN PHI = VAL(A$)
410  LOCATE 3,6: PRINT PHI; "        "
420 LOCATE 4,8: INPUT;A$
430  IF LEN(A$) <> 0 THEN D = VAL(A$)
440  LOCATE 4,4: PRINT D; "        "
450 GOSUB 490: ' Draw the cube from current viewpoint
460 GOTO 160: ' Display parameters, repeat
470 '==================================================
480 'Cube drawing subroutine
490 CLS: RESTORE
500 S1 = SIN(THETA): C1 = COS(THETA)
510 S2 = SIN(PHI): C2 = COS(PHI)
520 READ X,Y,Z: GOSUB 630: PSET (SX,SY)
530 FOR I = 1 TO 11
540  READ X,Y,Z: GOSUB 630: LINE - (SX,SY)
550 NEXT I
560 FOR I = 1 TO 2
570  READ X,Y,Z: GOSUB 630: PSET (SX,SY)
580  READ X,Y,Z: GOSUB 630: LINE - (SX,SY)
590 NEXT I
600 RETURN
610 '==========================================
620 'Perspective projection subroutine
630 XE = -X*S1 + Y*C1
640 YE = -X*C1*C2 - Y*S1*C2 + Z*S2
650 ZE = -X*S2*C1 - Y*S1*S2 - Z*C2 + RHO
```

```
660 SX = D*XE/ZE
670 SY = D*YE/ZE
680 RETURN
690 '=======================================
700 DATA 1,1,1, 1,-1,1, -1,-1,1, -1,1,1
710 DATA 1,1,1, 1,1,-1, 1,-1,-1
720 DATA -1,-1,-1, -1,1,-1, 1,1,-1
730 DATA 1,-1,1, 1,-1,-1, -1,-1,1
740 DATA -1,-1,-1, -1,1,1, -1,1,-1
```

Program P8-2 provides an opportunity to observe the effects of RHO, THETA, PHI, and D. The program accepts values for these variables, then uses the values to display a view of a cube. To help maintain orientation, a diagonal line has been placed on the side of the cube that faces in the direction of the positive X axis. Try the following combinations of values, then experiment with several choices of your own. (Note that the angles THETA and PHI are again measured in radians.)

RHO	30	15	15	15	15	15	15
THETA	.7	.7	1	1.7	.7	.7	.7
PHI	1.3	1.3	1.3	1.3	1	.2	1
D	10	20	20	20	20	20	20

Program P8-2 illustrates the role of RHO, THETA, PHI, and D. It also points out another concern: It is possible to see through the closer faces of the cube to the farther edges. While this may be acceptable in some cases and desirable in some others, it is a problem when it leads to optical illusions. In the next chapter we will discuss methods of eliminating hidden lines and surfaces from the display.

TRANSFORMATION OF IMAGES

Transformation matrices were introduced earlier and were used to establish a relationship between standard and eye coordinates of points. We will use them now to transform the points that define an object.

Program P8-3 generates images of three solids. The same data are used in drawing each of the objects; the only difference is that in each instance the data are subjected to different transformations before the object is drawn. Object number 1 is the cube of Program P8-2. Objects number 2 and 3 results from transformations applied to the points before screen coordinates are calculated.

OBJECT 2:

(a) Scale the object by multiplying the Z coordinates by 3. The transformation matrix is

$$A = \begin{pmatrix} 1 & 0 & 0 & 0 \\ 0 & 1 & 0 & 0 \\ 0 & 0 & 3 & 0 \\ 0 & 0 & 0 & 1 \end{pmatrix}$$

(b) Rotate the solid through 30° about the Z axis. The transformation matrix is

$$B = \begin{pmatrix} \cos 30^\circ & \sin 30^\circ & 0 & 0 \\ -\sin 30^\circ & \cos 30^\circ & 0 & 0 \\ 0 & 0 & 1 & 0 \\ 0 & 0 & 0 & 1 \end{pmatrix} \begin{pmatrix} .866 & .5 & 0 & 0 \\ -.5 & .866 & 0 & 0 \\ 0 & 0 & 1 & 0 \\ 0 & 0 & 0 & 1 \end{pmatrix}$$

(c) Translate the solid, placing its center at $(-1,4,2)$. The transformation matrix is

$$C = \begin{pmatrix} 1 & 0 & 0 & 0 \\ 0 & 1 & 0 & 0 \\ 0 & 0 & 1 & 0 \\ -1 & 4 & 2 & 1 \end{pmatrix}$$

Applying the successive transformations to a point P with coordinates (X,Y,Z) results in point P′ which has coordinates (X1,Y1,Z1) = (X,Y,Z)ABC =

$$(X,Y,Z,1) \begin{pmatrix} .866 & .5 & 0 & 0 \\ -.5 & .866 & 0 & 0 \\ 0 & 0 & 3 & 0 \\ -1 & 4 & 2 & 1 \end{pmatrix}$$

so that

$$\begin{aligned} X1 &= .866X - .5Y - 1 \\ Y1 &= .5X + .866Y + 4 \\ Z1 &= 3Z + 2 \end{aligned}$$

OBJECT 3:

(a) Scale X and Y coordinates by a factor of 2.
(b) Rotate the solid through 60° about the X axis.
(c) Rotate the solid through 15° about the Z axis.
(d) Translate the solid, placing its center at (4,2, −2).

For practice, write the transformation matrices of steps a, b, c, and d; multiply them to obtain the matrix

$$\begin{pmatrix} 1.93 & .518 & 0 & 0 \\ -.259 & .966 & 1.732 & 0 \\ .224 & -.836 & .5 & 0 \\ 4 & 2 & -2 & 1 \end{pmatrix}$$

As a result, the coordinates of the points of object 3 are described as

$$(X1,Y1,Z1,1) = (X,Y,Z,1)M$$

and

$$\begin{aligned} X1 &= 1.93X - .259Y + .224Z + 4 \\ Y1 &= .518X + .966Y - .836Z + 2 \\ Z1 &= 1.732Y + .5Z - 2 \end{aligned}$$

The entries of the transformation matrices for each of the three objects are given in the DATA statements in lines 580–710 of Program P8-3. Note that an identity matrix is provided for object 1 and that the fourth column of each matrix is missing; it doesn't contribute to the calculation of X1, Y1, Z1.

Lines 210–270 read the matrix components into an array M(I,J,K). I, which varies from 1 to 3, represents the number of the matrix, and corresponds to the object number. J represents the matrix row numbers, and K represents the matrix column numbers.

Lines 300–400 read the X, Y, Z coordinates of the objects and calls the subroutine which starts at line 430. The points are transformed by multiplication by the appropriate transformation matrix, then passed to the perspective projection routine. On return from the subroutine, the points are plotted.

Program P8-3: TRANSFORMED CUBE

```
10 'PROGRAM P8-3    (TRANSFORMED CUBE)
20 'Draws 3 images from 1 set of data
100 '=================================================
```

```
110 KEY OFF: SCREEN 2: CLS
120 WINDOW (-4,-3) - (4,3)
130 'Establish viewpoint and viewing parameters
140 RHO = 30: D = 10
150 THETA = .1: S1 = SIN(THETA): C1 = COS(THETA)
160 PHI = 1: S2 = SIN(PHI): C2 = COS(PHI)
170 '=====================================================
180 OPTION BASE 1
190 DIM M(3,4,3), V(3)
200 'Fill transformation matrices
210 FOR I = 1 TO 3
220  FOR J = 1 TO 4
230   FOR K = 1 TO 3
240    READ M(I,J,K)
250   NEXT K
260  NEXT J
270 NEXT I
280 '=====================================================
290 'Read data, draw cube
300 FOR I = 1 TO 3
310  READ X,Y,Z: GOSUB 440: PSET (SX,SY)
320  FOR L = 1 TO 11
330   READ X,Y,Z: GOSUB 440: LINE - (SX,SY)
340  NEXT L
350  FOR L = 1 TO 2
360   READ X,Y,Z: GOSUB 440: PSET (SX,SY)
370   READ X,Y,Z: GOSUB 440: LINE - (SX,SY)
380  NEXT L
390  RESTORE 730
400 NEXT I
410 END
420 '=====================================================
430 'Transformation of points
440 FOR K = 1 TO 3
450  V(K) = M(I,1,K)*X + M(I,2,K)*Y + M(I,3,K)*Z + M(I,4,K)
460 NEXT K
470 X = V(1): Y = V(2): Z = V(3)
480 '=====================================================
490 'Perspective projection calculation
500 XE = -X*S1 + Y*C1
510 YE = -X*C1*C2 - Y*S1*C2 + Z*S2
520 ZE = -X*S2*C1 - Y*S1*S2 - Z*C2 + RHO
530 SX = D*XE/ZE
540 SY = D*YE/ZE
550 RETURN
560 '=====================================================
570 'Data for matrix 1
580 DATA 1,  0,  0
590 DATA 0,  1,  0
600 DATA 0,  0,  1
610 DATA 0,  0,  0
620 'Data for matrix 2
```

```
630 DATA .866,   .5,   0
640 DATA -.5,   .866, 0
650 DATA 0,       0,   3
660 DATA -1,      4,   2
670 'Data for matrix 3
680 DATA 1.93,   .518,     0
690 DATA -.259, .966,   1.732
700 DATA  .224, -.836,   .5
710 DATA  4,       2,     -2
720 'Data for cube
730 DATA 1,1,1, 1,-1,1, -1,-1,1, -1,1,1
740 DATA 1,1,1, 1,1,-1, 1,-1,-1
750 DATA -1,-1,-1, -1,1,-1, 1,1,-1
760 DATA 1,-1,1, 1,-1,-1, -1,-1,1
770 DATA -1,-1,-1, -1,1,1, -1,1,-1
```

NOTES AND SUGGESTIONS

1. Modify Program P8-1 to generate images of other three-dimensional objects. Try pyramids, houses, furniture, and so forth. For each image you should make a rough sketch, keeping the three-dimensional coordinate system in mind. From the drawing you can make a listing of the coordinates of points to be displayed. For the present, if you wish to eliminate hidden lines and surfaces, leave the corresponding points out of your listing. With each selection of an object, it is usually necessary to experiment with choices of values for the viewing parameters RHO, THETA, PHI, and D to obtain a satisfactory image.

2. Modify program P8-1 so that it will draw your initials on the three faces of the cube.

3. For the imaginative: You may already have tried using values of D that position the viewer between the object and the display screen (try negative values of D). If you haven't, can you predict the result before trying it on the computer? While you are at it, what will happen if the viewer is placed within the object?

SURFACES OF THE FORM Z = F(X,Y)

Having developed the processes of generating three-dimensional images, we may apply them to a variety of surfaces (see Program P8-4). The program structure will be similar to that of Program P8-3. We must:

1. Provide rectangular coordinates (X,Y,Z) of points of the surface.

2. Transform these to screen coordinates (SX, SY); and
3. Plot the points and line segments.

Unlike the previous programs in this chapter, this one will not provide the coordinates of points as DATA in the program, but will have the points generated by a program segment.

Program P8-4: SURFACE

```
10 'PROGRAM P8-4   (SURFACE)
20 'Draws a surface Z = F(X,Y)
100 '=========================================
110 KEY OFF: SCREEN 2: CLS
120 WINDOW (-4,-3) - (4,3)
130 RHO = 30: D = 10
140 THETA = .3: S1 = SIN(THETA): C1 = COS(THETA)
150 PHI = 1: S2 = SIN(PHI): C2 = COS(PHI)
160 '=========================================
170 DEF FN F(X,Y) = COS(.1*(X*X + Y*Y))
180 FOR X = 10 TO -10 STEP -1
190  FL = 0
200  FOR Y = -10 TO 10
210   Z = FN F(X,Y): GOSUB 290
220   IF FL = 0 THEN FL = 1: PSET (SX,SY)
230   LINE - (SX,SY)
240  NEXT Y
250 NEXT X
260 END
270 '=========================================
280 'Perspective projection subroutine
290 XE = -X*S1 + Y*C1
300 YE = -X*C1*C2 - Y*S1*C2 + Z*S2
310 ZE = -X*S2*C1 - Y*S1*S2 - Z*C2 + RHO
320 SX = D*XE/ZE
330 SY = D*YE/ZE
340 RETURN
```

The program generates an image which represents the surface as a sequence of wire-frame curves. The curves are the intersections of the surface with vertical planes parallel to the YZ plane. We thus use two-dimensional curves to create a three-dimensional image. This is an example of a standard maxim of mathematics and computer science: When attacking a new problem, reduce it to a simpler form—one which you know how to handle.

The image obtained by the program obviously is dependent on the function selected (line 170). A pleasing image which shows the significant characteristics of the surface typically is the result of a time-consuming trial-and-error process. Don't expect to define a function at random and immediately obtain a satisfactory image. Minor changes in the definition of the function may affect the image significantly. You might experiment with minor variations in the above function. Try

```
DEF FN F(X,Y) = 3*COS(.4*(X*X + Y*Y))
```

or

```
DEF FN F(X,Y) = COS(.1*(X*X - Y*Y))
```

A smoother surface will result from calculating more points on each curve (decreasing the step size of the loop beginning in line 200). Of course, this will result in an increase in execution time.

While the image is dependent on the function, it is also severely affected by the choice of the viewing parameters RHO, THETA, PHI, and D. Try RHO = 40, or PHI = 2, or experiment with other choices. It is best to change only one of the viewing parameters at a time. Each time you make a change, try to predict the effect on the image before running the program.

As different viewing positions are selected, the image may become badly confused by overlapping curves. The program creates a transparent surface. We can see through the near parts of the surface to the farther parts that lie behind. This is sometimes desirable, but frequently it is a problem, leading to confused images and optical illusions. We might obtain images that are more pleasing if the closer portions of the surface were able to hide the more distant portions. In general, the development of effective hidden line algorithms is one of the most challenging problems in computer graphics. The next chapter provides some approaches to the problem.

Experiment with the graphs of the following functions. It usually will be necessary to adjust the viewing parameters and the domain (limits of the FOR–NEXT loops). Selection of larger values for the STEP size will result in faster program execution, but curves that are more angular.

1. DEF FN F(X,Y) = 3*EXP(−.1*(X*X+Y*Y))

2. DEF FN F(X,Y) = −7*EXP(−.1*(X*X+Y*Y))
3. DEF FN F(X,Y) = A*SIN(X/B)*SIN(Y/C) [Try a variety of values for A, B, and C.]
4. DEF FN F(X,Y) = .1*(X*X − Y*Y)
5. DEF FN F(X,Y) = .5*(Y*X^3 − X*Y^3)

Chapter 9

Hidden Line and Hidden Surface Routines

Figure 9.1

Faster than a speeding bullet!
More powerful than a locomotive!!
Able to leap tall buildings in a single bound!!!

Superman also had X-ray vision: He could see through objects. As ordinary people we might envy such an ability when we must make special efforts to identify a weak component in a mechanical device, or to study the inner workings of the human body, or when we are looking for lost car keys. However, uncontrolled X-ray vision would be inconvenient. An X-ray world, one in which all things are transparent or translucent, would be a very confusing place. We might then wish for the ability to look at an object and to turn it over as we study it, without being able to see through the closer surfaces to the farther surfaces and vertices.

Our previous attempts to provide images of three-dimensional objects resulted in an X-ray world. It will require some very special efforts on our part to bring it under control. We must develop methods for identifying those surfaces and line segments which are visible, or partly visible, and those which are not. We may then display the visible portions of an object and eliminate those portions which are hidden from view.

The elimination of hidden lines and surfaces is one of the most challenging problems of computer graphics. Hidden line algorithms require large amounts of computer time and memory.

Our present discussion is limited. We present the theory of operation of several techniques and provide sample programs that draw images of simple three-dimensional objects. A general-purpose hidden line subroutine would be very inefficient. It is much more effective for the programmer to adapt the techniques to each specific application.

The processes described in Chapter 8 permit the drawing of images of three-dimensional objects. If we want to avoid drawing the hidden lines and surfaces of objects it is necessary to have a method of distinguishing the visible lines from the hidden lines.

One obvious way to display only the visible portions of an object is to be careful that only the visible portions be identified to the computer. This was done in Program P8-1, which drew only the visible portions of a cube. Only the vertices of surfaces which were visible from the specified viewpoint were identified in the program. This technique requires the programmer to plan the view desired and to identify the points of the object which are visible from that view. The program is short and draws the image quickly. It is limited, however. If the image is to be drawn from a different viewpoint, it may be necessary to change the DATA statements and the program portion that draws the visible line segments.

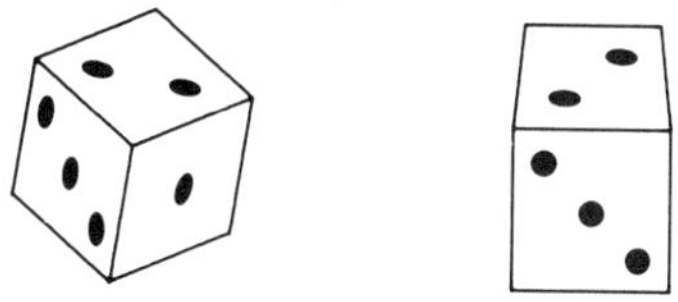

Figure 9.2

SURFACE ORIENTATION

The following method is more general. All parts of an object are defined in a program. The program determines which surfaces are facing the viewpoint and identifies these as the visible surfaces.

> **NOTE:** The following discussion assumes familiarity with vectors and the cross products and dot products of vectors. See Appendix 3 for a brief summary of these concepts.

As we look at a die, two or three of the faces are visible to us. The other faces are not visible since they are facing away from us (see Figure 9.2). It is the orientation, or facing direction, of a surface that we will use in our first hidden line technique.

With each face of a cube we can associate two normal (perpendicular) directions. One normal direction will point inward; the other will point outward, away from the cube. We represent these directions by normal vectors and take the outward pointing vector as the orientation vector of the surface. Three outward pointing normals of a cube are shown in Figure 9.3.

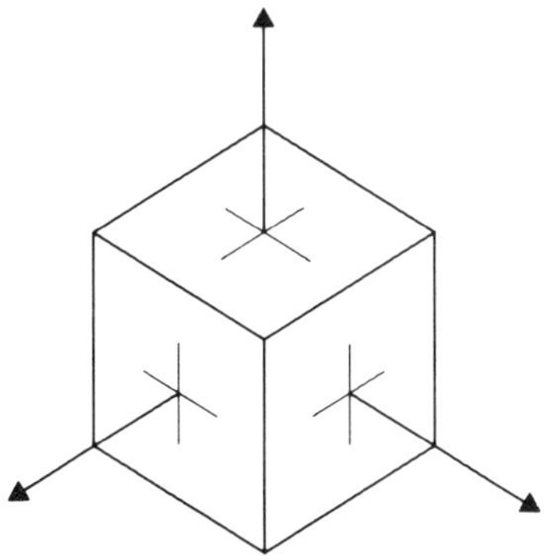

Figure 9.3

With each surface of an object we also associate a second vector, a line-of-sight vector. This is the vector directed from one of the vertices of the surface (any vertex) to the viewpoint (the location of the eye of the viewer).

For each surface we may measure the angle between the line-of-sight vector and the orientation vector. If this angle is between 0° and 90°, the surface is facing the viewer. It is visible and should be displayed. If the angle is between 90° and 180°, then the surface is facing away from the viewer. It is not visible and should not be displayed. (See Figure 9.4.)

ORIENTATION VECTOR

In Figure 9.5 we have numbered the vertices of one surface of a cube. The identification of vertex number 1 is arbitrary, but it is important that the numbering of the remaining vertices of the surface continue in a counterclockwise direction, as viewed from outside the cube, facing the surface. We then identify vector $\vec{u}$, directed from vertex number 1 to vertex number 2, and vector $\vec{v}$, directed from vertex number 1 to vertex number 3. The cross product, $\vec{n} = \vec{u} \times \vec{v}$, will be normal (perpendicular) to the face of the cube and will be directed outward. (The magni-

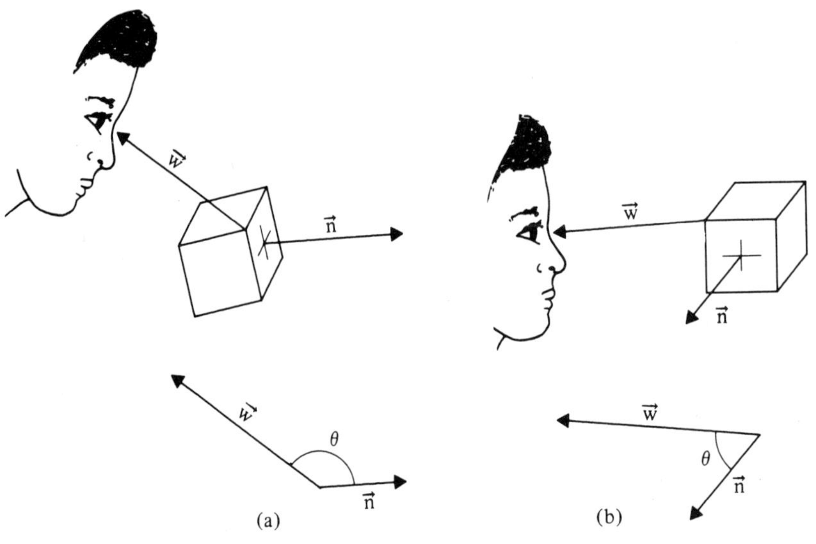

Figure 9.4

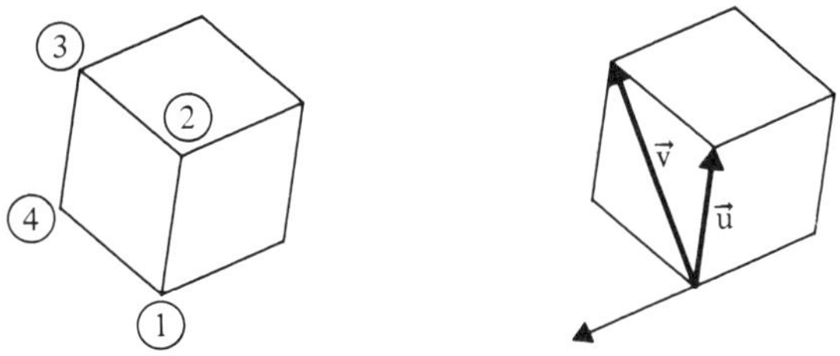

Figure 9.5

tude, or length, of the orientation vector $\vec{n}$ will not be of importance to us).

> **NOTE:** It is important that the vertices numbered 1, 2, 3, 4 on the surface be given in counterclockwise direction as seen from outside the cube, facing the surface. If the points are assigned in a clockwise direction, the vector $\vec{n} = \vec{u} \times \vec{v}$, as described above, will be pointing inward.

VISIBILITY

The dot product of vectors $\vec{w}$ and $\vec{n}$ has the property

$$\vec{w} \cdot \vec{n} = |w|\,|n| \cos\theta$$

where θ is the angle between $\vec{w}$ and $\vec{n}$. If θ is between 0° and 90°, the values of $\vec{w} \cdot \vec{n}$ will be positive. If θ is between 90° and 180°, $\vec{w} \cdot \vec{n}$ will be negative.

Using $\vec{w}$ to represent the line of sight vector of a surface, and $\vec{n}$ to represent the orientation vector, we have a visibility test. For a visible surface, such as the surface of Figure 9.4b, the angle between $\vec{w}$ and $\vec{n}$ is between 0° and 90°, and $\vec{w} \cdot \vec{n}$ is positive. For a hidden surface, such as in Figure 9.4a, the angle between $\vec{w}$ and $\vec{n}$ is between 90° and 180°, and $\vec{w} \cdot \vec{n}$ is negative.

AN EXAMPLE

To illustrate the use of surface orientation in eliminating hidden lines, we will discuss a program (P9-1) which draws a house. (The program which draws this object is a long one, so we will present it in five parts. The complete listing is given on pages 190–192.)

Program P9-1: HIDDEN LINES; HOUSE
Program P9-1a

```
10 'PROGRAM P9-1  (HIDDEN LINES: HOUSE)
20 'Surface orientation method
100 '==========================================
110 KEY OFF: SCREEN 2: CLS
120 OPTION BASE 1
130 WINDOW (-4,-3) - (4,3)
140 RHO = 80: D = 20
150 THETA = .9: S1 = SIN(THETA): C1 = COS(THETA)
160 PHI = 1.2: S2 = SIN(PHI): C2 = COS(PHI)
170 '==========================================
180 'Data for vertices
190 DATA 5,7,-5,  5,7,5,  5,-7,5, 5,-7,-5, -5,7,-5
200 DATA -5,-7,-5, -5,-7,5, -5,7,5, 0,7,8, 0,-7,8
210 'Fill vertex arrays
220 DIM V(10,3),SV(10,2)
230 FOR I = 1 TO 10
240  READ X,Y,Z
250  V(I,1) = X: V(I,2) = Y: V(I,3) = Z
260  XE = -X*S1 + Y*C1
270  YE = -X*C1*C2 - Y*S1*C2 + Z*S2
280  ZE = -X*S2*C1 - Y*S2*S1 - Z*C2 + RHO
290  SV(I,1) = D*XE/ZE: SV(I,2) = D*YE/ZE
300 NEXT I
```

The house is defined by seven surfaces: two roof components, the front, the back, two ends, and the bottom. Each surface is defined by four or five edges. The two ends have five edges each; the other surfaces have four edges each. The edges, in turn, are defined by endpoints, or vertices. For the house shown in Figure 9.6, there are ten vertices.

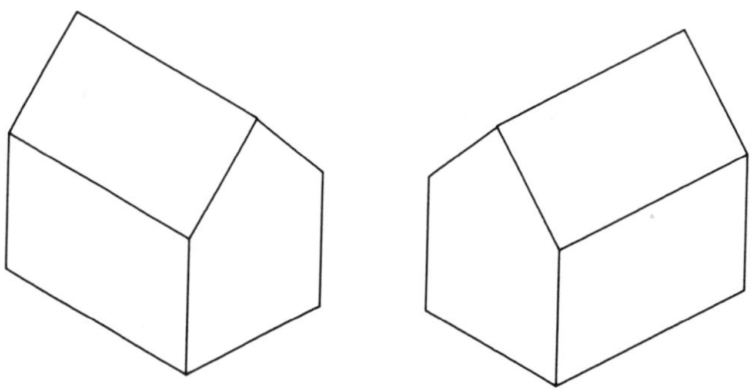

Figure 9.6

The Vertex Arrays

We begin by identifying the ten vertices of the house. For reference purposes they are numbered as shown in Figure 9.7.

Vertex	Coordinates		
1	5	7	−5
2	5	7	5
3	5	−7	5
4	5	−7	−5
5	−5	7	−5
6	−5	−7	5
7	−5	−7	5
8	−5	7	5
9	0	7	8
10	0	−7	8

The selection of a WINDOW and the viewing parameters (RHO, THETA, PHI, and D) are somewhat arbitrary, but the choices are interdependent. The selection of display screen is not important, but there is no immediate intent to use color graphics, so we may as well have the better resolution of SCREEN 2.

Program lines 230–300 load the vertex coordinates into a two-dimensional vertex array. For each array entry, V(I,J), I is the identification number of the vertex (between 1 and 10), while J is the number of the

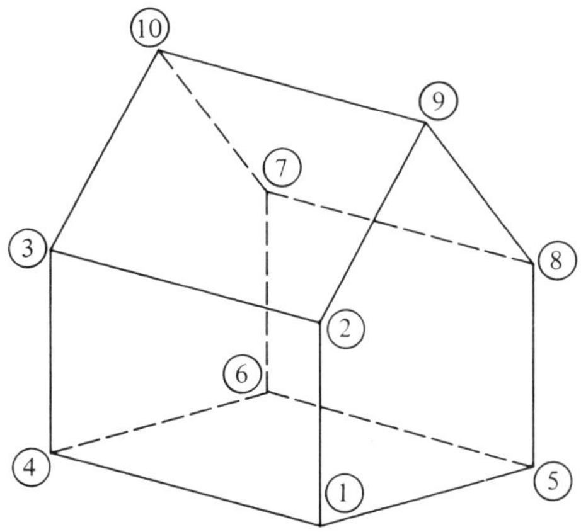

Figure 9.7

coordinate identified. For example, V(8,1) will be the first (x) coordinate of the eighth vertex, V(8,2) will be the second (y) coordinate of the eighth vertex, and V(8,3) will be the third (z) coordinate of the eighth vertex. Since vertex number 8 is (−5,7,5), we have

V(8,1) = −5
V(8,2) = 7
V(8,3) = 5

As the coordinates of the vertices are saved in the vertex array, the screen coordinates of each point are calculated for the screen vertex array SV(I,J). For each I, SV(I,1) and SV(I,2) are the screen coordinates SX and SY, respectively, of point number I.

The Surface Array

There are seven surfaces in the object (house) to be drawn. The surfaces are identified by number as shown in Figure 9.8.

Each surface may be drawn by connecting the appropriate vertices: for surface number 1, connect vertex 1 to 2 to 3 to 4 to 1; for surface 2, connect vertex 1 to 5 to 8 to 9 to 2 to 1 (see Figure 9.9). The other surfaces are defined in a similar manner.

The array S(I,J) identifies, for each surface I, the vertices that define the surface. Since the boundary of surface 1 connects vertices 1, 2, 3, 4, and 1, these numbers are saved as S(1,1), S(1,2), S(1,3), S(1,4), and S(1,5), respectively. Similarly, S(2,1) = 1, S(2,2) = 5, S(2,3) = 8, S(2,4) = 9, S(2,5) = 2, and S(2,6) = 1.

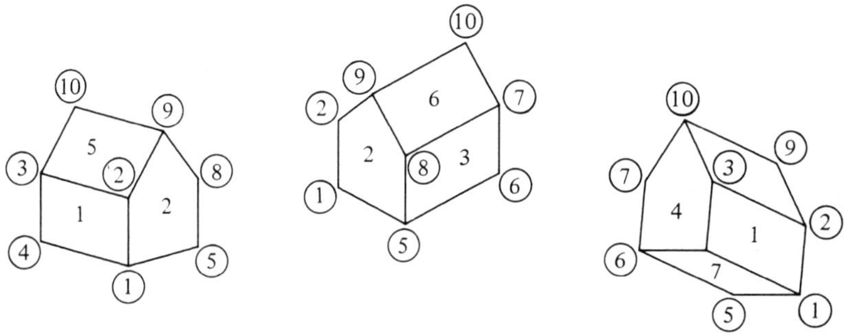

Figure 9.8

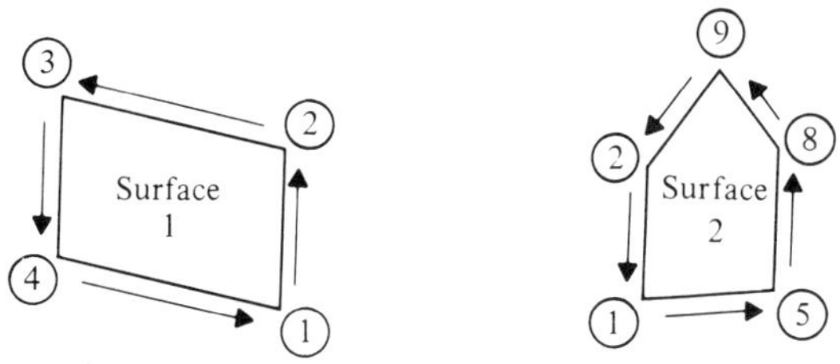

Figure 9.9

The complete array looks like this:

S(I,J)		J (points to be connected) 1	2	3	4	5	6
I (surface)	1	1	2	3	4	1	0
	2	1	5	8	9	2	1
	3	5	6	7	8	5	0
	4	4	3	10	7	6	4
	5	3	2	9	10	3	0
	6	7	10	9	8	7	0
	7	1	4	6	5	1	0

It is important, for each surface, that the vertices be identified in counterclockwise order as they appear from outside the object. You should verify that the points as listed in the surface array are in proper order. Refer to Figure 9.8 for outside views of each of the surfaces.

Program P9-1b

```
310 '==========================================
320 'Number of points (vertices) in each surface
330 DIM NPS(7)
340 DATA 5,6,5,6,5,5,5
350 FOR I = 1 TO 7
360  READ NPS(I)
370 NEXT I
380 'Surface array - pointers to vertices
390 DATA 1,2,3,4,1
400 DATA 1,5,8,9,2,1
410 DATA 5,6,7,8,5
420 DATA 4,3,10,7,6,4
```

```
430 DATA 3,2,9,10,3
440 DATA 7,10,9,8,7
450 DATA 1,4,6,5,1
460 'Fill surface array with vertex pointers
470 DIM S(7,6)
480 FOR I = 1 TO 7
490  FOR J = 1 TO NPS(I)
500   READ S(I,J)
510 NEXT J,I
```

The Normal Array

The surface orientation approach to hidden line elimination requires a vector which is normal (perpendicular) to each of the surfaces. These normals are calculated in Program P9-1C lines 550–650.

Program P9-1c

```
520 '============================================
530 'Calculate the vector that is normal to each surface
540 DIM N(7,3)
550 FOR I = 1 TO 7
560  U1 = V(S(I,2),1) - V(S(I,1),1)
570  U2 = V(S(I,2),2) - V(S(I,1),2)
580  U3 = V(S(I,2),3) - V(S(I,1),3)
590  V1 = V(S(I,3),1) - V(S(I,1),1)
600  V2 = V(S(I,3),2) - V(S(I,1),2)
610  V3 = V(S(I,3),3) - V(S(I,1),3)
620  N(I,1) = U2*V3 - V2*U3
630  N(I,2) = U3*V1 - V3*U1
640  N(I,3) = U1*V2 - V1*U2
650 NEXT I
```

The order in which points are listed in the surface array is important when the normal array is developed. This array contains the coordinates of outward-pointing vectors to the surfaces. N(1,1), N(1,2), and N(1,3) are the x, y, z components of an outward-pointing normal vector to surface 1. N(2,1), N(2,2), and N(2,3) are the components of an outward-pointing vector that is normal to surface 2.

The calculation of the normal vectors makes use of the fact that the cross product of two vectors is normal to the plane containing the two vectors. To identify a vector normal to a surface, we first choose vectors

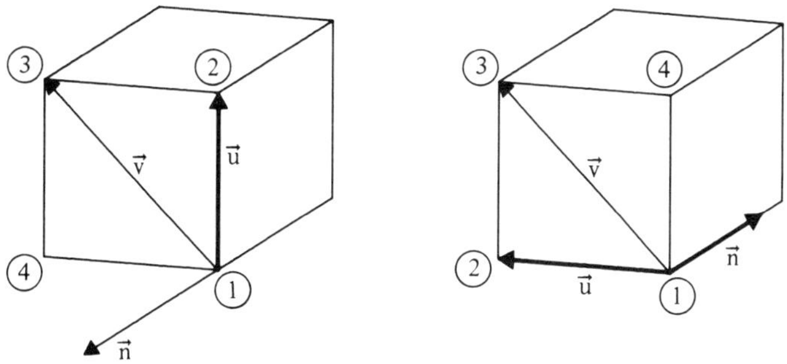

Figure 9.10

$\vec{u}$ and $\vec{v}$, which are parallel to the surface. Then $\vec{u} \times \vec{v}$ will yield a normal vector.

Each surface has either five or six vertices. Program lines 560–580 identify $\vec{u}$ as extending from the first to the second of these vertices. Vector $\vec{v}$ extends from the first to the third vertex (lines 590–610). Lines 620–640 calculate the components of the cross product of $\vec{u}$ and $\vec{v}$.

Notice how the order of the vertices affects the calculation of the normal vector. If the vertices of a surface are listed in a clockwise direction, then the relative orientation of $\vec{u}$ and $\vec{v}$ will be reversed, and $\vec{u} \times \vec{v}$ will be an inward-pointing normal vector, rather than an outward-pointing vector (see Figure 9.10).

The Visibility Test

We are now ready to apply the visibility test to each surface of the object. For each surface, we choose a line-of-sight vector $\vec{w}$ extending from a point (any point) on the surface to the viewpoint (XE,YE,ZE). The angle between $\vec{w}$ and the outward-pointing normal, $\vec{n}$, provides a visibility criterion. If the angle is between 0° and 90°, the surface faces the viewer. In this case the dot product $\vec{n} \cdot \vec{w}$ will be positive. If the angle is between 90° and 180°, the surface faces away from the viewer; $\vec{n} \cdot \vec{w}$ will be negative.

Program line 760 is the visibility filter. Those surfaces which face the viewer ($\vec{n} \cdot \vec{w} > 0$) will pass through the filter, eventually to be plotted. Those surfaces which do not face the viewer ($\vec{n} \cdot \vec{w} \leq 0$) will be rejected (see Program P9-1D).

Program P9-1d

```
660 '=========================================
670 'Determine visibility of each surface
680 'and collect visible edges in edge array
690 XE = RHO*S2*C1: YE = RHO*S2*S1: ZE = RHO*C2
700 DIM E(12,3): N = 1
710 FOR I = 1 TO 7
720  E1 = S(I,1)
730  WX = XE - V(E1,1)
740  WY = YE - V(E1,2)
750  WZ = ZE - V(E1,3)
760  IF N(I,1)*WX + N(I,2)*WY + N(I,3)*WZ <= 0 THEN 870
770  FOR J = 2 TO NPS(I)
780   E2 = S(I,J): K = 1
790   IF E(K,1) = E2 AND E(K,2) = E1 THEN 840
800   IF K = N THEN 820
810   K = K + 1: GOTO 790
820   E(N,1) = E1: E(N,2) = E2
830   N = N + 1
840   E1 = E2
850   E(K,3) = E(K,3) + 1
860  NEXT J
870 NEXT I
```

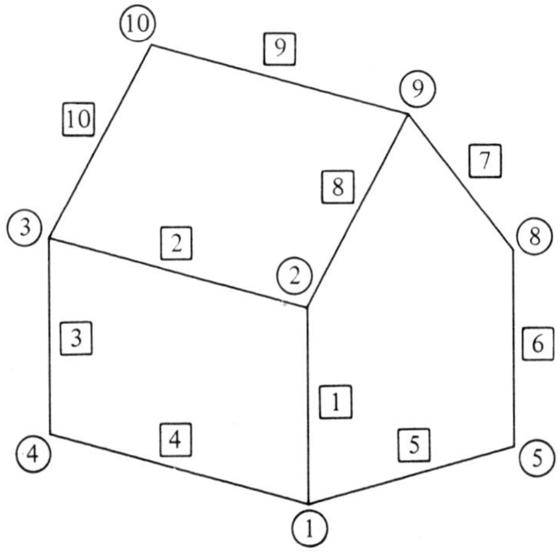

Figure 9.11

The Edge Array

Visible surfaces are decomposed into edges that are collected in the edge array, which has been dimensioned to accept as many as 12 edges (line 700).

Each of the edges that are put in the array is identified by a number I (between 1 and 12). For each edge I, three numbers are saved. E(I,1) and E(I,2) are the identification numbers of the two endpoints of the edge. E(I,3) is a tag, and identifies the number of visible surfaces for which the edge is a boundary. If the edge is a boundary of one visible edge, then the value of E(I,3) is 1. If the edge is a boundary of two visible edges, then the value of E(I,3) is 2.

Figure 9.11 illustrates the labelling of edges in the edge array. The labelling shown is that which is developed by the viewing parameters of Program P9-1.

Edge	Endpoints		Tag
1	1	2	2
2	2	3	2
3	3	4	1
4	4	1	1
5	1	5	1
6	5	8	1
7	8	9	1
8	9	2	2
9	9	10	1
10	10	3	1
11	0	0	0
12	0	0	0

Edges 11 and 12 are not needed for this view. The array provides more space than is necessary; no view of the object will show more than 12 edges.

Notice that the edges that are outer edges of the drawing (edges 3, 4, 5, 6, 7, 9, 10) all have tags with a value of 1. These edges are those which are a boundary of only one visible surface. The inner edges of the drawing (1, 2, 8) are those which bound two visible surfaces. Their tags are all equal to 2. The distinction between inner and outer edges becomes important when we consider the drawing of more than one object (Program P9-5).

Program lines 710–870 fill the edge array. The endpoints of each edge are read from the surface array (lines 720, 780) and stored in the edge array (line 850), and the tag is set to 1. If an edge is encountered for a second time, the tag is reset to 2 (lines 790, 850).

Plotting

It is now the time to draw the visible edges. Lines 900–940 of Program P9-1E identify the visible edges (those with nonzero tags), read the identification numbers of the corresponding endpoints, and plot the edges.

Program P9-1e

```
890 'Draw visible edges
900 FOR I = 1 TO 12
910  IF E(I,3) = 0 THEN 940
920  J = E(I,1): K = E(I,2)
930  LINE (SV(J,1),SV(J,2)) - (SV(K,1),SV(K,2))
940 NEXT I
```

Program P9-1: HIDDEN LINES; HOUSE

```
10 'PROGRAM P9-1  (HIDDEN LINES: HOUSE)
20 'Surface orientation method
100 '=======================================
110 KEY OFF: SCREEN 2: CLS
120 OPTION BASE 1
130 WINDOW (-4,-3) - (4,3)
140 RHO = 80: D = 20
150 THETA = .9: S1 = SIN(THETA): C1 = COS(THETA)
160 PHI = 1.2: S2 = SIN(PHI): C2 = COS(PHI)
170 '=======================================
180 'Data for vertices
190 DATA 5,7,-5,  5,7,5,  5,-7,5, 5,-7,-5, -5,7,-5
200 DATA -5,-7,-5, -5,-7,5, -5,7,5, 0,7,8, 0,-7,8
210 'Fill vertex arrays
220 DIM V(10,3),SV(10,2)
230 FOR I = 1 TO 10
240  READ X,Y,Z
250  V(I,1) = X: V(I,2) = Y: V(I,3) = Z
260  XE = -X*S1 + Y*C1
270  YE = -X*C1*C2 - Y*S1*C2 + Z*S2
280  ZE = -X*S2*C1 - Y*S2*S1 - Z*C2 + RHO
290  SV(I,1) = D*XE/ZE: SV(I,2) = D*YE/ZE
```

```
300 NEXT I
310 '===============================================
320 'Number of points (vertices) in each surface
330 DIM NPS(7)
340 DATA 5,6,5,6,5,5,5
350 FOR I = 1 TO 7
360  READ NPS(I)
370 NEXT I
380 'Surface array - pointers to vertices
390 DATA 1,2,3,4,1
400 DATA 1,5,8,9,2,1
410 DATA 5,6,7,8,5
420 DATA 4,3,10,7,6,4
430 DATA 3,2,9,10,3
440 DATA 7,10,9,8,7
450 DATA 1,4,6,5,1
460 'Fill surface array with vertex pointers
470 DIM S(7,6)
480 FOR I = 1 TO 7
490  FOR J = 1 TO NPS(I)
500   READ S(I,J)
510 NEXT J,I
520 '===============================================
530 'Calculate the vector that is normal to each surface
540 DIM N(7,3)
550 FOR I = 1 TO 7
560  U1 = V(S(I,2),1) - V(S(I,1),1)
570  U2 = V(S(I,2),2) - V(S(I,1),2)
580  U3 = V(S(I,2),3) - V(S(I,1),3)
590  V1 = V(S(I,3),1) - V(S(I,1),1)
600  V2 = V(S(I,3),2) - V(S(I,1),2)
610  V3 = V(S(I,3),3) - V(S(I,1),3)
620  N(I,1) = U2* V3 - V2*U3
630  N(I,2) = U3* V1 - V3*U1
640  N(I,3) = U1* V2 - V1*U2
650 NEXT I
660 '===============================================
670 'Determine visibility of each surface
680 'and collect visible edges in edge array
690 XE = RHO*S2*C1: YE = RHO*S2*S1: ZE = RHO*C2
700 DIM E(12,3): N = 1
710 FOR I = 1 TO 7
720  E1 = S(I,1)
730  WX = XE - V(E1,1)
740  WY = YE - V(E1,2)
750  WZ = ZE - V(E1,3)
760  IF N(I,1)*WX + N(I,2)*WY + N(I,3)*WZ <= 0 THEN 870
770  FOR J = 2 TO NPS(I)
780   E2 = S(I,J): K = 1
```

```
790     IF E(K,1) = E2 AND E(K,2) = E1 THEN 840
800     IF K = N THEN 820
810     K = K + 1: GOTO 790
820     E(N,1) = E1: E(N,2) = E2
830     N = N + 1
840     E1 = E2
850     E(K,3) = E(K,3) + 1
860    NEXT J
870   NEXT I
880   '============================================
890   'Draw visible edges
900   FOR I = 1 TO 12
910    IF E(I,3) = 0 THEN 940
920    J = E(I,1): K = E(I,2)
930    LINE (SV(J,1),SV(J,2)) - (SV(K,1),SV(K,2))
940   NEXT I
```

NOTES AND SUGGESTIONS

1. The viewpoint parameters are specified in lines 140–160. Try a variety of views. In general, you will want to change only THETA or PHI, but changing RHO and D will help in understanding their role in the development of the image.
2. Programming other convex solids will require obvious changes in the data for the vertex array and the surface array, and related changes in the limits of the various FOR–NEXT loops. Try objects such as cubes, pyramids, and prisms.
3. Once a surface is identified as being visible (facing the viewer), components within that surface may be assumed to be visible. To each of the four walls of the house add windows and doors, then draw these components whenever the corresponding surface is visible.
4. The image of Program P9-1 is produced on the high-resolution graphics screen. Have it drawn on the medium-resolution graphics screen (change line 110) and have the visible components PAINTed with various colors or paint tilings.

TWO OBJECTS; BLACKOUT

The methods described above permit the drawing of visible portions of a single convex object. In the pages ahead, methods will be presented that

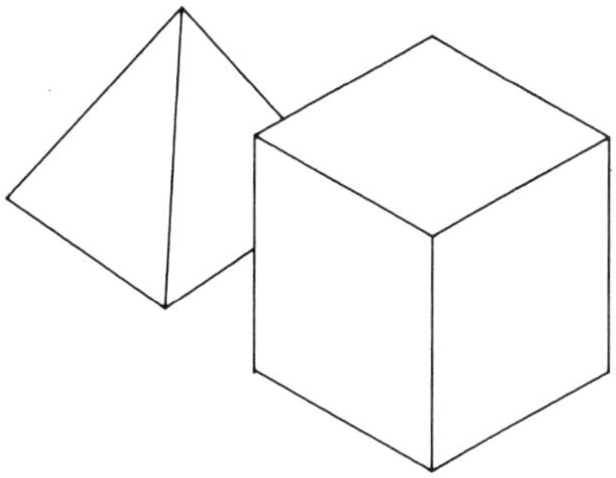

Figure 9.12

allow the drawing of the visible portions of several objects. In addition to being concerned about the identification of those portions of an object which face towards, or away from, the viewer, it will be necessary to identify those portions which are hidden by a closer object.

When we look around us, portions of objects are hidden by closer objects because of the inability of light to pass through an opaque substance. We could consider that the hidden proportions of an object have been drawn, but were erased by the drawing of a closer object (see Figure 9.12). This approach is used in Program P9-2.

Program P9-2: BLACKOUT

```
10 'PROGRAM P9-2  (BLACKOUT)
20 'Two objects; blackout
100 '=======================================
110 KEY OFF: SCREEN 2: CLS
120 WINDOW (-4,-3) - (4,3)
130 RHO = 40: D = 80
140 THETA = 1: S1 = SIN(THETA): C1 = COS(THETA)
150 PHI = 1.2: S2 = SIN(PHI): C2 = COS(PHI)
160 '=======================================
170 'Draw pyramid
180 N = 6: GOSUB 410
190 '=======================================
200 'Black out region to be occupied by cube
210 READ X,Y,Z: GOSUB 490: X1 = SX: Y1 = SY
```

```
220 X1 = PMAP(SX,0)
230 Y1 = PMAP(SY,1)
240 READ X,Y,Z: GOSUB 490: X2 = SX: Y2 = SY
250 X2 = PMAP(SX,0)
260 Y2 = PMAP(SY,1)
270 SLOPE = (Y1-Y2)/(X1-X2)
280 WINDOW
290 FOR XP = X1 TO X2
300  YP = SLOPE*(XP-X1) + Y1
310  LINE (XP,YP) - (XP,199),0
320 NEXT XP
330 WINDOW (-4,-3) - (4,3)
340 '=========================================
350 'Draw cube
360 N = 9: GOSUB 410
370 N = 2: GOSUB 410
380 END
390 '=========================================
400 'Drawing subroutine
410 FOR I = 1 TO N
420  READ X,Y,Z: GOSUB 490
430  IF I = 1 THEN PSET (SX,SY),1
440  LINE - (SX,SY)
450 NEXT I
460 RETURN
470 '=========================================
480 'Perspective projection subroutine
490 XE = -X*S1 + Y*C1
500 YE = -X*C1*C2 - Y*S1*C2 + Z*S2
510 ZE = -X*S2*C1 - Y*S2*S1 - Z*C2 + RHO
520 SX = D*XE/ZE: SY = D*YE/ZE
530 RETURN
540 '=========================================
550 'Data for pyramid
560 DATA 1,1,0,  0,0,1,  0,1,0
570 DATA 1,1,0,  1,0,0,  0,0,1
580 'Data for cube
590 DATA 1,1.5,1,  0,1.5,1,  0,2.5,1
600 DATA 1,2.5,1,  1,2.5,0,  0,2.5,0
610 DATA 0,2.5,1,  0,1.5,1,  1,1.5,1
620 DATA 1,1.5,0,  1,2.5,0,  1,2.5,1
630 DATA 1,1.5,1
```

The data in lines 560 through 630 identify the vertices of a cube and a pyramid as shown in Figure 9.12. The only vertices given are those which are part of a surface that faces the viewer. The more distant of the two objects (the pyramid) is drawn first (line 180). Before the closer object (the cube) is drawn, the hidden portions of the pyramid are removed from the screen. This is accomplished by using color 0 of the current palette (the background color) to draw over a portion of the screen occupied by the cube. The erasure of the hidden parts of the pyramid is handled in lines 210 through 320. Vertical black lines are drawn from the screen image of one of the cube edges to the bottom of the screen. When the erasure is complete, the cube is drawn (line 360).

This technique of hidden line elimination is fairly easy to use and gives nice results in short execution time. It is limited, however; the viewpoint must be planned well in advance. This planning is necessary in order that only the vertices of visible surfaces are provided, and so that the region to be blacked out may be identified. A change in viewpoint typically will require changes in DATA statements and changes in the blackout routine.

NOTE: Notice the use of PMAP and WINDOW in the above program. In order for the blackout routine (lines 290 to 320) to draw vertical black lines over an entire region, it is best to be drawing in the default WINDOW. For this reason, line 280 resets the window from that established by line 120. Lines 220, 230, and 250, 260 have identified physical coordinates which correspond to the endpoints of an edge of the cube. These physical coordinates are used to identify the vertical black lines that are to be drawn.

PAINTOUT

Program P9-3 presents an alternate to the blackout method. It makes use of the PAINT statement and requires three colors, so it cannot be used on the high-resolution graphics page. The basic structure of the program is the same as Program P9-2.

Program P9-3: PAINTOUT

```
10 'PROGRAM P9-3  (PAINTOUT)
20 'Two objects; paintout
```

```
100 '==========================================
110 KEY OFF: SCREEN 1,0: COLOR 0,1: CLS
120 WINDOW (-4,-3) - (4,3)
130 RHO = 40: D = 80
140 THETA = 1: S1 = SIN(THETA): C1 = COS(THETA)
150 PHI = 1.2: S2 = SIN(PHI): C2 = COS(PHI)
160 '==========================================
170 'Draw pyramid
180 N = 6: C = 3: GOSUB 380
190 '==========================================
200 'Draw cube
210 N = 9: C = 2: GOSUB 380
220 N = 2: C = 2: GOSUB 380
230 '==========================================
240 'Paint surfaces of the cube
250 FOR I = 1 TO 3
260  READ X,Y,Z: GOSUB 450
270  PAINT (SX,SY),3,2
280  PAINT (SX,SY),0,2
290 NEXT I
300 '==========================================
310 'Draw cube again, with color 3
320 RESTORE 560
330 N = 9: C = 3: GOSUB 380
340 N = 2: C = 3: GOSUB 380
350 END
360 '==========================================
370 'Drawing subroutine
380 FOR I = 1 TO N
390  READ X,Y,Z: GOSUB 460
400  IF I = 1 THEN PSET (SX,SY),C
410  LINE - (SX,SY),C
420 NEXT I
430 RETURN
440 '==========================================
450 'Perspective projection subroutine
460 XE = -X*S1 + Y*C1
470 YE = -X*C1*C2 - Y*S1*C2 + Z*S2
480 ZE = -X*S2*C1 - Y*S2*S1 - Z*C2 + RHO
490 SX = D*XE/ZE: SY = D*YE/ZE
500 RETURN
510 '==========================================
520 'Data for pyramid
```

```
530 DATA 1,1,0,   0,0,1,   0,1,0
540 DATA 1,1,0,   1,0,0,   0,0,1
550 'Data for cube
560 DATA 0,2.5,1,   1,2.5,1,   1,2.5,0
570 DATA 0,2.5,0,   0,2.5,1,   0,1.5,1
580 DATA 1,1.5,1,   1,1.5,0,   1,2.5,0
590 DATA 1,2.5,1,   1,1.5,1,   .5,2,1
600 DATA .5,2.5,.5,   1,2,.1
```

First, the pyramid is drawn (the object farthest from the viewer). Instead of erasing the part of the screen which is to be occupied by the cube, we have the cube drawn, with the hidden lines of the pyramid still visible. But while the pyramid was drawn in color 3 of the current palette, the cube is drawn in color 2.

When the cube is completed, each of its three visible surfaces is painted twice: once in color 3 of the current palette, then in color 0 (the background color). The first PAINT is done so that the second will extend throughout the region.

Painting in the background color effectively erases the hidden parts of the pyramid. Finally, the cube is drawn in color 3, so that the entire image is in a consistent color. (In order for PAINT to color the entire interior of each of the sides of the cube, it was necessary to have the cube drawn in a different color than the pyramid.)

The PAINTOUT method of erasing hidden lines is one of the easiest to use, and it works in a variety of settings. It is not universally useful, however. Note that it cannot be used on the high-resolution screen. Further, it cannot be used if the output is by digital plotter instead of the display screen. In the form presented here, it also is dependent on the viewpoint selected. Making it independent of viewpoint is possible; you might consider how to do so.

TWO OBJECTS; BINARY SEARCH

In Figure 9.13, the cube should block vertex H of the pyramid from view. Edge VH of the pyramid should be partly hidden, with only VT visible. The screen coordinates of vertex V are available, but the coordinates of T must be calculated. Since T is the point of intersection of cube edge PQ and pyramid edge VH, the coordinates of T could be calculated

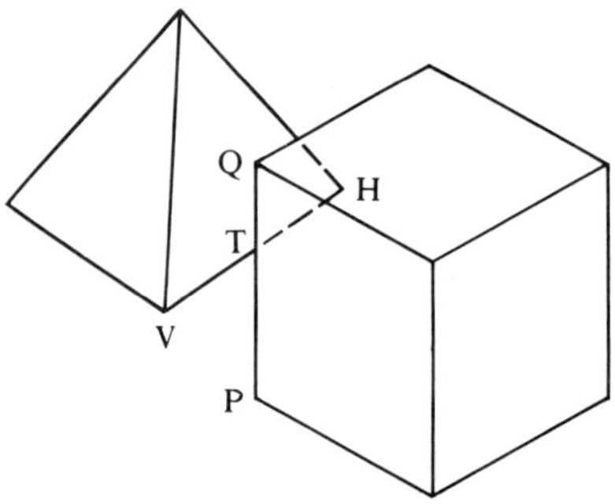

Figure 9.13

from the equation of lines VH and PQ. The algebra involved is straightforward, but not efficient. Instead, we will recommend a binary search to identify the coordinates of T (see Program P9-4).

Program P9-4: BINARY SEARCH

```
10 'PROGRAM P9-4  (BINARY SEARCH)
20 'Two objects; binary search
100 '========================================
110 KEY OFF: SCREEN 2: CLS
120 WINDOW (-4,-3) - (4,3)
130 RHO = 40: D = 80
140 THETA = 1: S1 = SIN(THETA): C1 = COS(THETA)
150 PHI = 1.2: S2 = SIN(PHI): C2 = COS(PHI)
160 '========================================
170 'Draw cube
180 N = 9: GOSUB 450
190 N = 2: GOSUB 450
200 'Parts of pyramid that are completely visible
210 N = 4: GOSUB 450
220 'Pyramid lines that are partly hidden
230 FOR J = 1 TO 2
240  READ X,Y,Z: GOSUB 530: XV = SX: YV = SY
250  READ X,Y,Z: GOSUB 530: XH = SX: YH = SY
260  READ X,Y,Z: GOSUB 530: XP = SX: YP = SY
270  READ X,Y,Z: GOSUB 530: XQ = SX: YQ = SY
280  V1 = (XH - XV)/2: V2 = (YH - YV)/2
290  U1 = XP - XQ: U2 = YP - YQ
```

```
300  XT = XV + V1: YT = YV + V2
310 '=========================================
320 'Binary search
330  FOR I = 2 TO 7
340   CROSS1 = U2*(XV - XQ) - U1*(YV - YQ)
350   CROSS2 = U2*(XT - XQ) - U1*(YT - YQ)
360   VI = SGN(CROSS1*CROSS2)
370   V1 = V1/2: V2 = V2/2
380   XT = XT + VI*V1: YT = YT+ VI*V2
390  NEXT I
400  LINE (XV,YV) -(XT,YT)
410 NEXT J
420 END
430 '=========================================
440 'Drawing subroutine
450 FOR I = 1 TO N
460  READ X,Y,Z: GOSUB 530
470  IF I = 1 THEN PSET (SX,SY)
480  LINE - (SX,SY)
490 NEXT I
500 RETURN
510 '=========================================
520 'Perspective projection subroutine
530 XE = -X*S1 + Y*C1
540 YE = -X*C1*C2 - Y*S1*C2 + Z*S2
550 ZE = -X*S2*C1 - Y*S2*S1 - Z*C2 + RHO
560 SX = D*XE/ZE: SY = D*YE/ZE
570 RETURN
580 '=========================================
590 'Data for cube
600 DATA 0,2.5,1,  1,2.5,1,  1,2.5,0
610 DATA 0,2.5,0,  0,2.5,1,  0,1.5,1
620 DATA 1,1.5,1,  1,1.5,0,  1,2.5,0
630 DATA 1,2.5,1,  1,1.5,1
640 'Visible parts of pyramid
650 DATA 1,1,0,  0,0,1
660 DATA 1,0,0,  1,1,0
670 'Partly visible lines
680 DATA 1,1,0,  0,1,0
690 DATA 1,1.5,0,  1,1.5,1
700 DATA 0,0,1,  0,1,0
710 DATA 1,1.5,1,  0,1.5,1
```

Lines 180, 190, and 210 plot the visible portions of the cube and edges of the pyramid that are completely visible. Lines 240 through 270 obtain the screen coordinates of points V, H, P, and Q. The calculation of the coordinates of point T is accomplished in lines 280 through 300. The binary search used to obtain T functions as follows.

1. Identify the vector (V1,V2), extending from point V(XV,YV) halfway to point H(XH,YH) (line 280).
2. Add (V1,V2) to (XV,YV) to obtain the midpoint (XT,YT) of the line segment from (XV,YV) to (XH,YH) (line 300).
3. Test (XT,YT) for visibility (lines 340 to 360).
4. Redefine (V1,V2) = (V1,V2)/2 (line 370).
5. If (XT,YT) is visible, then move toward (XH,YH) by redefining (XT,YT) = (XT,YT) + (V1,V2). If (XT,YT) is hidden, then move toward (XV,YV) by redefining (XT,YT) = (XT,YT) − (V1,V2) (line 380).
6. Return to step 3 (line 410).

To determine the visibility of T, we identify vector $\vec{u}$ extending from point Q to point P, the vector (XV − XQ,YV − YQ) extending from point Q to point V and the vector (XT − XQ,YT − YQ) extending from point Q to point T. If T is visible, then T must lie on the same side of line PQ as point V. If that is the case, the cross product of (XT − XQ,YT − YQ) and $\vec{u}$ will have the same sign as the cross product of (XV − XQ, YV − YQ) and vector $\vec{u}$. If T is not visible, the cross products will have opposite signs. (May we safely assume that neither cross product is zero?) Line 360 takes care of the comparison of the cross products.

The value of (XT,YT) is accepted after the seventh value has been calculated. The length of (V1,V2) is then 1/128th of the distance from (XV,YV) to (XH,YH). This provides acceptable accuracy for most images on the IBM display screen. Greater accuracy may be obtained by increasing the number of cycles through the loop.

On leaving the loop, the line segment from point V to point T is plotted. The procedure is then repeated for the second partially hidden line.

TWO OBJECTS; ARBITRARY VIEWPOINT

The previous three methods for eliminating hidden lines from images containing several convex objects place limits on the viewpoint. If it is preferred to have a more general method, we may extend the surface orientation method.

THEORY OF OPERATION

We will use the objects shown in Figure 9.14 to illustrate the calculations that are necessary.

From the angle of view provided in 9.14a, the cube lies closer to the viewer, hiding a part of the pyramid. In Figure 9.14b, the pyramid hides part of the cube. One of our concerns will be the assignment of a priority to each of the objects. When two objects are a part of a scene, the one that cannot be hidden by the other will be given first-priority status. The object which may be partly hidden will be assigned second-priority status. Assignment of priority can be made on the basis of distance from the viewpoint to the center of each object, with the closer object being assigned first-priority status.

A second method of assigning priority is based on a separating plane (a plane that separates the two objects). First priority is assigned to the object that lies on the same side of the separating plane as the viewpoint. Any plane which separates the objects may be chosen as the separating plane. (The separating plane may contain a point, an edge, or a surface of one or both of the objects.) If a change in separating planes causes a change in priority of the objects, we need not worry. In that case, neither object will hide the other.

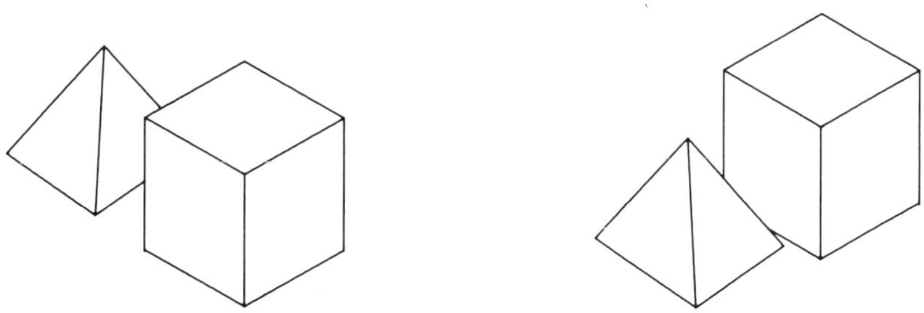

(a) (b)

Figure 9.14

Once the objects have been assigned priority, the first-priority object may be plotted. We will use the surface orientation process to draw only those surfaces which face the viewer.

The surface orientation process also will be applied to the second-priority object in order to identify those surfaces which face the viewer. Each edge of a visible surface then must be considered separately to determine whether either of its endpoints are hidden by the first-priority object. If neither endpoint is hidden, the edge may be plotted. If both endpoints are hidden, the edge is discarded. If exactly one endpoint is hidden, we must calculate the point of intersection of the screen image of the edge with the screen image of the boundary of the first-priority object. The visible portion of the edge is then plotted.

This problem presents challenges we have not faced before. We will illustrate them with a cube and an edge of a pyramid.

In Figure 9.15a, the hidden portions of two edges of the pyramid are shown as dashed lines. Since the visible portion of each of these edges extends from the visible endpoint to the intersection with an outside boundary of the cube image, we may simplify the diagram by discarding the inner cube boundaries (Figure 9.15b).

The orientation of the outside cube edges, inherited from the definition of the surface array entries, is shown in Figure 9.15c. In that drawing, note that point H of the pyramid edge, lying inside the cube boundaries and thus hidden by the cube, is in the left half-plane of each of the cube boundaries. Point V, which is not hidden by the cube, is in the left half-plane of several cube boundaries, and in the right half-plane of others. (See Appendix 3 for a discussion of half-planes.)

To identify the visible portions of the pyramid edge, we could move along the line from H to V, testing each point for visibility. Identify T as the first point which is found to lie in the right half-plane of at least

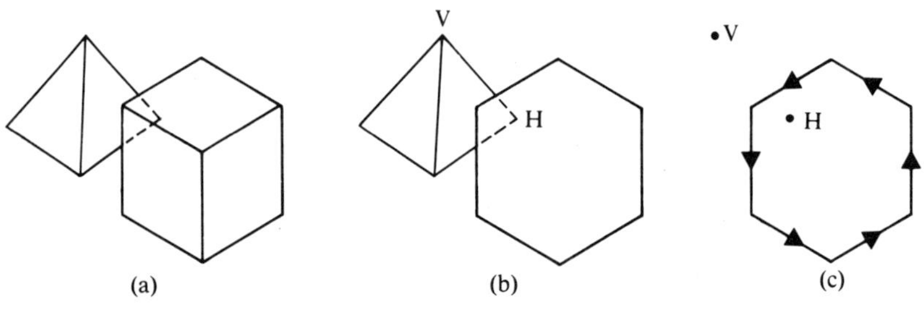

Figure 9.15

one cube boundary. Then the visible line segment from V to T may be plotted.

PROGRAM P9-5

The methods described above are illustrated in the following program (Program P9-5). To the house of Program P9-1, we will add a second object: a chimney. (Again, the program is a long one; it will be given in parts.)

The chimney is defined by six surfaces: the top, the bottom, and four sides. Every surface is defined by four edges, each of which is identified by its endpoints (vertices of the chimney).

In defining the two objects, the vertices of the house are retained as they were defined in Program P9-1 (Figure 9.16).

Vertex	Coordinates		
1	5	7	−5
2	5	7	5
3	5	−7	5
4	5	−7	−5
5	−5	7	−5
6	−5	−7	−5
7	−5	−7	5
8	−5	7	5
9	0	7	8
10	0	−7	8

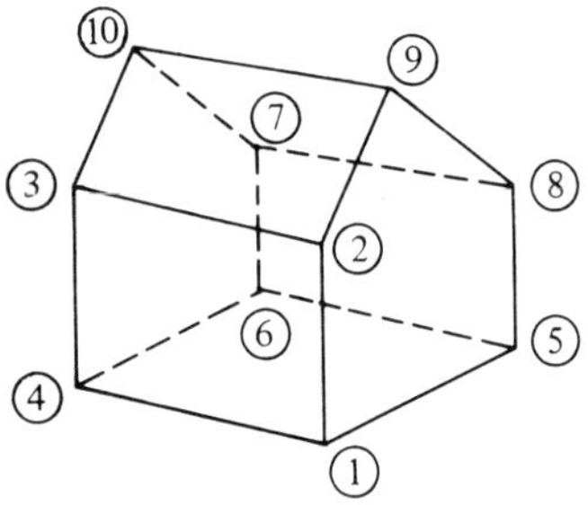

Figure 9.16

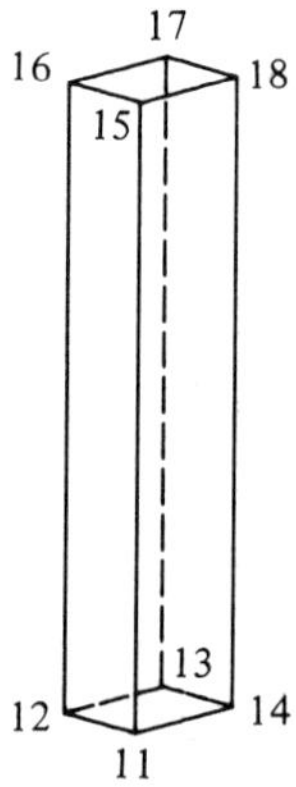

Figure 9.17

The vertices of the chimney are identified by number as shown in Figure 9.17.

Vertex	Coordinates		
11	−2	−7	−5
12	−2	−9	−5
13	−5	−9	−5
14	−5	−7	−5
15	−2	−7	9
16	−2	−9	9
17	−5	−9	9
18	−5	−7	9

The Vertex Arrays

Program lines 140 through 330 identify the viewpoint and screen parameters, and read the coordinates of the vertices into the vertex arrays. Arrays V(I,J) and SV(I,J) are dimensioned so that each accommodates the coordinates of 18 points. The vertex array V(I,J) serves the same function as before, with V(I,1), V(I,2), and V(I,3) identifying the x,y and z coordinates of vertex I.

Program P9-5: HIDDEN LINES; HOUSE AND CHIMNEY
Program P9-5a

```
10 'PROGRAM P9-5   (HIDDEN LINE; HOUSE AND CHIMNEY)
20 'Two objects; arbitrary viewpoint
```

```
100 '==============================================
110 KEY OFF: SCREEN 2: CLS
120 OPTION BASE 1
130 WINDOW (-4,-3) - (4,3)
140 RHO = 80: D = 20
150 THETA = .9: S1 = SIN(THETA): C1 = COS(THETA)
160 PHI = 1.2: S2 = SIN(PHI): C2 = COS(PHI)
170 '================================================
180 'Data for vertices of object 1 (house)
190 DATA 5,7,-5,  5,7,5,  5,-7,5, 5,-7,-5, -5,7,-5
200 DATA -5,-7,-5, -5,-7,5, -5,7,5, 0,7,8, 0,-7,8
210 'Data for vertices of object 2 (chimney)
220 DATA -2,-7,-5,  -2,-9,-5,  -5,-9,-5,  -5,-7,-5
230 DATA -2,-7,9,  -2,-9,9,  -5,-9,9,  -5,-7,9
240 'Fill vertex arrays
250 DIM V(18,3),SV(18,3)
260 FOR I = 1 TO 18
270  READ X,Y,Z
280  V(I,1) = X: V(I,2) = Y: V(I,3) = Z
290  XE = -X*S1 + Y*C1
300  YE = -X*C1*C2 - Y*S1*C2 + Z*S2
310  ZE = -X*S2*C1 - Y*S2*S1 - Z*C2 + RHO
320  SV(I,1) = D*XE/ZE: SV(I,2) = D*YE/ZE
330 NEXT I
```

The entries SV(I,1) and SV(I,2) are calculated as the values of V(I,1), V(I,2) and V(I,3) are identified. For each I, SV(I,1) and SV(I,2) identify the screen coordinates of the point (X,Y,Z). A third entry, SV(I,3), is available for each vertex I. Initially, each SV(I,3) is left equal to 0. Later, this entry will be changed in order to identify the status (visible or hidden) of some of the vertices.

Program P9-5b

```
340 '============================================
350 'Number of points (vertices) in each surface
360 DIM NPS(13)
370 DATA 5,6,5,6,5,5,5
380 DATA 5,5,5,5,5,5
390 FOR I = 1 TO 13
400  READ NPS(I)
410 NEXT I
420 'Surface array - pointers to vertices
430 DATA 1,2,3,4,1
440 DATA 1,5,8,9,2,1
450 DATA 5,6,7,8,5
460 DATA 4,3,10,7,6,4
470 DATA 3,2,9,10,3
480 DATA 7,10,9,8,7
```

```
490 DATA 1,4,6,5,1
500 DATA 11,12,13,14,11
510 DATA 15,18,17,16,15
520 DATA 11,14,18,15,11
530 DATA 12,16,17,13,12
540 DATA 11,15,16,12,11
550 DATA 14,13,17,18,14
560 'Fill surface arrays with vertex pointers
570 DIM S(13,6)
580 FOR I = 1 TO 13
590  FOR J = 1 TO NPS(I)
600   READ S(I,J)
610 NEXT J,I
```

The Surface Array

The surface array is the next to be filled (see Program P9-5B). The array is an enlargement of the one used in Program P9-1, identifying surfaces 1 through 7 as the surfaces of the house, and surfaces 8 through 13 as the surfaces of the chimney. Surfaces 8 and 9 are the top and bottom of the chimney; surfaces 10, 11, 12, and 13 are the four sides of the chimney. As before, the array entries V(I,1) through V(I,NPS(I)) identify the vertices of surface I, listed in counterclockwise order around the surface (as seen from outside the object).

When complete, the surface array looks like this:

	J (points to be connected)					
S(I,J)	1	2	3	4	5	6
I (surface) 1	1	2	3	4	1	0
2	1	5	8	9	2	1
3	5	6	7	8	5	0
4	4	3	10	7	6	4
5	3	2	9	10	3	0
6	7	10	9	8	7	0
7	1	4	6	5	1	0
8	11	12	13	14	11	0
9	15	18	17	16	15	0
10	11	14	18	15	11	0
11	12	16	17	13	12	0
12	11	15	16	12	11	0
13	14	13	17	18	14	0

The Normal Array

The normal array is calculated as before, with N(I,1), N(I,2), and N(I,3) identifying the three components of the outward-pointing normal vector to surface I (see Program P9-5C).

Program P9-5c

```
620 '===================================================
630 'Calculate the vector that is normal to each surface
640 DIM N(13,3)
650 FOR I = 1 TO 13
660  U1 = V(S(I,2),1) - V(S(I,1),1)
670  U2 = V(S(I,2),2) - V(S(I,1),2)
680  U3 = V(S(I,2),3) - V(S(I,1),3)
690  V1 = V(S(I,3),1) - V(S(I,1),1)
700  V2 = V(S(I,3),2) - V(S(I,1),2)
710  V3 = V(S(I,3),3) - V(S(I,1),3)
720  N(I,1) = U2* V3 - V2*U3
730  N(I,2) = U3* V1 - V3*U1
740  N(I,3) = U1* V2 - V1*U2
750 NEXT I
```

The Edge Array

In Program P9-1, the edge array provided space for the identification of the endpoints of as many as 12 visible edges of the house. The chimney adds 12 edges, no more than nine of which are visible from any given viewpoint.

Since some of the edges of the farther object may be partly hidden by the closer object, it is useful to classify each edge so that it may be referenced by object number. The edge array is dimensioned E(2,12,3). When referencing an entry in the edge array, E(I,J,K), I will have a value of 1 or 2, referring to an edge of object 1 or object 2 (house or chimney). For each I, J will have a value between 1 and 12, allowing as many as 12 visible edges for each object (at most, 12 are needed for the house; at most, nine for the chimney). For edge J of object I, E(I,J,1) and E(I,J,2) are pointers to vertices that are the endpoints of the edge. E(I,J,3) is a tag which identifies the number of visible surfaces for which the edge is a boundary.

Figure 9.18 shows the pattern of labelling the edges in the edge array. These are the values in the edge array when Program P9-5 is run with the specified viewpoint parameters (see Program P9-5D).

I = 1; object 1 (house)

Edge	Endpoints		Tag
1	1	2	2
2	2	3	2
3	3	4	1
4	4	1	1
5	1	5	1
6	5	8	1
7	8	9	1
8	9	2	2
9	9	10	1
10	10	3	1
11	0	0	0
12	0	0	0

I = 2; object 2 (chimney)

Edge	Endpoints		Tag
1	11	12	1
2	14	11	1
3	15	18	2
4	18	17	1
5	17	16	1
6	16	15	2
7	14	18	1
8	15	11	2
9	16	12	1
10	0	0	0
11	0	0	0
12	0	0	0

The contents of the edge array are dependent on the viewpoint selected. As the viewpoint changes, the number of edges will change, and the sequence of edges in the array and the tags will change.

Program P9-5d

```
760 '=================================================
770 'Determine visibility of each surface
780 'and collect visible edges in edge array
790 XE = RHO*S2*C1: YE = RHO*S2*S1: ZE = RHO*C2
800 DIM E(2,12,3): N = 1: OBJ = 1
810 FOR I = 1 TO 13
820  E1 = S(I,1)
830  WX = XE - V(E1,1)
840  WY = YE - V(E1,2)
850  WZ = ZE - V(E1,3)
860  IF N(I,1)*WX + N(I,2)*WY + N(I,3)*WZ <= 0 THEN 970
870  FOR J = 2 TO NPS(I)
880    E2 = S(I,J): K = 1
890    IF E(OBJ,K,1) = E2 AND E(OBJ,K,2) = E1 THEN 940
900    IF K = N THEN 920
910    K = K+1: GOTO 890
920    E(OBJ,N,1) = E1: E(OBJ,N,2) = E2
930    N = N + 1
940    E1 = E2
950    E(OBJ,K,3) = E(OBJ,K,3) + 1
960  NEXT J
970  IF I = 7 THEN N = 1: OBJ = 2
980 NEXT I
```

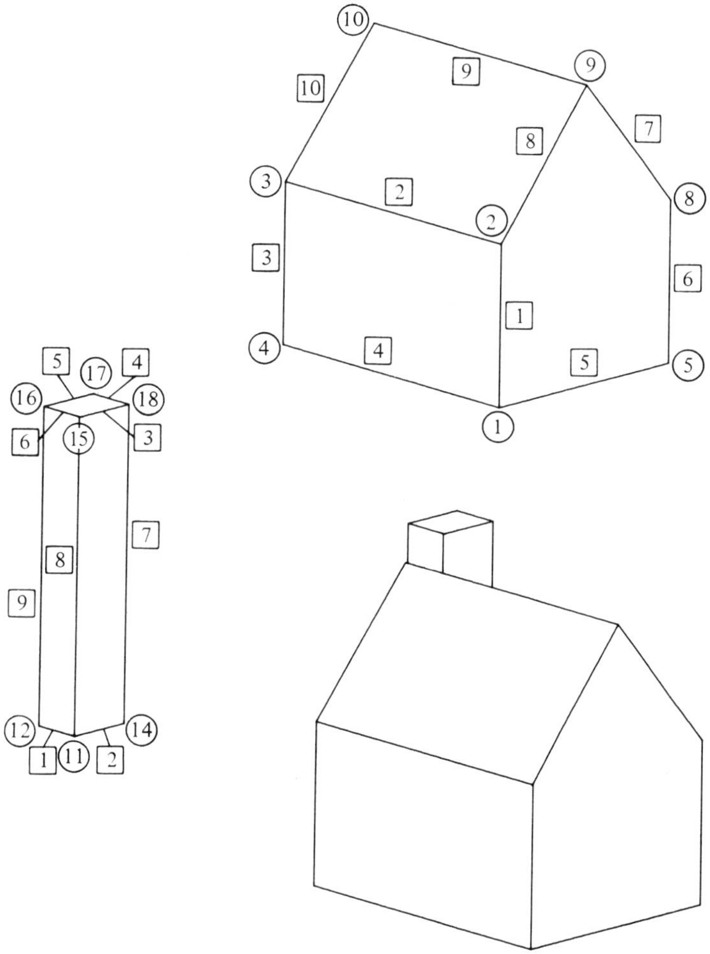

Figure 9.18

The identification of visible edges by the program is performed in essentially the same fashion as in Program P9-1. The surfaces of object 1 are considered first (line 800: OBJ = 1). Each surface of the object is tested for visibility in line 860 and the surfaces that face away from the viewpoint are discarded. Lines 870 through 960 then consider each of the edges of a visible surface. The endpoints of each edge are identified in lines 820 and 880, and collected in the edge array by line 920. The tag E(OBJ,N,3) is set to 1 in line 950. If an edge is encountered for a sec-

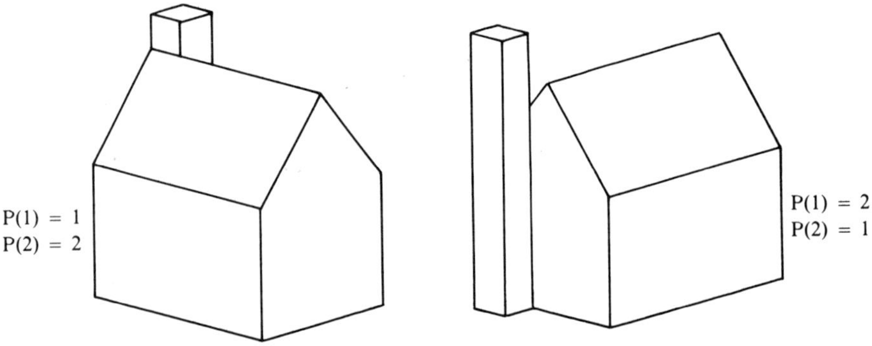

Figure 9.19

ond time (suggesting that it is a boundary of two visible surfaces), the tag E(OBJ,N,3) is set to 2 (again, line 950). When all surfaces of object 1 (the house) have been tested for visibility, the testing continues with the surfaces of object 2 (the chimney).

Object Priority

Since edges of the farther object may be partly hidden by the closer object, it is necessary to classify the objects by their relative positions. A separating plane has been used to establish the priority of the two objects. The plane Y = −7 is used as the separating plane, since the points of object 1 are either in the plane or on the side opposite the points of object 2.

If the viewpoint (XE,YE,ZE) lies on the same side of the separating plane as the house, then the visible edges of the house cannot be hidden by portions of the chimney. The house is given priority 1, while the chimney is given priority 2 (see Figure 9.19). If the viewpoint is on the same side of the separating plane as the chimney, then the chimney is given priority 1 and the house is given priority 2 (see Program P9-5E).

Program P9-5e

```
990 '====================================
1000 'Establish priority of objects
1010 IF YE >= -7 THEN P(1) = 1: P(2) = 2
1020 IF YE < -7 THEN P(1) = 2: P(2) = 1
```

Priority-One Edges

The visible edges of the object having first priority may now be drawn. Each of the edges is a boundary of a surface which has passed the surface orientation test for visibility. Since the edges are associated with the object having first priority, they could not be hidden (partly or completely) by the other object (see Program P9-5F).

Program P9-5f

```
1030 '============================================
1040 'Draw visible edges of first priority object
1050 FOR I = 1 TO 12
1060  IF E(P(1),I,3) = 0 THEN 1090
1070  J = E(P(1),I,1): K = E(P(1),I,2)
1080  LINE (SV(J,1),SV(J,2)) - (SV(K,1),SV(K,2))
1090 NEXT I
```

Priority-Two Edges

The edges associated with the second object must be scrutinized more carefully. An edge which is in the edge array may be partly or completely hidden by the priority-one object.

To illustrate, consider the view of the house and chimney shown in Figure 9.20.

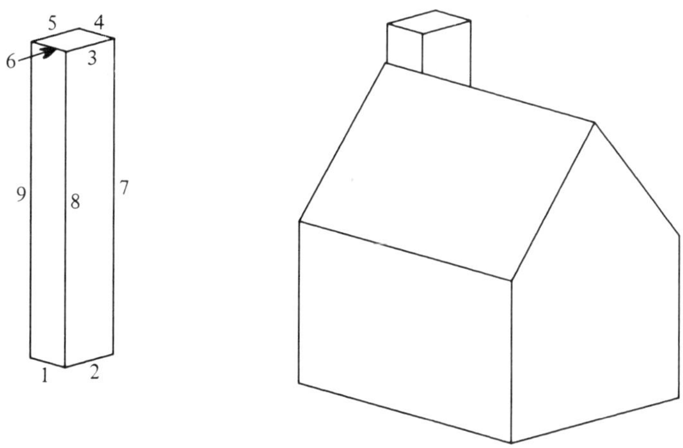

Figure 9.20

Edges 1 and 2 of the chimney are boundaries of the sides of the chimney that have passed the surface orientation test for visibility. However, these edges are completely hidden by the house. They should not be plotted. Edges 3, 4, 5, and 6 are completely visible and should be plotted. On the other hand, edges 7, 8, and 9 are only partly visible. For each of these edges it will be necessary to determine at what point the edge becomes visible, and then plot only the visible portion.

There are, then, three types of edges associated with the visible surfaces of the object which has second priority. Some edges are completely hidden by a closer object, some are only partly hidden, and others are completely visible (see Program P9-5G).

Program P9-5g

```
1100 '=========================================================
1110 'Test each edge of second priority object for visibility
status
1120 'Draw visible edges and visible parts of edges
1130 FOR E = 1 TO 12
1140  IF E(P(2),E,3) = 0 THEN 1220
1150  I = E(P(2),E,1): J = E(P(2),E,2)
1160 XT = SV(I,1): YT = SV(I,2): GOSUB 1390: SV(I,3) = VI
1170 XT = SV(J,1): YT = SV(J,2): GOSUB 1390: SV(J,3) = VI
1180 IF SV(I,3) + SV(J,3) = -2 THEN 1210
1190 IF SV(I,3) + SV(J,3) = 0 THEN 1240
1200 LINE (SV(I,1),SV(I,2)) - (SV(J,1),SV(J,2))
1210 NEXT E
1220 END
```

Program lines 1130 through 1210 oversee the disposition of the priority two edges. As each edge is considered, the screen array entries SV(I,3), which have been ignored up to now, will be used to indicate the visibility status of the endpoints (identified in line 1150). Lines 1160 and 1170 use the subroutine beginning at line 1390 (discussed below) to determine the visibility status of each endpoint. If endpoint I is visible, then SV(I,3) is set equal to 1. If endpoint I is hidden, then SV(I,3) is set equal to -1.

An edge with vertices I and J as endpoints is identified as hidden if SV(I,3) + SV(J,3) = -2; such an edge is discarded (line 1180).

If SV(I,3) + SV(J,3) = 0 (line 1190), then one endpoint is visible and one is hidden. The endpoints are turned over to the routine beginning at line 1240, which identifies and plots the visible portion of the edge.

If SV(I,3) + SV(J,3) = 2, then both endpoints are visible; the edge may be plotted (line 1200).

Clipping Edges That Are Partly Hidden

If an edge has one vertex hidden and one visible, it is necessary to clip the line segment so as to display only the visible portion. Program line 1190 refers such edges to a routine beginning at line 1250. There, the point that is visible is identified as (XV,YV) and the hidden point is labelled as (XH,YH).

Program lines 1270 through 1340 use a binary search to locate the point (XT,YT) that divides the line segment in two parts: a visible segment from (XV,YV) to (XT,YT), and a hidden portion from (XT,YT) to (XH,YH). The binary search was used with Program P9-4. Here is a summary of its operation in the current situation:

1. Identify the vector (V1,V2) extending from (XV,YV) halfway to (XH,YH) (line 1270).
2. Add (V1,V2) to (XV,YV) to obtain the midpoint (XT,YT) of the line segment from (XV,YV) to (XH,YH) (line 1280).
3. Test (XT,YT) for visibility (line 1300).
4. Redefine (V1,V2) = (V1,V2)/2 (line 1310).
5. If (XT,YT) is visible, then move toward (XH,YH) by redefining (XT,YT) = (XT,YT) + (V1,V2). If (XT,YT) is hidden, then move toward (XV,YV) by redefining (XT,YT) = (XT,YT) − (V1,V2) (lines 1320, 1330).
6. Return to 3 (line 1340).

The test for visibility of (XT,YT) (line 1300) uses the classification subroutine beginning at line 1390. As before, the routine returns with VI = +1 if (XT,YT) is visible or with VI = −1 if (XT,YT) is hidden. The value of VI then determines whether the next (XT,YT) is obtained by moving toward (XH,YH) (if VI = +1), or by moving toward (XV,YV) (if VI = −1).

The exit from the loop of steps 3 through 5 occurs when the seventh value of (XT,YT) has been calculated. The length of (V1,V2) then is 1/128th of the distance between (XV,YV) and (XH,YH). This resolution is adequate for most images on the IBM display screen. Of course, greater

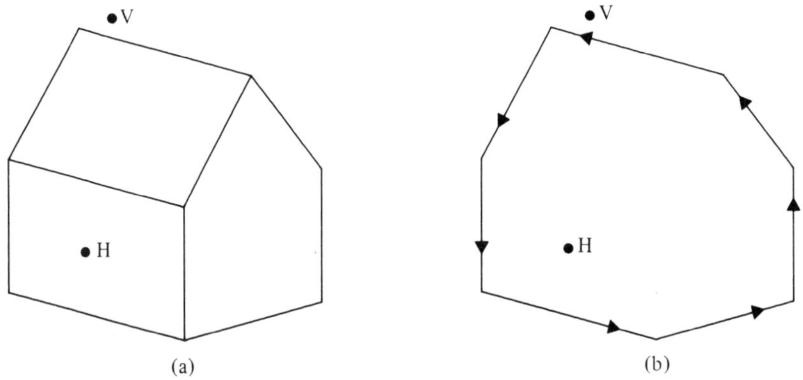

Figure 9.21

resolution may be obtained by increasing the number of cycles through the loop.

On leaving the loop, the line segment from (XV,YV) to (XT,YT) is plotted. Program control is then returned to line 1210 in order to begin consideration of another edge (see Program P9-5H).

Program P9-5h

```
1230 '=====================================================
1240 'Plot visible portion of edges which are partly hidden
1250 IF SV(I,3) = 1 THEN XV = SV(I,1): YV = SV(I,2):
XH = SV(J,1): YH = SV(J,2)
1260 IF SV(J,3) = 1 THEN XV = SV(J,1): YV = SV(J,2):
XH = SV(I,1): YH = SV(I,2)
1270 V1 = (XH - XV)/2: V2 = (YH - YV)/2
1280 XT = XV + V1: YT = YV + V2
1290 FOR I = 2 TO 7
1300  GOSUB 1390
1310 V1 = V1/2: V2 = V2/2
1320 XT = XT + VI*V1
1330 YT = YT + VI*V2
1340 NEXT I
1350 LINE (XV,YV) - (XT,YT)
1360 GOTO 1210
```

Visibility Status of Edge Endpoints

Program lines 1390 through 1470 form a subroutine which is used to classify points as visible or hidden. Figure 9.21 will be used to illustrate the process used for endpoint classification.

In Figure 9.21a, the visible surfaces of the house have been plotted and endpoints of one edge of the chimney are shown. Note that endpoint H, which should be hidden by the house, is inside the outer boundary of the house (Figure 9.21b), while point V is outside. Since the outside house boundaries have a counterclockwise orientation (specified in the surface array and preserved in the edge array), an inside point H is identified as such because it lies in the left half-plane of each component of the boundary. The point V is identified as an outside point by noting that it is in the right half-plane of at least one boundary component (see Program P9-5I). (For a discussion of half-planes, see Appendix 3.)

Program P9-5i

```
1370 '==================================================
1380 'Classify endpoints of edges as visible or hidden
1390 VI = -1
1400 FOR L = 1 TO 12
1410  IF E(P(1),L,3) <> 1 THEN 1460
1420  P = E(P(1),L,1): Q = E(P(1),L,2)
1430  R1 = SV(Q,1) - SV(P,1): R2 = SV(Q,2) - SV(P,2)
1440 U1 = XT - SV(P,1): U2 = YT - SV(P,2)
1450 IF U1*R2 - U2*R1 > 9.999999E-06 THEN VI = 1: L = 12
1460 NEXT L
1470 RETURN
```

The intent of the classification subroutine is to establish the value of the visibility variable VI as +1 for a visible endpoint (a point outside the house boundary) or −1 for a hidden endpoint (a point inside the house boundary). To this end, we assume that each point is hidden (line 1390: VI = −1) until it is proven visible.

Since a point is visible if it is in the right half-plane of at least one boundary component, the loop 1400 through 1460 compares point (XT,YT) with each visible edge of the house. In order to obtain an inside or outside classification, only those edges which are outside boundaries need be considered. Line 1410 skips over all others.

For each outside edge PQ of the house, two vectors are calculated. As shown in Figure 9.22, vector $\vec{r}$ extends from P to Q. Vector $\vec{u}$ extends from P to (XT,YT), the point to be classified. If (XT,YT) is in the right half-plane of line PQ (thus visible), then $\vec{u} \times \vec{r}$ is a negative multiple of (0,0,1) (see Appendix 3). In this case, program line 1450 will change the value of VI to 1, then return from the subroutine.

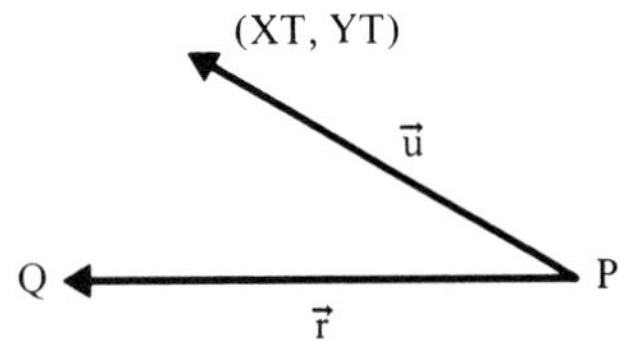

Figure 9.22

> **Note:** The visibility of a point is determined by the sign of $\vec{u} \times \vec{r}$. But, rather than compare $\vec{u} \times \vec{r}$ with $\vec{0}$, we have compared it with (0,0,9.99999E-06). The reason is this: If $\vec{r}$ and $\vec{u}$ lie on the same line, then $\vec{r} \times \vec{u}$ should be zero; but, because the computer is working in binary, the result may not be exactly zero, only very close. We will want (XT,YT) to be considered hidden in such cases, so we compare with a number that is positive, but very close to zero.

If the endpoint (XT,YT) is in the left half-plane of each of the outside edges of the house, then we will return from the subroutine with VI = −1. We reproduce below Program P9-5, in its entirety.

Program P9-5

```
10 'PROGRAM P9-5  (HIDDEN LINE; HOUSE AND CHIMNEY)
20 'Two objects; arbitrary viewpoint
100 '==============================================
110 KEY OFF: SCREEN 2: CLS
120 OPTION BASE 1
130 WINDOW (-4,-3) - (4,3)
140 RHO = 80: D = 20
150 THETA = .9: S1 = SIN(THETA): C1 = COS(THETA)
160 PHI = 1.2: S2 = SIN(PHI): C2 = COS(PHI)
170 '===============================================
180 'Data for vertices of object 1 (house)
190 DATA 5,7,-5,  5,7,5,  5,-7,5, 5,-7,-5, -5,7,-5
200 DATA -5,-7,-5, -5,-7,5, -5,7,5, 0,7,8, 0,-7,8
210 'Data for vertices of object 2 (chimney)
220 DATA -2,-7,-5,  -2,-9,-5,  -5,-9,-5,  -5,-7,-5
230 DATA -2,-7,9,  -2,-9,9,  -5,-9,9,  -5,-7,9
240 'Fill vertex arrays
250 DIM V(18,3),SV(18,3)
260 FOR I = 1 TO 18
270  READ X,Y,Z
280  V(I,1) = X: V(I,2) = Y: V(I,3) = Z
290  XE = -X*S1 + Y*C1
```

```
300  YE = -X*C1*C2 - Y*S1*C2 + Z*S2
310  ZE = -X*S2*C1 - Y*S2*S1 - Z*C2 + RHO
320  SV(I,1) = D*XE/ZE: SV(I,2) = D*YE/ZE
330 NEXT I
340 '=========================================
350 'Number of points (vertices) in each surface
360 DIM NPS(13)
370 DATA 5,6,5,6,5,5,5
380 DATA 5,5,5,5,5,5
390 FOR I = 1 TO 13
400  READ NPS(I)
410 NEXT I
420 'Surface array - pointers to vertices
430 DATA 1,2,3,4,1
440 DATA 1,5,8,9,2,1
450 DATA 5,6,7,8,5
460 DATA 4,3,10,7,6,4
470 DATA 3,2,9,10,3
480 DATA 7,10,9,8,7
490 DATA 1,4,6,5,1
500 DATA 11,12,13,14,11
510 DATA 15,18,17,16,15
520 DATA 11,14,18,15,11
530 DATA 12,16,17,13,12
540 DATA 11,15,16,12,11
550 DATA 14,13,17,18,14
560 'Fill surface arrays with vertex pointers
570 DIM S(13,6)
580 FOR I = 1 TO 13
590  FOR J = 1 TO NPS(I)
600   READ S(I,J)
610 NEXT J,I
620 '=====================================================
630 'Calculate the vector that is normal to each surface
640 DIM N(13,3)
650 FOR I = 1 TO 13
660  U1 = V(S(I,2),1) - V(S(I,1),1)
670  U2 = V(S(I,2),2) - V(S(I,1),2)
680  U3 = V(S(I,2),3) - V(S(I,1),3)
690  V1 = V(S(I,3),1) - V(S(I,1),1)
700  V2 = V(S(I,3),2) - V(S(I,1),2)
710  V3 = V(S(I,3),3) - V(S(I,1),3)
720  N(I,1) = U2* V3 - V2*U3
730  N(I,2) = U3* V1 - V3*U1
740  N(I,3) = U1* V2 - V1*U2
750 NEXT I
760 '====================================================
770 'Determine visibility of each surface
780 'and collect visible edges in edge array
790 XE = RHO*S2*C1: YE = RHO*S2*S1: ZE = RHO*C2
800 DIM E(2,12,3): N = 1: OBJ = 1
810 FOR I = 1 TO 13
820  E1 = S(I,1)
```

```
830   WX = XE - V(E1,1)
840   WY = YE - V(E1,2)
850   WZ = ZE - V(E1,3)
860   IF N(I,1)*WX + N(I,2)*WY + N(I,3)*WZ <= 0 THEN 970
870   FOR J = 2 TO NPS(I)
880     E2 = S(I,J): K = 1
890     IF E(OBJ,K,1) = E2 AND E(OBJ,K,2) = E1 THEN 940
900     IF K = N THEN 920
910     K = K+1: GOTO 890
920     E(OBJ,N,1) = E1: E(OBJ,N,2) = E2
930     N = N + 1
940     E1 = E2
950     E(OBJ,K,3) = E(OBJ,K,3) + 1
960   NEXT J
970   IF I = 7 THEN N = 1: OBJ = 2
980 NEXT I
990 '==================================
1000 'Establish priority of objects
1010 IF YE >= -7 THEN P(1) = 1: P(2) = 2
1020 IF YE < -7 THEN P(1) = 2: P(2) = 1
1030 '========================================
1040 'Draw visible edges of first priority object
1050 FOR I = 1 TO 12
1060  IF E(P(1),I,3) = 0 THEN 1090
1070  J = E(P(1),I,1): K = E(P(1),I,2)
1080  LINE (SV(J,1),SV(J,2)) - (SV(K,1),SV(K,2))
1090 NEXT I
1100 '=================================================
1110 'Test each edge of second priority object for visibility
status
1120 'Draw visible edges and visible parts of edges
1130 FOR E = 1 TO 12
1140  IF E(P(2),E,3) = 0 THEN 1220
1150  I = E(P(2),E,1): J = E(P(2),E,2)
1160 XT = SV(I,1): YT = SV(I,2): GOSUB 1390: SV(I,3) = VI
1170 XT = SV(J,1): YT = SV(J,2): GOSUB 1390: SV(J,3) = VI
1180 IF SV(I,3) + SV(J,3) = -2 THEN 1210
1190 IF SV(I,3) + SV(J,3) = 0 THEN 1240
1200 LINE (SV(I,1),SV(I,2)) - (SV(J,1),SV(J,2))
1210 NEXT E
1220 END
1230 '=================================================
1240 'Plot visible portion of edges which are partly hidden
1250 IF SV(I,3) = 1 THEN XV = SV(I,1): YV = SV(I,2):
XH = SV(J,1): YH = SV(J,2)
1260 IF SV(J,3) = 1 THEN XV = SV(J,1): YV = SV(J,2):
XH = SV(I,1): YH = SV(I,2)
1270 V1 = (XH - XV)/2: V2 = (YH - YV)/2
1280 XT = XV + V1: YT = YV + V2
1290 FOR I = 2 TO 7
1300  GOSUB 1390
1310 V1 = V1/2: V2 = V2/2
1320 XT = XT + VI*V1
```

```
1330 YT = YT + VI*V2
1340 NEXT I
1350 LINE (XV,YV) - (XT,YT)
1360 GOTO 1210
1370 '==============================================
1380 'Classify endpoints of edges as visible or hidden
1390 VI = -1
1400 FOR L = 1 TO 12
1410  IF E(P(1),L,3) <> 1 THEN 1460
1420  P = E(P(1),L,1): Q = E(P(1),L,2)
1430  R1 = SV(Q,1) - SV(P,1): R2 = SV(Q,2) - SV(P,2)
1440 U1 = XT - SV(P,1): U2 = YT - SV(P,2)
1450 IF U1*R2 - U2*R1 > 9.999999E-06 THEN VI = 1: L = 12
1460 NEXT L
1470 RETURN
```

NOTES AND SUGGESTIONS

1. The techniques described are not without flaws. For example, if the endpoints of an edge of a second-priority object are both outside the image of the first-priority object, the edge is drawn. This may result in the drawing of edges that should be partly hidden. To illustrate, edge AB of the prism in Figure 9.23 would be drawn, even though a portion of it is hidden by the cube. From certain viewpoints, Program P9-5 can draw hidden parts of lines.

2. Modify the data and the limits in the loops of the program in order to draw other images. For example, try the pyramid and cube of Figure 9.14.

3. The techniques described here may be extended to images containing three or more objects. Of course, the program's complexity will increase, and program execution will take longer.

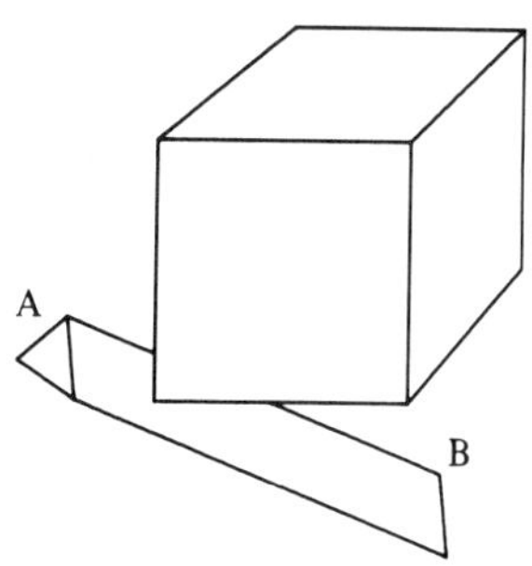

Figure 9.23

HIDDEN LINE ELIMINATION FOR SURFACES OF THE FORM Z = F(X,Y)

Toward the end of Chapter 8, a program was given as an example of a means of generating images of the form Z = F(X,Y). The program was brief, and drew the surface quickly. Unfortunately, no provision was made for hidden line elimination. The result was an image that could be confusing. We intend to correct the situation so that we might draw only the visible parts of such surfaces.

Before turning to the hidden line calculations, we will review the earlier program in Program P9-6:

Program P9-6: SURFACE

```
10 'PROGRAM P9-6   (SURFACE)
20 'Repeat of Program P8-4
100 '=========================================
110 KEY OFF: SCREEN 2: CLS
120 WINDOW (-4,-3) - (4,3)
130 RHO = 30: D = 10
140 THETA = .3: S1 = SIN(THETA): C1 = COS(THETA)
150 PHI = 1: S2 = SIN(PHI): C2 = COS(PHI)
160 '=========================================
170 DEF FN F(X,Y) = COS(.1*(X*X + Y*Y))
180 FOR X = 10 TO -10 STEP -1
190  FL = 0
200  FOR Y = -10 TO 10
210   Z = FN F(X,Y): GOSUB 290
220   IF FL = 0 THEN FL = 1: PSET (SX,SY)
230   LINE - (SX,SY)
240  NEXT Y
250 NEXT X
260 END
270 '=========================================
280 'Perspective projection subroutine
290 XE = -X*S1 + Y*C1
300 YE = -X*C1*C2 - Y*S1*C2 + Z*S2
310 ZE = -X*S2*C1 - Y*S1*S2 - Z*C2 + RHO
320 SX = D*XE/ZE
330 SY = D*YE/ZE
340 RETURN
```

Program lines 110 through 170 identify the viewing parameters, the screen parameters, and the function to be plotted. The nested loops in lines 180 through 250 generate the coordinates of points on the surface and send the points to the perspective projection subroutine. There, the screen coordinates (SX,SY) are calculated. On return from the subroutine, the calculated coordinates are plotted. The first point of a wire-frame curve (FL=0) results in plotting via PSET (SX,SY). Otherwise, a line segment which connects the point with the one most recently plotted (line 230) is plotted.

Program P9-7 is an extension of the above program to include hidden line capabilities. The initialization is similar to the beginning of Program P9-6, establishing the viewing and screen parameters and a function to be

Program P9-7: HIDDEN SURFACE

```
10 'PROGRAM P9-7   (HIDDEN SURFACE)
20 'Hidden line elimination for surfaces Z = F(X,Y)
100 '==================================================
110 KEY OFF: SCREEN 2: CLS
120 RHO = 40: D = 800
130 THETA = .3: S1 = SIN(THETA): C1 = COS(THETA)
140 PHI = 1: S2 = SIN(PHI): C2 = COS(PHI)
150 DEF FN F(X,Y) = 2*COS(.1*(X*X + Y*Y))
160 DIM YMIN(639),YMAX(639)
170 FOR I = 0 TO 639: YMIN(I) = 199: NEXT I
180 '==================================================
190 'Point generating loop
200 FOR X = 10 TO -10 STEP -1
210  FL = 0
220  FOR Y = -10 TO 10
230   Z = FN F(X,Y): GOSUB 290
240  NEXT Y
250 NEXT X
260 END
270 '==================================================
280 'Perspective projection calculation
290 XE = -X*S1 + Y*C1
300 YE = -X*C1*C2 - Y*S1*C2 + Z*S2
310 ZE = -X*S2*C1 - Y*S1*S2 - Z*C2 + RHO
320 SX = D*XE/ZE + 320
330 SY = -5*D*YE/ZE/12 + 100
340 '===============================================
350 'Hidden line routine
```

```
360 IF SX < 0 OR SX > 639 THEN 480
370 IF FL = 0 THEN FL = 1: F = 0: GOTO 480
380 DX = OLDX - SX: IF DX = 0 THEN DX = 1
390 SL = (OLDY - SY)/DX
400 YP = OLDY
410 '----------------------------------
420 FOR XP = INT(OLDX) + 1 TO SX
430  YP = YP + SL
440  IF YP <= YMIN(XP) THEN 500
450  IF YP >= YMAX(XP) THEN 550
460  F = 0
470 NEXT XP
480 OLDX = SX: OLDY = SY: RETURN
490 '----------------------------------
500 YMIN(XP) = YP
510 IF F = 0 THEN PSET (XP,YP): F = 1
520 LINE - (XP,YP)
530 IF YP < YMAX(XP) THEN 470
540 '----------------------------------
550 YMAX(XP) = YP
560 IF F = 0 THEN PSET (XP,YP): F = 1
570 LINE - (XP,YP)
580 GOTO 470
```

plotted (note that we have not established a WINDOW). Then, in lines 160 and 170, two arrays are defined. These are for use by the hidden line routine. The intent of the arrays is as follows:

> YMAX(XP) identifies, for each horizontal screen coordinate XP, the maximum (lowest on screen) vertical screen coordinate encountered.
> YMIN(XP) identifies, for each horizontal screen coordinate XP, the minimum (highest on screen) vertical screen coordinate encountered.

Inititally, the value of each YMAX(I) is zero and the value of each YMIN(I) is 199. As points (XP,YP) are plotted, the values of YMAX(XP) and YMIN(XP) are reset. As each (XP,YP) is considered for plotting, YP is compared with YMAX(XP) and YMIN(XP). If YP lies between YMAX(XP) and YMIN(XP) the point (XP,YP) is classified as hidden. Otherwise it is assumed to be visible. The function of the arrays is shown in Figure 9.24.

This use of arrays requires that the wire-frame curves representing the surface be generated sequentially, beginning with the one closest to the

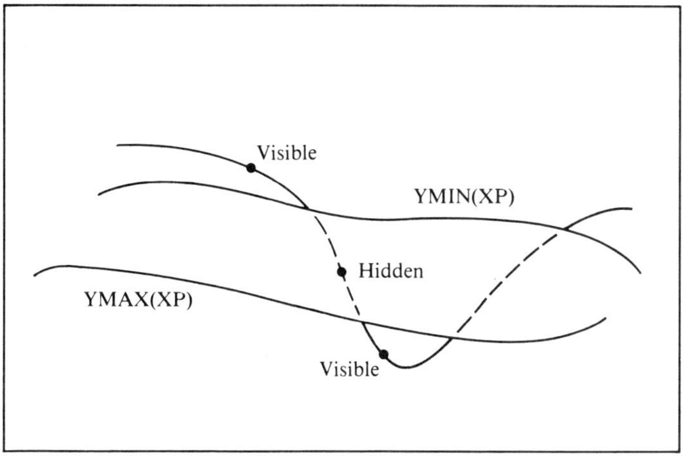

Figure 9.24

viewer. The point-generating loop (lines 200–250) provides that this is the case.

As each point (X,Y,Z) is generated, it is passed to the hidden line subroutine, where the corresponding screen coordinates (SX,SY) are calculated.

The point (SX,SY) could be tested for visibility [is SY < = YMIN(SX), or is SY > = YMAX(XP)?]. However, that would not be adequate. It is necessary to determine the status of each point (XP,YP) along the line segment connecting (SX,SY) with the point previously calculated (OLDX,OLDY). If (XP,YP) is hidden, it is not plotted. If (XP,YP) is visible, it is plotted and the corresponding array entry [YMAX(XP) or YMIN(XP)] is updated. No WINDOW was used by the program so that it would be easier to consider each XP between OLDX and SX.

The hidden line subroutine uses two variables as flags to signal actions within the program:

1. FL: If the point (SX,SY) is the first of a wire-frame curve, then FL = 0; otherwise, FL = 1.

2. F: If F = 0, the statement **PSET (XP,YP)** should be used to plot the next visible point (XP,YP). If F = 1, then the statement **LINE–(XP,YP)** should be used.

The first point on a wire-frame curve is marked by setting FL = 0 (line 210). Within the subroutine, this is taken (line 370) as a signal to define (OLDX,OLDY) as the newly calculated (SX,SY), and the program returns to the point-generating loop.

If FL = 1, the points on the line segment from (OLDX,OLDY) to (SX,SY) will be tested for visibility. Lines 380 and 390 identify the slope of the line segment. Line 420 begins a loop that steps through the integers XP (screen coordinates) between OLDX and SX. After YP is calculated (line 430), it is compared with the array values YMIN(XP) and YMAX(XP) (lines 440, 450, and 530).

If YMIN(XP) < YP < YMAX(XP), then the point (XP,YP) is not visible; F is set to 0 (line 460) and the next point is considered.

If YP ≤ YMIN(XP), then YP is no larger than any previous vertical screen coordinate associated with XP. The point (XP,YP) is visible, appearing above the previously plotted portion of the surface. Array value YMIN(XP) is reset to YP(line 500), and the point (XP,YP) is plotted (lines 510 and 520).

If YP > = YMAX(XP) (line 450 and 530), then YP is as large as any previous vertical screen coordinate associated with XP. The point (XP,YP) is visible, appearing below the previously plotted portion of the surface. The array value YMAX(XP) is reset to YP (line 550), and the point (XP,YP) is plotted (lines 560 and 570).

When all integral values of XP along the line segment from (OLDX,OLDY) to (SX,SY) have been considered, (OLDX,OLDY) is redefined as (SX,SY), and the program returns to the point-generating loop (line 480).

NOTES AND SUGGESTIONS

1. Program P9-7 assumes that each wire-frame curve is generated in a left to right direction on the screen. A more versatile subroutine results from adding a line such as

```
395 ST = SGN(SX - OLDX)
```

changing line 420 to read

```
420 FOR XP = INT(OLDX) + ST TO SX STEP ST
```

and changing line 430 to read

```
430 YP = YP + ST*SL
```

2. Some points (XP,YP) will identify new screen maximum values [(YP > = YMAX(XP))] and also new screen minimum values [YP < = YMIN(XP)]. This properly will result in resetting both YX(XP) and YN(XP). However, it also will result in plotting the point or line segment twice (lines 510, 520, 560, and 570). No harm is done by replotting, although some small amount of time is wasted. Can you correct this?

3. Several hidden line techniques have been discussed in this chapter. Adapt them to generate other images (the cube and prism of Figure 9.23, for example).

4. Program P9-7 draws a surface that could be thought of as a rubber sheet that had been stretched into the shape of the specified function. Modify the program to make it appear that the top and bottom of the rubber sheet are of different colors.

5. To reiterate the statement made at the beginning of this chapter:

   The elimination of hidden lines and surfaces is one of the most challenging problems of computer graphics.

This is a problem that has received a lot of attention; many hidden line techniques have been developed. Those given here constitute a brief introduction. The reader interested in pursuing the subject should consult texts such as *Principles of Interactive Computer Graphics* by Newman and Sproull (McGraw Hill), or *Fundamentals of Interactive Computer Graphics* by Foley and Van Dam (Addison-Wesley).

Appendix 1

Binary, Decimal, and Hexadecimal Number Systems

It is said to be an accident of nature that we use a base 10 number system. If our ancestors had six fingers on each hand, we might be using base 12. If they had one finger on each hand, perhaps we would calculate in base 2. We might then have less trouble communicating with a computer. The conversion between base 2 and base 10 is one of the inconveniences we must live with in order to get the most out of a computer.

The structure of a number system is the same, regardless of the base used. The number 243.72 (base 10) represents

$$2(10)^2 + 4(10)^1 + 3(10)^0 + 7(10)^{-1} + 2(10)^{-2}$$

If we write a number $a_1a_2a_3.a_4a_5$ (base b), it is assumed that the number represents

$$a_1(b)^2 + a_2(b)^1 + a_3(b)^0 + a_4(b)^{-1} + a_5(b)^{-2}$$

Thus, 423.51 (base 7) represents

$$4(7)^2 + 2(7)^1 + 3(7)^0 + 5(7)^{-1} + 1(7)^{-2}$$

and 13.423 (base 5) represents

$$1(5)^1 + 3(5)^0 + 4(5)^{-1} + 2(5)^{-2} + 3(5)^{-3} \text{ [8.904 (base 10)]}$$

It is necessary to be familiar with three number systems in order to communicate properly with the IBM PC. We assume that you are familiar with base 10 (decimal). The other two systems we will use are base 2 (binary) and base 16 (hexadecimal). Base 2 is the native language of digital computers; base 16 happens to be convenient for conversation between people and computers. Base 16 is convenient because it is, in a way, a shorthand base 2 notation. This will be apparent later.

BINARY

When working in base 10 we have the ten symbols 0, 1, 2, 3, 4, 5, 6, 7, 8, and 9 with which to represent numbers. In base 2 we have only two symbols: 0 and 1. Any number may be represented in base 2 as a pattern of 0s and 1s. For example, the binary 1011011 represents (starting from the left):

$$1(2)^6 + 0(2)^5 + 1(2)^4 + 1(2)^3 + 0(2)^2 + 1(2)^1 + 1(2)^0$$
$$= 64 + 0(32) + 16 + 8 + 0(4) + 2 + 1 = 91$$

Thus the binary number 1011011 represents the number we write as 91.

Similarly, the binary 110111 represents the decimal 55, since

$$1(2)^5 + 1(2)^4 + 0(2)^3 + 1(2)^2 + 1(2)^1 + 1(2)^0 = 55$$

Conversion of a number from decimal to binary representation is accomplished through subtraction of powers of 2, starting with the largest possible power. To write the number 237 in binary form, we note that $128 = 2^7$ is the largest power of two which can be subtracted from 237 ($237 = 128 + 109$). We then turn to 109. The largest power of 2 which can be subtracted from 109 is $2^6 = 64$ ($109 = 64 + 45$). Thus, $237 = 128 + 64 + 45$. Since $45 = 32 + 13$, and $13 = 8 + 4 + 1$, we may write:

$$237 = 128 + 64 + 32 + 8 + 4 + 1$$
$$= 1(2)^7 + 1(2)^6 + 1(2)^5 + 0(2)^4 + 1(2)^3 + 1(2)^2 + 0(2)^1 + 1(2)^0$$
$$= 11101101 \text{ (base 2)}$$

The memory available for the computer to use is configured in blocks of eight. Each eight-bit unit is referred to as a byte. A half-byte is called a nybble. The number 10111110 (decimal 190) is one byte. The lower, or less significant, nybble is 1110, and the higher, more significant, nybble is 1011.

You may have figured that the largest number that can be represented as an eight-bit binary is decimal 255 (11111111). That doesn't prevent the computer from considering larger numbers (or fractions). It simply breaks the number up into components and stores the parts in several bytes.

HEXADECIMAL

The hexadecimal (or hex) notation for a number is the base 16 representation of the number. In this numeration system, the number 235 refers to $2(16)^2 + 3(16)^1 + 5(16)^0 = 565$. In order to avoid confusing the hex number 235 with the decimal number 235, it is common practice to add a &H prefix to the hex notation. Thus, &H235 = 565. (Actually, there are several commonly used ways to designate hexadecimal notation. We use &H because it has been adopted in the IBM PC manuals.)

In base 10, ten symbols are available to represent numbers. Base 2 provides only the symbols 0 and 1. For work with hexadecimal notation, we need 16 symbols. It is conventional to use the symbols 0 through 9 for their normal duty, and the symbols A, B, C, D, E, and F to represent the decimal numbers 10, 11, 12, 13, 14, and 15.

If we were counting in hex, our count would go like this: &H1, &H2, &H3, &H4, &H5, &H6, &H7, &H8, &H9, &HA, &HB, &HC, &HD, &HE, &HF, &H10, &H11, &H12, &H13, &H14, &H15, &H16, &H17, &H18, &H19, &H1A, &H1B, &H1C, &H1D, &H1E, &H1F, &H20, &H21 . . . .

Note: It is considered poor form to refer to &H24 as "hex twenty-four," since "twenty-four" implies decimal. Proper reading of &H24 is "hex-two-four."

To convert &H2A3E to decimal, we write

$$\begin{aligned}\&H2A3E &= 2(16)^3 + 10(16)^2 + 3(16)^1 + 14(16)^0\\ &= 2(4096) + 10(256) + 3(16) + 14(1)\\ &= 8192 + 2560 + 48 + 14\\ &= 10814\end{aligned}$$

Similarly,

$$\begin{aligned}\&HE38F &= 14(16)^3 + 3(16)^2 + 8(16)^1 + 15(16)^0\\ &= 57344 + 768 + 128 + 15\\ &= 58255\end{aligned}$$

Table A.1

	16^3	16^2	16^1	16^0	
&H1	4096	256	16	1	&H1
&H2	8192	512	32	2	&H2
&H3	12288	768	48	3	&H3
&H4	16384	1024	64	4	&H4
&H5	20480	1280	80	5	&H5
&H6	24576	1536	96	6	&H6
&H7	28672	1792	112	7	&H7
&H8	32768	2048	128	8	&H8
&H9	36864	2304	144	9	&H9
&HA	40960	2560	160	10	&HA
&HB	45056	2816	176	11	&HB
&HC	49152	3027	192	12	&HC
&HD	53248	3328	208	13	&HD
&HE	57344	3584	224	14	&HE
&HF	61440	3840	240	15	&HF

Table A.1 may be used to save calculation time. Using the table, we read

&H1111 as 4096 + 256 + 16 + 1 = 4369
&H2202 as 8192 + 512 + 0 + 2 = 8706
&H253B as 8192 + 1280 + 48 + 11 = 9531
&HEB29 as 57344 + 2816 + 32 + 9 = 60201

To convert the decimal 29143 to hex notation, we first must identify the largest multiple of the largest power of 16 that may be subtracted from 29143. That number is 7(16) = 28672. Subtracting yields 29143 − 28672 = 471. Next, identify the largest multiple of the largest power of 16 that may be subtracted from 471. That number is 1(16) = 256. Subtracting yields 471 − 256 = 215. Continuing, the largest multiple of (16) that may be subtracted from 215 is 13(16) = 208, and 215 − 208 = 7. Thus,

$$\begin{aligned} 29143 &= 28672 + 471 \\ &= 7(16)^3 + 256 + 215 \\ &= 7(16)^3 + 1(16)^2 + 208 + 7 \\ &= 7(16)^3 + 1(16)^2 + 13(16)^1 + 7 \\ &= \&H71D7 \end{aligned}$$

Similarly,

$$
\begin{aligned}
43618 &= 40960 + 2658 \\
&= 10(4096) + 2560 + 98 \\
&= 10(16^3) + 10(256) + 96 + 2 \\
&= 10(16^3) + 10(16^2) + 6(16^1) + 2(16^0) \\
&= \&HAA62
\end{aligned}
$$

RELATIONSHIP OF HEX TO BINARY

Each of the decimal numbers from 0 to 15 may be represented by a four-bit binary (0000 through 1111), or by a one-digit hex (&H0 through &HF). The decimal numbers from 0 through 255 have one byte (eight-bit) binary representation (00000000 through 11111111) and two-digit hex representation (&H00 through &HFF).

The decimal 181 is represented by binary 10110101, and by the hex &HB5. Note here that the lower nybble 0101 has hex value &H5, while the upper nybble has hex value &HB. This association is not an accidental occurrence. To convert between binary and hex representations of a number, we may associate hex digits with binary nybbles.

EXAMPLE: Write &H6C in binary form.

Since &H6 = 0110 (binary) and &HC = 1100 (binary),
then &H6C = 01101100 (binary).

EXAMPLE: Write 10111101 in hex notation.

The upper nybble, 1011, has hex equivalent &HB;
the lower nybble, 1101, has hex equivalent &HD.
Thus, 10111101 (binary) = &HBD.

Appendix 2
Memory Addressing

The memory locations in the IBM PC are numbered consecutively, beginning with 0. In a 64K machine the addresses range from 0 to 65535 (64 * 1024 − 1). In a 256K computer the addresses range from 0 to 262143 (256 * 1024 − 1). Addresses can be given in either decimal or hexadecimal form, but the hexadecimal form is more common and makes it easier to understand how memory addresses are read by the computer.

> *Note:* There is little likelihood that a number like 1B might be misread as a decimal number, but a number like 82 might be intended as a decimal or as a hexadecimal number. It is necessary to have a means of distinguishing hex and decimal numbers. Since decimal notation is firmly entrenched in our language, we will not tamper with it but will specially designate the hex notation of numbers. There are several common ways of doing this. We will use the notation adopted in the PC manuals: identifying hex numbers by a prefix of &H. This way we can easily distinguish between the hex number &H82 and the decimal number 82.

Although it is possible to have a large amount of memory in the PC, the processor has an address range of only 64K consecutive bytes. This is a limitation we must deal with. The specific 64K bytes of memory that are accessed can be varied. For example, it is possible to access the memory units from &H0–&HFFFF (0–65535) or the memory units from &HA0–&H1009F (160–65695).

The identification of the memory units that can be accessed is controlled by establishing a *base address* for the 64K memory segment. If the base address is set at &H0, then the computer can access memory from &H0 to &HFFFF. If the base address is set at &HA0, then the computer can access memory from &HA0 to &H1009F.

As various operations are performed by the computer, it will change the base address. This occurs without the knowledge of the BASIC programmer. On those occasions when a BASIC program accesses memory directly (e.g., PEEK, POKE, BSAVE, BLOAD, CALL), it is necessary to identify the 64K memory segment to be used. This is done by using the DEF SEG statement. When a memory segment is identified by a DEF SEG statement, the computer will reference that segment when a BASIC statement directly accesses memory.

The statement

DEF SEG = n

identifies 16 * n as the beginning address of the 64K memory segment to be accessed by BASIC statements.

For example, the sequence

```
DEF SEG = 0
PRINT PEEK (25)
```

will print the contents of memory location 25, whereas

```
DEF SEG = 20
PRINT PEEK (25)
```

will print the contents of memory location 345 (= 25 + 16 * 20.)

Since this book is directed at graphics, the part of memory which is of prime interest is the graphics page (&HB8000–&HBBFFF). If we wish to access this region of memory from BASIC (using POKE or BLOAD, for example), we would do so by specifying a memory segment which includes the graphics page of memory. The easiest choice is

```
DEF SEG = &HB800
```

We can then turn on all graphics screen pixels (after graphics display has been selected) with the statements

```
FOR I = 0 TO 16383
POKE I, 255
NEXT I
```

Memory location &HB8000 is affected when I = 0; location &HB8010 is affected when I = 16 (&H10), etc.

In the above example, I is referred to as the *offset*. In general, the offset is the difference between the address of a memory location and the base address of the current memory segment. When referring to a specific memory location we can name the base address and the offset together; for example, &HB800:0A. Here the number which precedes the colon is taken as the base segment; the number which follows the colon is the offset.

Since the offset is dependent on the specification of a memory segment, any given memory location can be specified by a range of base address/offset combinations. For example, the contents of location &HB8030 are read by each of the following:

```
DEF SEG = &HB800
PRINT PEEK (48)

DEF SEG = &HB801
PRINT PEEK (32)

DEF SEG = &HB803
PRINT PEEK (0)
```

Once a memory segment is identified by a DEF SEG statement, it is retained until another DEF SEG statement is encountered. The segment is not changed, even by the RUN command. For this reason it is best to use DEF SEG immediately before a direct access of memory is to be made by a BASIC statement.

BASIC'S DATA SEGMENT

When BASIC is first entered, it establishes a default memory segment, referred to as the BASIC *Data Segment*. The base address of this memory segment will vary with the version of BASIC being used, and it is not important that you know what that address is. This data segment is used for direct access of memory from BASIC unless a DEF SEG = n statement is used to designate another segment. If another segment has been specified, DEF SEG (with no address given) resets the base address to BASIC's Data Segment.

Within the BASIC Data Segment, memory locations are addressed sequentially from &H0 through &HFFFF. The memory map on page I-2 of the IBM PC BASIC manual shows how this segment of memory is used by BASIC.

If it is necessary to have a section of memory available for use by a machine language program, or to store a table (for example, a character table—see Program 5-4), it is possible to reserve a region at the upper reaches of the Data Segment. The command CLEAR ,n limits BASIC to the use of the first n bytes of the Data Segment. For example, CLEAR ,&HF000 will reserve locations &HF000–&HFFFF.

Appendix 3
Vectors

For our purposes, a vector may be considered to be a directed line segment. For points P and Q, the vector extending from P to Q may be represented by $\overrightarrow{PQ}$ or by a single character, $\vec{v}$. If the coordinates are provided for P and Q, say P(a,b) and Q(c,d), then the vector $\vec{v}$ may be identified by its components. The x-component of the vector is $v_x = c - a$, and $v_y = d - b$ is the y-component.

For P(−3,1) and Q(4,6), as shown in Figure A3.1, vector $\vec{v} = \overrightarrow{PQ}$ has components $v_x = 7$ and $v_y = 5$. It is customary to write $\vec{v} = (7,5)$.

Although the notation (3,7) is used to specify the point P(3,7) and also to identify the vector extending from Q(0,0) to P, the ambiguity should not be a problem to us.

Vector addition (see Figure A3.2) is easily defined in terms of com-

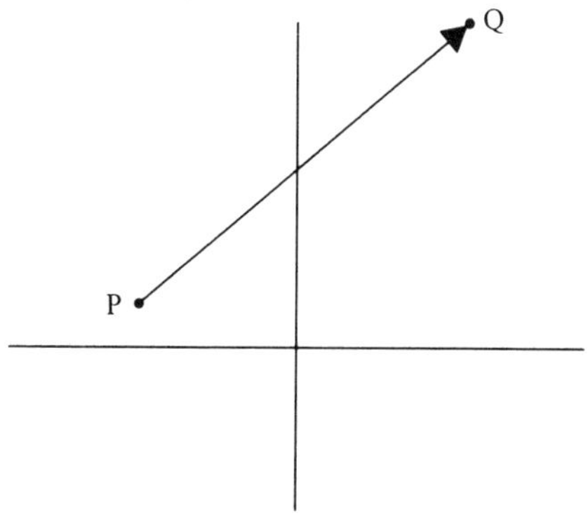

FIGURE A3.1

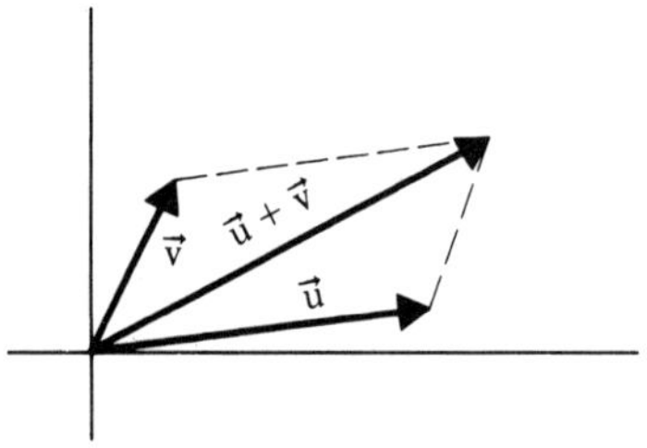

FIGURE A3.2

ponents. For $\vec{u} = (a,b)$ and $\vec{v} = (c,d)$, we define
$\vec{u} + \vec{v} = (a + c, b + d)$.

Vector subtraction (see Figure A3.3) follows from the definition of addition: for $\vec{u} = (a,b)$ and $\vec{v} = (c,d)$, $\vec{u} - \vec{v} = (a - c, b - d)$.

SCALAR MULTIPLES OF VECTORS

The multiplication of a vector by a number (scalar) is referred to as scalar multiplication. For $\vec{u} = (a,b)$, the product $t\vec{u}$ is defined as $t\vec{u} = t(a,b) = (ta,tb)$. Multiplication of a vector by a positive scalar has the effect of multiplying the length of the vector by the scalar, without affecting the direction of the vector. Multiplication of a vector by a negative scalar multiplies the length of the vector by the absolute value of the scalar, while reversing the direction of the vector. (See Figure A3.4.)

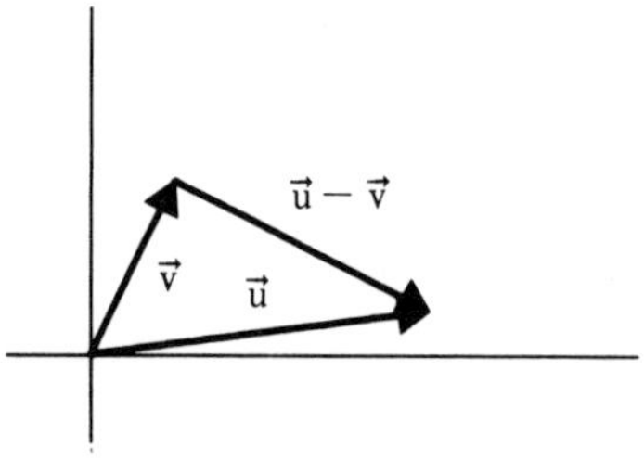

FIGURE A3.3

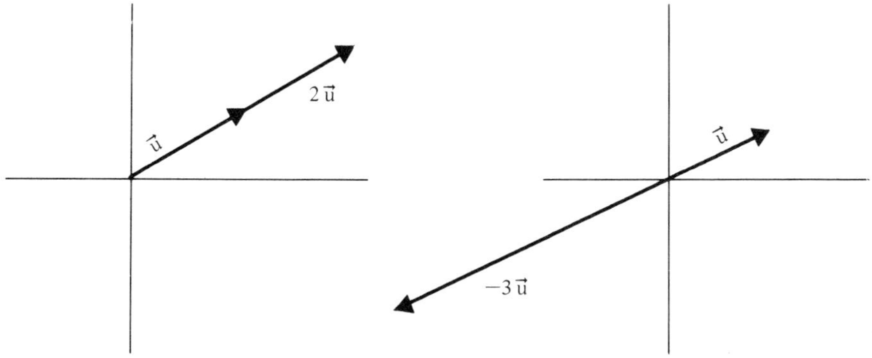

FIGURE A3.4

VECTOR REPRESENTATION OF LINES

If $\vec{v}$ and $\vec{w}$ are vectors extending from O(0,0) to points P and Q, then $\vec{u} = \vec{w} - \vec{v}$ is a vector extending from P to Q. If $\vec{x}$ is another vector which extends from O(0,0) to a point on the line containing P and Q, then $\vec{x} - \vec{v}$ will be a multiple of $\vec{u}$: $\vec{x} - \vec{v} = t\vec{u}$, or $\vec{x} = \vec{v} + t\vec{u}$ (see Figures A3.5 and A3.6).

To illustrate, let $\vec{v} = (10,3)$ and $\vec{w} = (1,7)$ (see Figure A3.6). Then, $\vec{u} = \vec{w} - \vec{v} = (1,7) - (10,3) = (-9,4)$. For any choice of $\vec{x} = (x,y)$ lying on the line PQ, then $\vec{x} = \vec{v} + t\vec{u}$, or $(x,y) = (10,3) + t(-9,4)$.

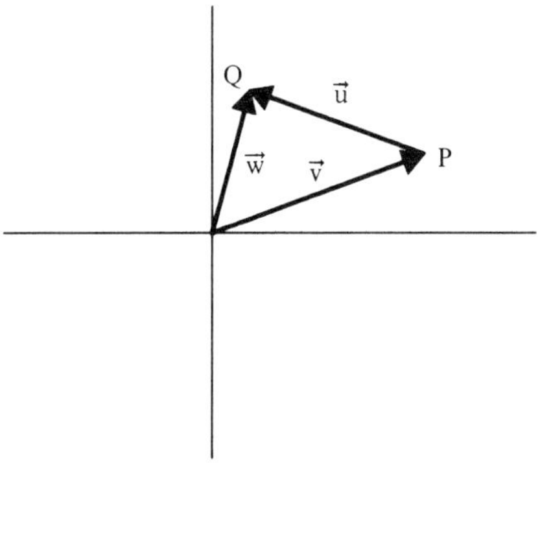

FIGURE A3.5

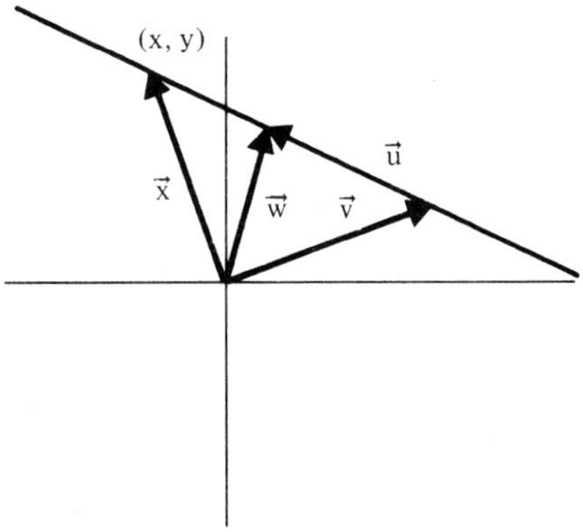

FIGURE A3.6

Each choice of a value for t will result in a specific pair of values (x,y) that identifies a point on the line PQ (see Figure A3.7). For example,

t	x	y
1	1	7
2	−8	11
3	−17	15
0	10	3
−1	19	−1
−2	28	−5

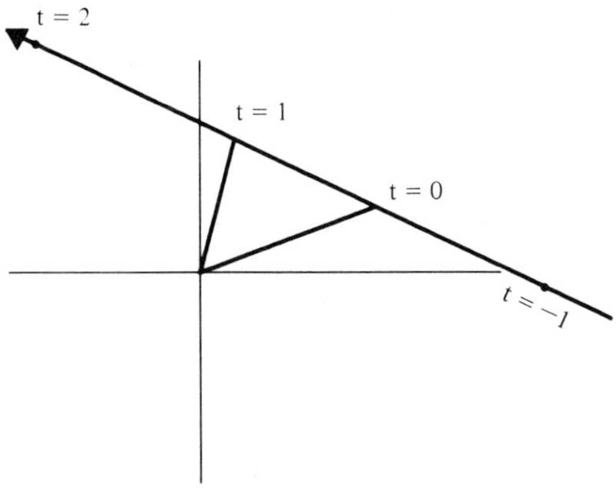

FIGURE A3.7

Notice that the line has positive and negative directions, inherited from the positive and negative directions of the vector $\vec{u}$.

VECTORS IN THREE-DIMENSIONAL SPACE

The previous discussion of vectors, based on two-dimensional space, is easily extended to higher dimensions. Most of our needs for vectors will be for three-dimensional calculations. For vectors $\vec{v} = (2,1,7)$ and $\vec{w} = (3,2,-5)$ we calculate

$$\vec{v} + \vec{w} = (2,1,7) + (3,2,-5) = (5,3,2)$$

$$\vec{v} - \vec{w} = (2,1,7) - (3,2,-5) = (-1,-1,12)$$

$$4\vec{v} = 4(2,1,7) = (8,4,28)$$

The line passing through the points $(2,1,7)$ and $(3,2,-5)$ may be represented as $\vec{x} = \vec{v} + t\vec{u}$, where $\vec{u} = \vec{w} - \vec{v} = (3,2,-5) - (2,1,7) = (1,1,-12)$. Thus the vector form of the equation of the line is $(x,y,z) = (2,1,7) + t(1,1,-12)$.

DOT PRODUCTS OF VECTORS

We define the dot product of vector $\vec{u} = (a,b,c)$ and $\vec{v} = (d,e,f)$ to be $\vec{u} \cdot \vec{v} = (a,b,c) \cdot (d,e,f) = ad + be + cf$. For example, if $\vec{u} = (9,1,2)$ and $\vec{v} = (3,-5,7)$, then $\vec{u} \cdot \vec{v} = (9,1,2) \cdot (3,-5,7) = 27 - 5 + 14 = 36$.

For two-dimensional vectors, the definition of the dot product is similar: $(a,b) \cdot (c,d) = ac + bd$. For example, $(3,5)\ (7,-3) = 21 - 15 = 6$.

While these two definitions provide an easy means of calculating the dot product of two vectors, no hint is given of the significance of the dot product. It can be shown that $\vec{u} \cdot \vec{v} = |\vec{u}||\vec{v}| \cos\theta$. Here $|\vec{u}|$ refers to the magnitude, or length, of $\vec{u}$. The length of $\vec{v}$ is $|\vec{v}|$, and θ is the angle between $\vec{u}$ and $\vec{v}$. Many useful applications may be derived from this interpretation of the dot product, but we shall require only one: If the angle between $\vec{u}$ and $\vec{v}$ is between 0° and 90°, the dot product of $\vec{u}$ and $\vec{v}$ is positive. If the angle is between 90° and 180°, the dot product is negative.

The value of θ may be calculated from the dot product:
Since

$$\vec{u} \cdot \vec{v} = |\vec{u}||\vec{v}| \cos\theta$$

then

$$\cos\theta = \frac{\vec{u} \cdot \vec{v}}{|\vec{u}||\vec{v}|}$$

and

$$\theta = \text{Arc cos}\left(\frac{\vec{u} \cdot \vec{v}}{|\vec{u}||\vec{v}|}\right)$$

Since $\vec{u}$ and $\vec{v}$ are always positive, the sign of $\vec{u} \cdot \vec{v} = |\vec{u}||\vec{v}| \cos\theta$ is the sign of $\cos\theta$. The truth of the above statement thus rests on the characteristics of cosine. If θ is between 0° and 90°, then $\cos\theta$ is positive. If θ is between 90° and 180°, $\cos\theta$ is negative.

To illustrate, if $\vec{u} = (1,3)$, $\vec{v} = (3,-5)$, and $\vec{w} = (-1,-6)$ (see Figure A3.8), then $\vec{u} \cdot \vec{v} = (1,3) \cdot (3,-5) = 3 - 15 = -12$ is negative because the angle between $\vec{u}$ and $\vec{v}$ is between 90° and 180°; and $\vec{u} \cdot \vec{w} = (1,3)\,(-1,-6) = -1 - 18 = -19$. Again, the angle is between 90° and 180°. But $\vec{v} \cdot \vec{w} = (3,-5) \cdot (-1,-6) = -3 + 30 = 27$ is positive; the angle is between 0° and 90°.

CROSS PRODUCTS OF VECTORS

The definition of the cross product is more cumbersome than that of the dot product. For u = (a,b,c) and v = (d,e,f), we have $\vec{u} \times \vec{v} = (bf -$

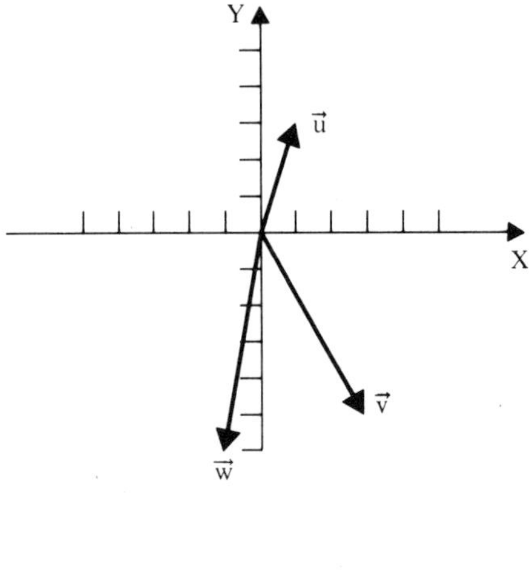

FIGURE A3.8

ce,cd − af,ae − bd). Note that while $\vec{u} \cdot \vec{v}$ is a number, $\vec{u} \times \vec{v}$ is a vector. Further, while $\vec{u} \cdot \vec{v}$ may be calculated for two- or three-dimensional vectors, $\vec{u} \times \vec{v}$ is defined only for three-dimensional vectors. For $\vec{u} = (1,9,8)$ and $\vec{v} = (3,0,7)$,

$$\begin{aligned}\vec{u} \times \vec{v} &= (1,9,8) \times (3,0,7)\\ &= (63 - 0,24 - 7,0 - 27)\\ &= (63,17,-27)\end{aligned}$$

What is the significance of the cross product? Only one application is of interest to us: In a right-hand coordinate system the cross product of vectors $\vec{u}$ and $\vec{v}$ will yield a vector $\vec{w}$ which is normal (perpendicular) to the plane of $\vec{u}$ and $\vec{v}$. The orientation of $\vec{w} = \vec{u} \times \vec{v}$ is such that if the index and second finger of the right hand are pointing in the direction of $\vec{u}$ and $\vec{v}$, respectively, then $\vec{w}$ has the direction of the thumb.

Note that $\vec{v} \times \vec{u}$ and $\vec{u} \times \vec{v}$ have opposite directions. For vectors $\vec{u} = (1,3,0)$ and $\vec{v} = (-3,7,0)$, lying on the xy plane, $\vec{u} \times \vec{v}$ is a positive multiple of (0,0,1).

In a left-hand coordinate system (such as the IBM PC display screen), when the index finger and second fingers of the left hand point in the direction of $\vec{u}$ and $\vec{v}$, respectively, $\vec{u} \times \vec{v}$ will be normal to the plane of $\vec{u}$ and $\vec{v}$, having the direction of the thumb.

HALF-PLANES

The line (x,y) = (a,b) + t(c,d) divides the xy plane into two half-planes. When facing in the direction of the vector $\vec{v} = (c,d)$, the half-plane on the left is referred to as the *left half-plane,* while the half-plane on the right is called the *right half-plane*. Note that the designation of the left and right half-planes rests on the orientation of the vector $\vec{v} = (c,d)$.

For example, the line (x,y) = (2,5) = t(−1,3) divides the plane as shown in Figure A3.9b. The line (x,y) = (2,5) + t(1,−3) (same line, opposite orientation) divides the plane as shown in Figure A3.9a.

Our concern with half-planes arises in Chapter 9, when we must determine which half-plane contains a given point. For the half-planes determined by the line $\vec{x} = \vec{u} + t\vec{v}$, the left and right half-planes are as indicated in Figure A3.10. To determine which half-plane contains point P(a,b), we will define vector $\vec{r} = (a,b)$ and vector $\vec{w} = \vec{r} - \vec{u}$. If P is in the left half-plane, then $\vec{v} \times \vec{w}$ will be a positive multiple of (0,0,1).

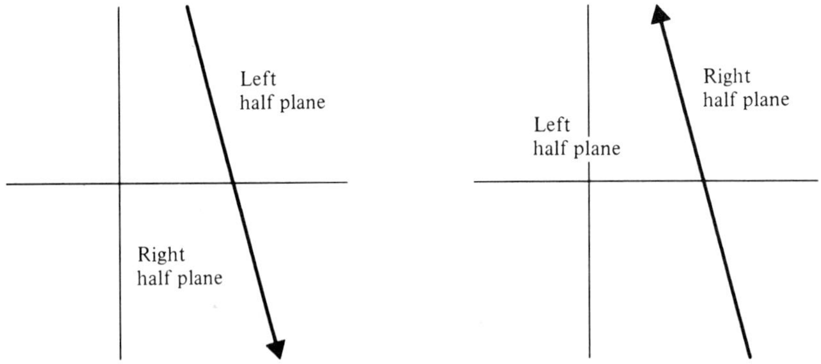

FIGURE A3.9

To illustrate, consider line (x,y) = (2,5) + t(1, −3) and point P(4,8). Then

$$\vec{u} = (2,5,0),\ \vec{v} = (1,-3,0),\ \vec{r} = (4,8,0)$$
$$\vec{w} = \vec{r} - \vec{u} = (4,8,0) - (2,5,0) = (2,3,0)$$

and

$$\begin{aligned}\vec{v} \times \vec{w} &= (1,-3,0) \times (2,3,0)\\ &= (0,0,3 + 6)\\ &= (0,0,9) = 9(0,0,1)\end{aligned}$$

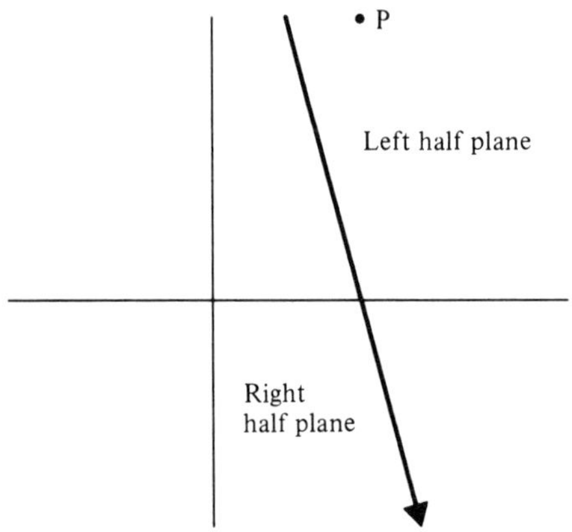

FIGURE A3.10

which is a positive multiple of (0,0,1). We can see from Figure A3.10 that P is indeed in the left half-plane.

> *Note:* The test above for location of a point in either the left or right half-plane is valid for points located in a right-hand coordinate system, which is a conventional context for calculation. However, the IBM PC display screen has a left-hand coordinate system. When working with points and half-planes on the IBM display screen, the rule above must be modified: With $\vec{u}$, $\vec{v}$, $\vec{r}$, $\vec{w}$, and P as defined above, we will find that P is in the left half-plane if $\vec{v} \times \vec{w}$ is a negative multiple of (0,0,1); but P is in the right half-plane if $\vec{v} \times \vec{w}$ is a positive multiple of (0,0,1). Of course, the display screen can be established as a right-hand coordinate system through the use of the WINDOW statement.

Appendix 4

Matrices

A matrix is a rectangular array of numbers, such as

$$\begin{pmatrix} 3 & -9 \\ 4 & 2 \end{pmatrix} \quad \text{or} \quad \begin{pmatrix} 5 & 8 \\ 2 & 1 \\ 3 & 4 \end{pmatrix}$$

Matrices have a wide range of applications, and a large number of matrix formulas and techniques have been developed. Our interest in the use of matrices for representing transformations will require only a very basic knowledge of matrices and matrix products.

The labelling and referencing of the elements of a matrix is illustrated by

$$A = \begin{pmatrix} a_{11} & a_{12} & a_{13} & a_{14} \\ a_{21} & a_{22} & a_{23} & a_{24} \\ a_{31} & a_{32} & a_{33} & a_{34} \end{pmatrix}$$

The subscripts of an element identify the row and column position of that element. Thus a_{24} is the second row, fourth column, and a_{31} is in the third row, first column. A matrix such as A, which has three rows and four columns, is referred to as a 3×4 matrix.

PRODUCTS OF MATRICES

The following example illustrates matrix multiplication:

$$\begin{matrix} A & B & = & C \end{matrix}$$

$$\begin{pmatrix} a_{11} & a_{12} \\ a_{21} & a_{22} \end{pmatrix} \begin{pmatrix} b_{11} & b_{12} \\ b_{21} & b_{22} \end{pmatrix} = \begin{pmatrix} a_{11}b_{11} + a_{12}b_{21} & a_{11}b_{12} + a_{12}b_{22} \\ a_{21}b_{11} + a_{22}b_{21} & a_{21}b_{12} + a_{22}b_{22} \end{pmatrix}$$

Note that in obtaining the matrix product AB = C, each entry c_{ij} of the product is the sum of the products of the entries of the ith row of A with the corresponding entries of the jth column of B. Thus c_{21} is the sum of the products of the second row of A(a_{21},a_{22}) with corresponding entries of the first column of B(b_{11},b_{21}).

Because of this definition of matrix product, AB is defined only if each row of A has as many entries as a column of B. Thus, if A is an $m \times n$ matrix and B is a $p \times q$ matrix, the product AB is possible only if $n = p$. We may then expect the product to have as many rows as A and as many columns as B; AB will be an $m \times q$ matrix. For example:

$$\begin{pmatrix} 1 & 4 & 2 \\ 3 & 0 & -1 \\ 1 & 5 & 2 \end{pmatrix} \begin{pmatrix} 4 & 9 & 8 \\ 3 & -4 & -7 \\ -5 & 0 & 6 \end{pmatrix} = \begin{pmatrix} 6 & -7 & -8 \\ 17 & 27 & 18 \\ 9 & -11 & -15 \end{pmatrix}$$

$$(2,1,3) \begin{pmatrix} 4 & 2 & -5 \\ 8 & 9 & 3 \\ 1 & -4 & 7 \end{pmatrix} = (19,1,14)$$

We note without proof that matrix multiplication in general is not commutative (AB = BA) but is associative (A(BC) = (AB)C).

The coordinates of a point may be considered to form a 1×2 matrix. The product

$$(x,y) \begin{pmatrix} 4 & 2 \\ 8 & 9 \end{pmatrix} = (4x + 8y, 2x + 9y)$$

shows that multiplication by the matrix

$$\begin{pmatrix} 4 & 2 \\ 8 & 9 \end{pmatrix}$$

provides a means of associating each point (x,y) with a second point (4x + 8y,2x + 9y). For example:

$$(1,-1)\begin{pmatrix}4 & 2\\ 8 & 9\end{pmatrix} = (-4,-7) \quad \text{and} \quad (-2,1)\begin{pmatrix}4 & 2\\ 8 & 9\end{pmatrix} = (0,5)$$

In a similar manner, any matrix

$$\begin{pmatrix}a & b\\ c & d\end{pmatrix}$$

may be considered to provide a means of associating the point (x,y) with the point (ax + cy,bx + dy). We speak of transforming the point (x,y) to the point (ax + cy,bx + dy), and refer to

$$\begin{pmatrix}a & b\\ c & d\end{pmatrix}$$

as being the matrix of the transformation.

Appendix 5

Radian Measure of Angles

There are several units available for measuring angles. While degree measurement is commonly used, it is not the preferred system for work in science or engineering; nor is it used by computers. Measurement of angles in radians is more conventional.

Figure A5.1 shows a unit circle (radius 1) and an angle (APB) with its vertex at the center of the circle. The radian measure of angle APB is the length of the arc AB. Thus, radian measure is defined in terms of arc length measured on a circle of radius 1.

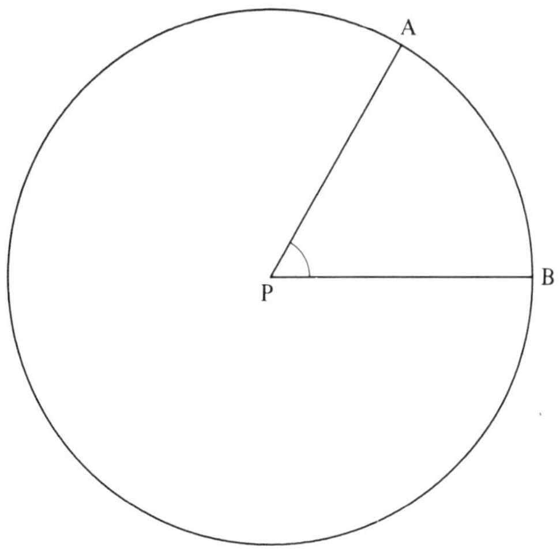

FIGURE A5.1

The association between degrees and radians is established by noting that the circumference of a unit circle is given by $C = 2\pi r = 2\pi(1) = 2\pi$. Thus, an angle of 360° has a radian equivalent of 2π. As a result, an angle of 1° has a radian measure of $2\pi/360$.

The following converts degrees to radians:

```
RADIANS = DEGREES (π/180)
```

to convert from radians to degrees:

```
DEGREES = RADIANS (180/π)
```

The following table shows the degree-radian equivalence of some commonly used angles

Degrees	**Radians**	
0	0	
30	$\pi/6$	.5236
45	$\pi/4$	.7854
60	$\pi/3$	1.0472
90	$\pi/2$	1.5708
180	π	3.1416
270	$3\pi/2$	4.7124
360	2π	6.2832

To use radian measure within a program it usually is convenient to provide the value of π. This may be done by defining the variable as

```
PI = 3.141593
```

or, since $\tan(45°) = \tan(\pi/4) = 1$,

```
PI = 4 * ATN(1)
```

Appendix 6

Additional Program Listings

In the following pages we provide listings of the programs which draw the images used on the cover of this book. In addition we list the program which draws the image of Figure 7.1. Each of the programs is accompanied by a brief description which references pertinent chapters. The documentation of the programs is brief, and assumes familiarity with the concepts and programs discussed in the related chapters.

FRONT COVER, UPPER LEFT

Although this program is long, it is quite simple in structure. The length is due to the large number of points which must be individually identified.

In planning the program, approximate measurements (in inches) were taken from an IBM PC system unit, monitor, and keyboard, using the lower left rear corner of the system unit as the reference point. This point becomes the origin of the X, Y, Z axis system. The measurements are provided in DATA statements and read as needed in the program.

The program uses the perspective projection subroutine of lines 1060–1110 to obtain the screen coordinates of points to be plotted. The subroutine was introduced in Chapter 8 and used in the programs of Chapters 8 and 9.

The hidden line elimination is handled in the subroutine of lines 860–1030, using the binary search method described in Chapter 9.

When the first image is completed, lines 610–690 define a viewport which fits inside the screen of the monitor which was drawn. Then the program draws a second image (using the same data as before) within this viewport.

Program A6-1: IBM

```
10 'PROGRAM A6.1  (IBM)
20 'Front cover; upper left
100 '============================================
110 RHO = 100: D = 1500
120 THETA = .5: S1 = SIN(THETA): C1 = COS(THETA)
130 PHI = 1.25: S2 = SIN(PHI): C2 = COS(PHI)
140 KEY OFF: SCREEN 2: CLS: C = 3: SC = 5/12
150 WINDOW SCREEN (0,0) - (639,199)
160 '------------------------------
170 FOR IMAGE = 1 TO 2
180  'System unit
190  GOSUB 750: GOSUB 750: GOSUB 860
200  ST = .3: IF IMAGE = 2 THEN ST = .9
210  FOR Y = .75 TO 5.85 STEP ST
220   X = 15.75: Z = 2.5
230   GOSUB 1060: PSET (SX,SY)
240   X = 16: Z = 1
250   GOSUB 1060: LINE - (SX,SY)
260  NEXT Y
270 '--------------------------------------
280 'Disk drives
290  GOSUB 750
300  X = 15: Y = 12: Z = 2
310  GOSUB 1060: PAINT (SX,SY)
320  C = 0: GOSUB 750: GOSUB 750
330  READ X,Y,Z: GOSUB 1060: PAINT (SX,SY),0,0
340  READ X,Y,Z: GOSUB 1060: PAINT (SX,SY),0,0
350  GOSUB 750: GOSUB 750: GOSUB 750: C = 3
360 '--------------------------------------
370 'Box for IBM logo
380  GOSUB 750
390 'Power switch
400  GOSUB 750
410  X = 1: Y = 19.5: Z = 2.5
420  GOSUB 1060: PAINT (SX,SY)
430 'Monitor
440  GOSUB 750: GOSUB 750
450  X = 13: Y = 15.5: Z = 12
460  GOSUB 1060: CIRCLE (SX,SY),6
470  Z = 10: GOSUB 1060: CIRCLE (SX,SY),6
480  Z = 13.5: GOSUB 1060: CIRCLE (SX,SY),2
490  GOSUB 750: GOSUB 750
500 '------------------------------------
```

```
510 'Keyboard
520  GOSUB 750
530  FOR X = 19 TO 23
540   Y = 1.5: Z = .75
550   GOSUB 1060: PSET (SX,SY)
560   Y = 16.5: GOSUB 1060: LINE - (SX,SY)
570  NEXT X
580  IF IMAGE = 2 THEN 710
590 '-----------------------------------
600 'Set viewport
610  X = 13: Y = 3: Z = 15
620  GOSUB 1060 : PX = SX
630  X = 13: Y = 14: Z = 15
640  GOSUB 1060: PY = SY
650  X = 14: Y = 14: Z = 6.5
660  GOSUB 1060: QX = SX
670  X = 14: Y = 3: Z = 6.5
680  GOSUB 1060: QY = SY
690  VIEW (PX,PY) - (QX,QY)
700  RESTORE
710 NEXT IMAGE
720 END
730 '=====================================
740 'Line drawing subroutine
750 READ N
760 READ X,Y,Z: X = X+X1: Y = Y+Y1: Z = Z+Z1
770 GOSUB 1060: PSET (SX,SY),C
780 FOR I = 1 TO N
790  READ X,Y,Z: X = X+X1: Y = Y+Y1: Z = Z+Z1
800  GOSUB 1060
810  LINE - (SX,SY),C
820 NEXT I
830 RETURN
840 '=====================================
850 'Hidden lines - binary search
860  FOR J = 1 TO 3
870   READ X,Y,Z: GOSUB 1060: XV = SX: YV = SY
880   READ X,Y,Z: GOSUB 1060: XH = SX: YH = SY
890   READ X,Y,Z: GOSUB 1060: XP = SX: YP = SY
900   READ X,Y,Z: GOSUB 1060: XQ = SX: YQ = SY
910   V1 = (XH - XV)/2: V2 = (YH - YV)/2
920   U1 = XP - XQ: U2 = YP - YQ
930   XT = XV + V1: YT = YV + V2
940   FOR I = 2 TO 7
950    CROSS1 = U2*(XV-XQ) - U1*(YV-YQ)
960    CROSS2 = U2*(XT-XQ) - U1*(YT-YQ)
970    VI = SGN(CROSS1*CROSS2)
980    V1 = V1/2: V2 = V2/2
990    XT = XT + VI*V1: YT = YT + VI*V2
1000  NEXT I
```

```
1010  LINE (XV,YV) - (XT,YT)
1020 NEXT J
1030 RETURN
1040 '========================================
1050 'Perspective projection subroutine
1060 XE = -X*S1 + Y*C1
1070 YE = -X*C1*C2 - Y*S1*C2 + Z*S2
1080 ZE = -X*S2*C1 - Y*S1*S2 - Z*C2 + RHO
1090 SX = D*XE/ZE + 310
1100 SY = 110 - SC*D*YE/ZE
1110 RETURN
1120 '=========================================
1130 'System unit
1140 DATA 5, 0,19.5,5.5, 15,19.5,5.5, 16,19.5,0
1150 DATA 0,19.5,0, 0,19.5,5.5, 0,17.5,5.5
1160 DATA 1, 15,19.5,5.5, 15,0,5.5
1170 'Hidden line data
1180 DATA 15,0,5.5,  0,0,5.5
1190 DATA 12.75,2,16.5, 14.5,2,5.5
1200 DATA 15,0,5.5, 16,0,0
1210 DATA 17,0,1, 17,18,1
1220 DATA 16,19.5,0, 16,0,0
1230 DATA 17,18,1, 17,18,0
1240 'Disk drives
1250 DATA 4, 15,6.5,1, 15,6.5,4.5, 15,18.5,4.5
1260 DATA 15,18.5,1, 15,6.5,1
1270 DATA 4, 15,9,3.75, 15,10,3.75, 15,10,1.75
1280 DATA 15,9,1.75, 15,9,3.75
1290 DATA 4, 15,15,3.75, 15,16,3.75, 15,16,1.75
1300 DATA 15,15,1.75, 15,15,3.75
1310 DATA 15,9.5,2.5, 15,15.5,2.5
1320 DATA 1, 15,7,2.75, 15,12,2.75
1330 DATA 1, 15,13,2.75, 15,18,2.75
1340 DATA 1, 15,12.5,4.5, 15,12.5,1
1350 'IBM logo
1360 DATA 4, 15.5,1,4.5, 15.5,2,4.5, 15.5,2,3.5
1370 DATA 15.5,1,3.5, 15.5,1,4.5
1380 'Power switch
1390 DATA 3, 0,19.5,1.5, 2,19.5,1.5, 2,19.5,3.5
1400 DATA 0,19.5,3.5
1410 'Monitor
1420 DATA 10, 12.75,2,16.5, 12.75,17.5,16.5, 0,17.5,16.5
1430 DATA 0,0,16.5, 12.75,2,16.5, 14.5,2,5.5
1440 DATA 14.5,17.5,5.5, 0,17.5,5.5, 0,17.5,16.5
1450 DATA 12.75,17.5,16.5, 14.5,17.5,5.5
1460 DATA 4, 13,3,15.5, 13,14,15.5, 14,14,6.5
1470 DATA 14,3,6.5, 13,3,15.5
1480 DATA 4, 13,15,15, 13,16,15, 13,16,14.5
1490 DATA 13,15,14.5, 13,15,15
```

```
1500 DATA 4, 14,14.5,7, 14,16.5,7, 14,16.5,7.5
1510 DATA 14,14.5,7.5, 14,14.5,7
1520 'Keyboard
1530 DATA 10, 17,18,1, 17,0,1, 25,0,.5
1540 DATA 25,18,.5, 17,18,1, 17,18,0
1550 DATA 25,18,0, 25,0,0, 25,0,.5
1560 DATA 25,18,.5, 25,18,0
1570 DATA 1, 18,1,.75, 18,17,.75
1580 DATA 24,17,.75, 18,1,.75
```

FRONT COVER, UPPER RIGHT

Program A6-2 is almost the same as Program 9-6. The differences lie in the function being used to define the surface in the viewpoint selected and in the limits used in the FOR–NEXT loops which generate points of the surface. Be patient; the computer is doing a lot of calculation, so the program takes a while to complete the surface.

Program A6-2: 3-D SURFACE

```
10 'PROGRAM A6-2    (3-D SURFACE)
20 'Front cover; upper right
100 '==============================================
110 KEY OFF: SCREEN 2: CLS
120 RHO = 100: D = 2000
130 THETA = .1: S1 = SIN(THETA): C1 = COS(THETA)
140 PHI = 1.3: S2 = SIN(PHI): C2 = COS(PHI)
150 DEF FNF(X,Y) = 14*EXP(-.04*W)*COS(.15*W)
160 DIM YMIN(639),YMAX(639)
170 FOR I = 0 TO 639: YMIN(I) = 199: NEXT I
180 '==============================================
190 'Point generating loop
200 FOR X = 12 TO -12 STEP -.5
210  FL = 0
220  FOR Y = -12 TO 12 STEP .2
230   W = X*X + Y*Y
240   Z = FN F(X,Y): GOSUB 300
250  NEXT Y
260 NEXT X
270 END
280 '==============================================
290 'Perspective projection calculation
300 XE = -X*S1 + Y*C1
310 YE = -X*C1*C2 - Y*S1*C2 + Z*S2
```

```
320 ZE = -X*S2*C1 - Y*S1*S2 - Z*C2 + RHO
330 SX = D*XE/ZE + 320
340 SY = -5*D*YE/ZE/12 + 120
350 '===========================================
360 'Hidden line routine
370 IF SX < 0 OR SX > 639 THEN 490
380 IF FL = 0 THEN FL = 1: F = 0: GOTO 490
390 DX = OLDX - SX: IF DX = 0 THEN DX = 1
400 SL = (OLDY - SY)/DX
410 YP = OLDY
420 '---------------------------------
430 FOR XP = INT(OLDX) + 1 TO SX
440  YP = YP + SL
450  IF YP <= YMIN(XP) THEN 510
460  IF YP >= YMAX(XP) THEN 560
470  F = 0
480 NEXT XP
490 OLDX = SX: OLDY = SY: RETURN
500 '---------------------------------
510 YMIN(XP) = YP
520 IF F = 0 THEN PSET (XP,YP): F = 1
530 LINE - (XP,YP)
540 IF YP < YMAX(XP) THEN 480
550 '---------------------------------
560 YMAX(XP) = YP
570 IF F = 0 THEN PSET (XP,YP): F = 1
580 LINE - (XP,YP)
590 GOTO 480
```

FRONT COVER, LOWER LEFT

This image illustrates some of the concepts of multivariable calculus (partial derivative, directional derivative). However, in addition to being useful, it is an interesting one.

Much of the program is similar to Program A6-2. The function which defines the surface is more complex (see lines 150–190), but the point calculation and hidden line calculation are essentially the same. The program first draws the closer part of the surface, then the vertical plane, and finally the farther part of the surface. A separate projection subroutine is used for the plane and the hidden line array update is handled differently than for the surface (line 480). The reason for the difference is that the array YMAX(I) does not need to be updated when the plane is being drawn.

Be patient; the program requires a substantial amount of time to draw the image.

Program A6-3: SURFACE/PLANE

```
10 'PROGRAM A6-3  (SURFACE/PLANE)
20 'Draws lower left image on front cover
100 '=============================================
110 KEY OFF: SCREEN 1,0: COLOR 0,0: CLS
120 RHO = 150: D = 1500
130 THETA = .4: S1 = SIN(THETA): C1 = COS(THETA)
140 PHI = 1.3: S2 = SIN(PHI): C2 = COS(PHI)
150 DEF FN R(X,Y) = 3*EXP(-.02*(X+10)^2 - .08*(Y+10)^2)
160 DEF FN S(X,Y) = 4*EXP(-.1*(X+10)^2 - .1*(Y-6)^2)
170 DEF FN T(X,Y) = 4*EXP(-.02*(X-10)^2 - .1*(Y+8)^2)
180 DEF FN U(X,Y) = -7*EXP(-.08*(X-5)^2 - .08*(Y-7)^2)
190 DEF FN F(X,Y) = FN R(X,Y) + FN S(X,Y) + FN T(X,Y)
+ FN U(X,Y)
200 DIM YMIN(319),YMAX(319)
210 X1 = 8: Y1 = -8: X2 = -9: Y2 = 8
220 SLP = (Y2-Y1)/(X2-X1)
230 FOR I = 0 TO 319: YMIN(I) = 199: NEXT I
240 '=============================================
250 'Closer part of the surface
260 FOR X = 14 TO -18 STEP -1
270  FL = 0: C = 3
280  YSTART = Y1 + (X-X1)*SLP
290  FOR Y = YSTART TO 17 STEP .5
300   W = X*X + Y*Y
310   Z = FN F(X,Y): GOSUB 640
320  NEXT Y
330 NEXT X
340 '---------------------------------------
350 'Curve of intersection
360 FL = 0: C = 2
370 FOR X = 14 TO -18 STEP -.4
380  Y = Y1 + (X - X1)*SLP
390  Z = FN F(X,Y): GOSUB 640
400 NEXT X
410 '---------------------------------------
420 'Plane
430 FOR X = 14 TO -18 STEP -.4
440  Y = Y1 + (X - X1)*SLP: Z = 5
450  FL = 0: GOSUB 960
460  IF SX <= 3 OR SX > 319 THEN 530
470  LINE (SX,SY) - (SX,YMIN(SX)-2),1
480  FOR I = PX TO SX: YMIN(I) = SY: NEXT I
490  Z = -8: FL = 1: GOSUB 960
500  IF SY <= YMAX(SX) + 2 THEN 520
```

```
510  LINE (SX,SY) - (SX,YMAX(SX)+2),1
520  PX = SX
530 NEXT X
540 '----------------------------------------
550 'Farther part of surface
560 FOR X = -5 TO -18 STEP -1
570 FL = 0: C = 3: YSTOP = Y1 + (S - X1)*SLP
580  FOR Y = -13 TO YSTOP
590   Z = FN F(X,Y): GOSUB 640
600 NEXT Y,X
610 END
620 '======================================
630 'Perspective projection calculation
640 XE = -X*S1 + Y*C1
650 YE = -X*C1*C2 - Y*S1*C2 + Z*S2
660 ZE = -X*S2*C1 - Y*S1*S2 - Z*C2 + RHO
670 SX = D*XE/ZE + 160
680 SY = -D*YE/ZE + 100
690 '======================================
700 'Hidden line routine
710 IF SX < 0 OR SX > 319 THEN 830
720 IF FL = 0 THEN FL = 1: F = 0: GOTO 830
730 DX = OLDX - SX: IF DX = 0 THEN DX = 1
740 SL = (OLDY - SY)/DX
750 YP = OLDY
760 '-------------------------------------
770 FOR XP = INT(OLDX) + 1 TO SX
780  YP = YP + SL
790  IF YP <= YMIN(XP) THEN 850
800  IF YP >= YMAX(XP) THEN 900
810  F = 0
820 NEXT XP
830 OLDX = SX: OLDY = SY: RETURN
840 '-------------------------------------
850 YMIN(XP) = YP
860 IF F = 0 THEN PSET (XP,YP),C: F = 1
870 LINE - (XP,YP),C
880 IF YP < YMAX(XP) THEN 820
890 '-------------------------------------
900 YMAX(XP) = YP
910 IF F = 0 THEN PSET (XP,YP),C: F = 1
920 LINE - (XP,YP),C
930 GOTO 820
940 '======================================
950 'Plane projection subroutine
960 XE = -X*S1 + Y*C1
970 YE = -X*C1*C2 - Y*S1*C2 + Z*S2
980 ZE = -X*S2*C1 - Y*S1*S2 - Z*C2 + RHO
990 SY = -D*YE/ZE + 100
1000 IF FL = 1 THEN 1020
1010 SX = D*XE/ZE + 160
1020 RETURN
```

FRONT COVER, LOWER RIGHT

This image is produced by Program 4-2. Although the image is intended to look like it is three-dimensional, no perspective projection is used; the 3-D effect is illusory. See Chapter 4 for a discussion.

BACK COVER, LEFT

This image is drawn by Program 4-5. See Chapter 4 for a discussion of the program.

BACK COVER, RIGHT

This program is the basis of Figure 9.1, which was drawn by a digital plotter. The program which was used to draw Figure 9.1 differs from this one in that the graphics commands (PSET, LINE) used here were replaced with corresponding plotter commands.

This program is long but simple. The coordinates of the line endpoints are provided in DATA statements. As these are needed they are passed to one of several subroutines. Each uses the perspective projection subroutine (lines 870–910). The hidden line calculations are handled by the subroutine of lines 690–840, using the binary search method.

The data elements provided and the hidden line technique used limit the selection of a viewpoint. You could try some other values for RHO, THETA, and PHI, but be careful: the range of choices is limited.

Program A6-4: HOUSE

```
10 'PROGRAM A6-4  (HOUSE)
20 'Back cover; upper right
100 '========================================
110 RHO = 100: D = 900
120 THETA = .7: S1 = SIN(THETA): C1 = COS(THETA)
130 PHI = 1.3: S2 = SIN(PHI): C2 = COS(PHI)
140 KEY OFF: SCREEN 2: CLS: SC = 5/12
150 '-----------------------------
160 'Visible lines
170 FOR K = 1 TO 8
180  GOSUB 590
190 NEXT K
200 'Hidden lines
210 FOR K = 1 TO 6
```

```
220  GOSUB 690
230 NEXT K
240 'Windows
250 FOR K = 1 TO 5
260  GOSUB 350
270 NEXT K
280 'Garage doors
290 FOR K = 1 TO 2
300  GOSUB 470
310 NEXT K
320 END
330 '================================================
340 'Window subroutine
350 READ X,Y,Z: GOSUB 870: PSET (SX,SY)
360 Y = Y + 4: GOSUB 870: LINE - (SX,SY)
370 Z = Z + 5.5: GOSUB 870: LINE - (SX,SY)
380 Y = Y - 4: GOSUB 870: LINE - (SX,SY)
390 Z = Z - 5.5: GOSUB 870: LINE - (SX,SY)
400 Y = Y + 2: GOSUB 870: PSET (SX,SY)
410 Z = Z + 5.5: GOSUB 870: LINE - (SX,SY)
420 Y = Y - 2: Z = Z - 2.75: GOSUB 870: PSET (SX,SY)
430 Y = Y + 4: GOSUB 870: LINE - (SX,SY)
440 RETURN
450 '================================================
460 'Garage door subroutine
470 READ X,Y,Z: GOSUB 870: PSET (SX,SY)
480 Z = Z + 7: GOSUB 870: LINE - (SX,SY)
490 Y = Y - 7.5: GOSUB 870: LINE - (SX,SY)
500 Z = Z - 7: GOSUB 870: LINE - (SX,SY)
510 Z = Z + 5: Y = Y + 1: GOSUB 870: PSET (SX,SY)
520 Z = Z + 1: GOSUB 870: LINE - (SX,SY)
530 Y = Y + 5.5: GOSUB 870: LINE - (SX,SY)
540 Z = Z - 1: GOSUB 870: LINE - (SX,SY)
550 Y = Y - 5.5: GOSUB 870: LINE -(SX,SY)
560 RETURN
570 '================================================
580 'Line drawing subroutine
590 READ N
600 READ X,Y,Z: X = X+X1: Y = Y+Y1: Z = Z+Z1
610 GOSUB 870: PSET (SX,SY)
620 FOR I = 1 TO N
630  READ X,Y,Z: X = X+X1: Y = Y+Y1: Z = Z+Z1
640  GOSUB 870: LINE - (SX,SY)
650 NEXT I
660 RETURN
670 '================================================
680 'Hidden lines - binary search
690  READ X,Y,Z: GOSUB 870: XV = SX: YV = SY
700  READ X,Y,Z: GOSUB 870: XH = SX: YH = SY
```

```
710  READ X,Y,Z: GOSUB 870: XP = SX: YP = SY
720  READ X,Y,Z: GOSUB 870: XQ = SX: YQ = SY
730  V1 = (XH - XV)/2: V2 = (YH - YV)/2
740  U1 = XP - XQ: U2 = YP - YQ
750  XT = XV + V1: YT = YV + V2
760  FOR I = 2 TO 7
770   CROSS1 = U2*(XV-XQ) - U1*(YV-YQ)
780   CROSS2 = U2*(XT-XQ) - U1*(YT-YQ)
790   VI = SGN(CROSS1*CROSS2)
800   V1 = V1/2: V2 = V2/2
810   XT = XT + VI*V1: YT = YT + VI*V2
820 NEXT I
830 LINE (XV,YV) - (XT,YT)
840 RETURN
850 '==================================================
860 'Perspective projection subroutine
870 XE = -X*S1 + Y*C1
880 YE = -X*C1*C2 - Y*S1*C2 + Z*S2
890 ZE = -X*S2*C1 - Y*S1*S2 - Z*C2 + RHO
900 SX = D*XE/ZE + 220
910 SY = 160 - SC*D*YE/ZE
920 RETURN
930 '==================================================
940 'Visible lines
950 DATA 10, -11,-20,23, 6,-20,9, 6,-20,0
960 DATA     6,32,0, 0,32,0, 0,32,20
970 DATA     0,0,20, 0,0,13, 0,32,13
980 DATA     6,32,9, 6,-20,9
990 DATA 1, 6,32,0, 6,32,9
1000 DATA 1, 6,0,0, 6,0,9
1010 DATA 2, 0,32,0, 0,0,0, 6,0,0
1020 DATA 9, 0,32,0, -11.5,32,0, -11.5,33.5,0
1030 DATA    -16.5,33.5,0, -16.5,33.5,33, -11.5,33.5,33
1040 DATA    -11.5,33.5,0, -11.5,32,0, -11.5,32,33
1050 DATA    -11.5,33.5,33
1060 DATA 1, -14,0,31.5, 0,0,20
1070 DATA 1, -28,32,0, -28,32,20
1080 DATA 3, 0,6,0, 0,6,6.5
1090 DATA    0,9,6.5, 0,9,0
1100 'Hidden lines
1110 DATA -14,0,31.5, -14,32,31.5
1120 DATA -11.5,32,33, -11.5,32,0
1130 DATA 0,32,20, -14,32,31.5
1140 DATA -11.5,32,33, -11.5,32,0
1150 DATA -11,-20,23, -11,0,23
1160 DATA -14,0,31.5, 0,0,20
1170 DATA -28,32,20, -14,32,31.5
1180 DATA -16.5,33.5,33, -16.5,33.5,0
1190 DATA -28,32,0, -16.5,32,0
```

```
1200 DATA -16.5,33.5,33, -16.5,33.5,0
1210 DATA 0,0,0, 0,0,10
1220 DATA 6,-20,9, 6,32,9
1230 'Window locations
1240 DATA 0,5,13.5, 0,14,13.5, 0,23,13.5
1250 DATA 0,14,2, 0,23,2
1260 'Garage door locations
1270 DATA 6,-11,0, 6,-1.5,0
```

FIGURE 7.1

The microcomputer cannot directly draw a curve. We have achieved curves by drawing sequences of short straight line segments. This program shows how a sequence of curves (circles) can approximate another curve (cardioid).

The program draws individual circles, each having its center on a reference, or base, circle. Further, each of the circles passes through a common point P on the base circle. The centers of the circles are spaced at equal intervals around the base circle. The base circle is not drawn.

The centers of the individual circles are identified in lines 160 and 170, using the recursive method of calculating points on a circle (see Chapter 7). As a circle center (XN,YN) is calculated, it is used to draw the circle. The value of YN is then used to identify a second circle having its center at (XN,YL). In this way the symmetry of the circle centers is used. We calculate the centers of only the upper circles and use them for drawing both the upper and lower circles.

Figure 7.1 was drawn by a slightly different program than this one. The figure was drawn by a digital plotter, requiring the graphics statements to be replaced by corresponding plotter commands.

Program A6-5: CARDIOID

```
10 'PROGRAM A6-5  (CARDIOID)
20 'Approximates a cardioid with a sequence of circles
30 'Draws image of Figure 7.1
100 '=================================================
110 KEY OFF: SCREEN 2: CLS
120 WINDOW (-160,-120) - (160,120)
130 XN = 40: YN = 0
140 C1 = COS(.314): S1 = SIN(.314)
150 FOR I = 1 TO 10
160  T = XN*C1 - YN*S1
```

```
170  YN = XN*S1 + YN*C1: XN = T
180  RAD = SQR((XN - 40)^2 + YN^2)
190  CIRCLE (XN,YN), RAD
200  YL = -YN
210  CIRCLE (XN,YL), RAD
220 NEXT I
```

Index